AMERICA'S
100
BEST
GROWTH
STOCKS

SECOND EDITION

AMERICA'S

100

BEST
GROWTH
STOCKS

SECOND EDITION

Thomas R. Drey, Jr.

BOB ADAMS, INC.
Holbrook, Massachusetts

Published by Bob Adams, Inc.
260 Center Street, Holbrook, MA 02343

ISBN: 1-55850-393-5

Printed in the United States of America.

J I H G F E D C B A

Library of Congress Cataloging-in-Publication Data
Drey, Thomas R.
    America's 100 best growth stocks / Thomas R. Drey, Jr., — 2nd ed.
        p.   cm.
    Includes bibliographical references and index.
    ISBN 1-55850-393-5
        1. Stocks—United States—Statistics. 2. Corporations—United States—Finance—Directories. I.
Title. II. Title: America's one hundred best growth stocks. III. Title: Growth stocks.
    HG4963.D73   1994
    332.63'22—dc20   94-15471
                                                                              CIP

This publication is designed to provide accurate and authoritative information with regard to the
subject matter covered. It is sold with the understanding that the publisher is not engaged in render-
ing legal, accounting, or other professional advice. If legal advice or other expert assistance is required, the services of a competent professional person should be sought.
— From a *Declaration of Principles* jointly adopted by a Committee of the American Bar Association
and a Committee of Publishers and Associations

This book is available at quantity discounts for bulk purchases.
For information, call 1-800-872-5627.

To my late uncle James Drey,
who introduced me to the stock market
and the Kirstein Business Library in Boston,
when I was in High School.

Contents

contact lenses

Introduction

During the past decade and the turbulent eras preceding, few stocks have shown as relatively high a degree of stability as those of the growth stock group. Throughout the years, in peace and war, in boom and recession, under Democrats and Republicans, growth stocks have, better than any other group, weathered the undulation of the business cycle.

The most reliable indicator of growth is a record of consistent, above-average gains in sales and earnings. Prominent among growth issues are business forms manufacturers, consumer food-oriented companies, pharmaceutical companies, and a number of regional banks. Growth industries are less vulnerable to recessions than cyclical ones such as steel, chemical, textile, and automobile companies. While growth companies may be found in a variety of industries, they have in common a number of characteristics: strong profit margins, a commitment to research and development, an above-average return on equity, modest dividend payouts, and expanding sales.

A number of parameters were used in selecting equities for inclusions in this book.

- First, the equity must have a *Standard & Poors* rating of A+, A, A-, B+, or B.
- Second, the corporation must have a minimum of at least a $100 million in assets, which means that only established growth stocks are included.
- Third, the corporation must have a public track record of at least ten years.
- Fourth, the corporation must have experienced a consistent long-term uptrend in assets, revenues, and operating earnings.
- Finally, and most important, the company must give indication that it can extend into the future, its upward momentum in sales, earnings, and dividends.

INVESTMENT FUNDAMENTALS

The stock market is a confluence of many factors including economic, monetary, technical, political, and international consideration. In almost no other area can performance be so objectively measured as in investing. Success in the market is heavily dependent upon what Robert Kirby, chairman of Capital Guardian Trust, calls "instinct," or knowing how.

There are basically two types of learning situations, namely, *"knowing that"* (about something) and *"knowing how."* Knowing about the stock market comes from studying books, magazine articles, newspapers, brokerage reports, etc. Knowing how to make money in the stock market comes from the ability to analyze the track record of a company and from actual experience in buying and selling. The successful investor should have a knowledge of both, but it is more often the latter "knowing how" that is lacking.

Franklin D. Roosevelt once remarked that "people don't eat in the long term"; similarly, investors do not achieve their objectives in the short term. History has established that the stock market moves in cycles. Money is made by individuals who single out a few undervalued rapid-growth stocks and stick with them over a long period of time. Stock selection is basically a search for value. Despite the emphasis on quantitative and technical analysis, successful investing remains more of an art than a science.

The most difficult aspect of learning about the stock market or individual stocks is obtaining sound, objective information. While much is written about the market and individual stocks, most of the authors have some vested interest in what they write about. For example, many brokerage firms are either underwriting or making a market in the equities they are writing about. Many books about the stock market are written by the proprietors of investment advisory letters, whose objective is to prove their thesis of how to beat the market.

The most objective information about individual equities usually can be obtained from the financial review section of annual reports, the 10-K Forms filed with the Securities and Exchange Commission, and sources such as *Standard & Poors*, *Moody's*, *Value Line*, and other publications from which much of the factual information in this book has been gleaned. The most objective education information about learning the *how* of the stock market is *Better Investing* and other publications of the National Association of Investment Clubs. Their *Stock Selection Guide* format is indispensable for someone interested in learning how to evaluate the track record and intrinsic value of individual equities. One does not need to be a member of an investment club to purchase their publications. The association's address is P.O. Box 220, Royal Oak, MI 48068. In addition, for someone interested in entering investments as a profession, I would recommend the publications and correspondence courses of the New York Institute of Finance, 70 Pine Street, New York, NY 10270.

A corporation can raise capital four ways:

- By borrowing it;
- By selling bonds, which yield a fixed rate of return either to call or to maturity;

- By issuing preferred stock with a fixed dividend and prior rights to dividends; and
- By selling equities (common stock).

Invariably, a corporation will opt for the equities route because it does not obligate the company to future payments for the use of capital. This is especially true if a company pays little or no dividend. However, equities cannot always be sold. In times of gloom, doom, recession, and low-stock prices, it is almost impossible to market new issues of equities, so corporations choose to borrow, issue preferred stock, or sell bonds. In times of economic euphoria, prosperity, and cheap money, corporations usually sell equities to raise capital.

When a corporation decides to take the equity route, it usually sells shares wholesale to an investment banker or a group of investment bankers (also usually brokers). The investment bankers then retail the shares for a pre-determined price. Very often, new issues include shares of existing inside stockholders, who purchased them for a few cents and are unloading them onto the public for considerable profit.

If the new issue involves an established major company, the broker can often sell the shares to institutions or substantial customers. On the other hand, if the new issue is an unseasoned, new, or fledgling company, the broker must sell the shares to the "gullible" public, knowing full well that institutional investors will not touch them with a ten-foot pole. For example, if the new issue is a fledgling cosmetic firm, the broker will send a prospectus and research report to potential customers. The research report contains a narrative about the industry and statistics concerning the company. The narrative will probably focus on the bright future prospects for the cosmetic industry without mentioning that the new firm will be competing with such giants as Proctor & Gamble, Revlon, Colgate Palmolive, and Alberto Culver. Whether the new issues represent a substantial or fledgling corporation, they usually come to market during a period of price euphoria and are, historically, overpriced.

It is possible to prove almost any investment thesis, either by citing specific examples or using a definitive time parameter. For example, one could establish that a low price-earnings ratio is the key to investment success by citing a variety of low price-earnings ratio issues that have substantially appreciated. One could also establish that new issues are the key to investment success by establishing a time parameter favorable to new issues. During the early seventies, it was almost impossible to establish any thesis except perhaps short selling. Most growth stocks then continued to increase earnings and assets, but their prices declined from their highs in the astronomical sixties. Basically, what happened was that interest rates began a long historic climb, making fixed-income investments, such as bonds, more attractive, and thus placing a lower price-earnings value of equities.

The automobile industry was a rapid-growth industry for over fifty years. There were as many as three hundred and fifty automobile companies in the United States at one time or another, yet only a handful survived. Most went bankrupt and some were merged. In order to have made money in automobile equities, one would have to have invested in General Motors or Chrysler or one of the companies which amalgamated with them. (Ford was not a public company until the 1950s.) The high-tech industry will be an expanding and developing industry for the next twenty-five or more years. However, I can't help but feel that, ultimately, only a small number of high-tech firms will survive; rest assured that IBM, AT&T, and Raytheon will be among them.

The wild inflationary boom of the twenties ended in a massive bust and long-term depression largely because the Federal Reserve, instead of putting on the brakes slowly, jammed them on suddenly. In 1929, the Federal Reserve not only tightened money but also raised bank reserve requirements, forcing the banks to call in loans. That meant that construction firms immediately owed money, which they could not pay, to the bank. The construction firms went bankrupt and laid off workers, banks ended up owning partially completed projects and homes, which they could not sell. Idle construction workers and engineers were the first dominoes that lead to an unemployment rate which reached as high as 25 percent. The debacle of 1929 was followed by the 1930 Hawley-Smoot Tariff Act, a protectionist measure, which raised U.S. tariff rates almost 50 percent and effectively stifled world trade.

During the twenties, banks and brokers sold securities on a low (10 percent) margin; and on that fateful day when the Federal Reserve increased bank reserve requirements, millions of stockholders ended up owing more than they owned. The Glass-Steagall Act (1933) highly regulated banks and effectively put them out of the stock brokerage business. Now, sixty years later, under guise of deregulation, the banks are once again getting back into the brokerage business. Could a 1929 style economic collapse occur again?

The answer is "yes," but probably for entirely different reasons. Like all big busts, it will occur completely unheralded. For example, a collapse of the world banking system or the bombing of American cities could trigger a massive collapse. While the Federal Deposit Insurance Corporation (FDIC) insurance on bank deposits can cover problems here and there, it could never sustain a massive run on banks. The banking system is based on confidence, and no bank, however financially sound, could sustain a large run on its deposits. Increasing banks' mandated reserves for real and imagined losses and increasing capital requirements, when banks are weak, are just the ways to erode confidence. The moral to the story is, don't buy stocks on margin or buy equities with money you can't afford to lose. (In passing, let me note that the so-called meltdown on October 19, 1987 was basically technical rather than economic.)

Now a word about those old reliable investment "advisors," who consistently make more money dispensing advice than their constituents make following it. Most market forecasters are correct—only their timing is off. The question is not whether the market will go up or down, but *when?* The flamboyant Joseph Granville is an excellent technician, but when, 1982, he became very specific in urging his clients to sell out, he lost face with the investment community.

Investment letters also often score more winners than their subscribers, because they recommend a large number of equities. An investor usually owns between five and twenty individual securities at a time, whereas many advisors' letters recommend anywhere from ten to twenty equities a month. Market letters often proclaim their success by using favorable time parameters. For example, if the market has just jumped 20 percent, a letter will advertise its winners in that time parameter and ignore previous recommendations. A number of market letters only superficially recommend equities, providing a list of stocks expected to increase earnings next year or a list of stocks selling below $25.00. The well-known advisory letters usually discuss large companies with wide investment appeal and active trading. The smaller, lesser-known advisory letters often concentrate on small companies with a small float (number of shares available for trading) and high betas (strong leverage on the upside and little resistance on the downside). In choosing a market letter one should know the basic philosophy of its author. Most market letters recommend stocks as trading vehicles; very few are recommending equities for long-term holding, such as five, ten, or twenty-five years.

The analysts in large brokerage firms tend to specialize in certain designated industries. While they recommend what they believe to be the best buys in their appointed industry, the individual investor is usually interested in acquiring the best value, irrespective of industry. The best investment letters or advisory services are probably those which are long on information and short on recommendations.

The stock market closely parallels money-rate fluctuations and anticipates future business trends by about six or nine months. There are basically two types of market analysts:

- the technician who bases his or her decisions on the reading and interpretation of statistics and charts, and
- the fundamentalist who bases his or her decisions upon such factors as economic conditions, level of interest rates, earnings history, dividends, supply and demand, management, labor problems, and the product itself.

While technicians claim to be more objective, the interpretation of charts and other technical data is highly subjective.

Many macro economic factors affect the price of an individual equity. Some of these are the level of interest rates, money supply, commercial bank loans, general economic conditions for business as a whole and, for specific industries in particular, short sales ratio, margin requirements, and strength of the dollar. Interest rates are one of the more important macro economic factors. As interest rates rise, they tend to cause money to flow out of equities into more attractive, higher-yielding alternative investments such as bonds and bank certificates of deposit. This results in equities being valued at a lower price-earnings ratio and a lower nominal price. Conversely, a decrease in the level of interest rates causes money to flow out of bonds and other fixed income securities into equities, and thus results in a rise in the stock market. The direction of interest rates can be determined by observing the average maturity of money fund loans: When their average maturity lengthens, interest rates are headed lower; when their average maturity shortens, interest rates are headed higher.

When commercial bank loans rise rapidly, the Federal Reserve tends to tighten the money supply (sells securities). On the other hand, when commercial bank loans rapidly decrease, the Federal Reserve moves to increase the money supply (buys securities). These actions by the Federal Reserve tend to dampen an overheated market and to stimulate a depressed market. A high short-sale ratio in the market as a whole or in a particular equity creates buying power because, ultimately, the shorts "must cover" buying the stocks. The increase and decrease of margin requirements contribute, likewise, to the ebb and flow of the market. If the dollar is weak, currency translation expands the foreign earnings of American companies; conversely, if the dollar is strong, currency translation contracts the foreign profits of American companies.

Some micro economic factors affecting the price of individual equities are management, earnings, dividends, the ratio of current assets to current liabilities, the float, institutional ownership, and funded debt. The history of the earnings of a company determines whether a company is fast growth, moderate growth, slow growth, or cyclical. A high dividend yield on an equity usually indicates that it has little growth or is cyclical. Growing companies tend to have low dividend yields and comparatively higher price-earnings ratios. The ratio of current assets to liabilities is a major determinant of the financial soundness of a company. For small- and medium-sized companies (under one billion in assets) the ratio should be at least two to one. In large companies (over one billion in assets) the ratio should be at least one to one. The float is the number of shares that are actually available for public trading. A large float aids price stability; a small float tends to accentuate price movements both up and down. Institutional ownership can be both good and bad. Purchases of large blocks of a particular equity by institutions moves the price per share up. Conversely, if institutions sour on an issue, massive blocks of an equity suddenly become for sale, depressing it's market price. The debt of a company determines to what extent the profits of a company will be divided, first to the debtor and, secondly, to the common stockholder.

In analyzing individual equities, historical track record and value are paramount. The investor should study the earnings and price movements at least for the prior ten years, and should especially note the earnings and price performance during the previous recession. Note that traditional growth stocks such as those of drug and publishing sell at higher comparative price-earnings ratios than other usually cyclical equities such as paper, metals, and housing. While a history of long-term increase in earnings and dividends is a chronicle of the past, it is the single most reliable prelude to the future, particularly if earnings and dividends have increased during the previous recession. However, there must be sound reasons for growth to continue.

The hallmarks of a quality company are:

- a small amount of debt as a percentage of total capitalization,
- a good current ratio,
- a high return on equity,
- a high profit margin,
- a low break-even point, and
- a consistent pattern of growth.

While the quality of a company is not directly related to its price, there are many more lemons available at $10.00 per share than are available at $40.00 per share. While there are many excellent shares selling at low prices, the risks of selection are much greater as price per share decreases.

The quantitative analysis of stock market trends began early in the twentieth century through the writings of Charles H. Dow and William Peter Hamilton in their evolutionary development of the Dow Theory. The Dow Industrials in their present form are more of an index than an average. Quantitative analysis came to fruition in the writings of Benjamin Graham, with *Security Analysis* (1934) and *The Intelligent Investor* (1949). Today technical analysis of the market utilizes many indicators such as the cash holdings of mutual funds, odd-lot short-sale ratio, moving averages, high-low differential, volume momentum, and many others. What one tends to get from an analysis of indicators is so many positives and so many negatives. Also, the indicators do not carry equal weightings in various market cycles. Picking tops and bottoms, with any degree of consistency, has eluded the technical experts. This, however, is not too important, because the tops and bottoms of specific industries and equities rarely coincide with the indicators. For example, when the Dow Industrial Average hits bottom, many individual equities have already hit bottom and are on the way up; conversely, many individual equities are still topping out and have yet to hit bottom. In short, while many indicators such as the short-sale ratio and cash in brokers' accounts are valuable tools for interpreting the market, no one indicator or group of indicators rings a bell when the market hits a high or a low.

A number of regional banks are included in this book. Because for them analysis is quite different than for industrial companies, a discussion of them is imperative. Many regional banks afford excellent growth at relatively low price-earnings ratios. Because regional banks are often local in both operation and ownership, with a small equity float, the prices of their equities rarely will be bid up too high, expanding price-earnings ratios. In singling out individual growth banks, the individual must guard against so-called innovative bankers such as Parsons of Bank of the Commonwealth (now merged with Comerica). Basically, what Parsons did was perfectly legitimate but unsound. In the mid-sixties, when interest rates began to rise, Parsons locked up the bank's assets in long-term bonds. He thought that long-term interest rates would fall, but instead they continued to rise, depressing the value of the bank's assets, making the bank highly illiquid and ultimately insolvent.

A quality bank is distinguished by an aggressive marketing and a conservative credit policy. A consistent positive return on assets is the single most important indicator of a bank's performance, preferably at least 1 percent for a small bank and slightly less for a large bank. For example, a return on assets of 1 percent means that the bank earned $1.00 for each $100.00 of assets. It is also preferable that the bank have a high ratio of consumer assets to total liabilities. The deposits of individual consumers are considered more stable than those of businesses or large depositors, who will flee more quickly for higher rates. The key financial figures to look for in a bank's statement are, first, the ratio of capital to assets. The Federal Government requires 7 percent, but the higher the better. Second in importance is the ratio of delinquent loans to assets, preferably below 2 percent, but the lower the better. A potentially excellent bank stock is one with a good price-earnings ratio, selling at or below book value with a consistent above average-return on assets. *The Bank Quarterly Rating & Analysis,* published by Sheshunoff Information Services, 505 Barton Springs Road, Austin, TX 78711, represents a good summary of statistical information on the nation's banking companies.

Property and casualty insurance companies, likewise, do not lend themselves to easy analysis. Not many property and casualty companies qualify as growth equities, because their earnings are subject to the fluctuations of the underwriting cycle. Long-term success can be obtained by restricting investment to those companies, which consistently demonstrate loss and expense ratios that are comparatively lower than their competitors. Best's *Property & Casualty Insurance* and Best's *Life Insurance* directories are the bibles of the insurance industry and can be very helpful in evaluating choices in this area.

INTELLIGENT INVESTING

There are no universal rules, systems or formulae for investment success. Equity market movement is a composite of many diverse internal and external forces. Rather than trying to forecast the highs and lows in the market, it is more important to distinguish values among individual equities. Investment management consists of three elements:

- learning about individual issues,
- relating values to the market, and
- recognizing one's own goals and limitations.

Moreover, it is important to remember no one is right all the time.

The investor must be aware that both the market and groups within the market move in cycles. Every cycle has a beginning and an end. It is when the public becomes convinced of the evolutionary character of a cycle that it collapses. Witness the boom in energy issues in the late seventies and their subsequent collapse in the early eighties. Every decade has at least one triumph and one washout. Clearly there are times when security prices are too high and, conversely, times when they are too low. The investor should wait for the bargain, even if the wait is several years.

Growth stocks

A growth stock should have a proven record of earnings, be a well-seasoned equity, and operate in an industry of above-average potential. The investor should focus on long-term investments in companies where management's performance indicates that they will be worth substantially more in five or ten years. Robert Kirby, chairman of Capital Guardian Trust, stated in the "Money Manager" discussion in the *Wall Street Transcript* (June 4, 1984) that, "People get rich not by anticipating interim market swings, but by investing in the right companies and staying there. You rarely see a large fortune that arose out of trading. Fortunes come from a few holdings in the right companies held over a long period of time. We think selection is 95 percent of successful investing and market timing is 5 percent."

The more an investor concentrates on short-term expectations, the more likely he will insulate himself from long-term appreciation. The ideal growth stock is a very successful company with over one hundred million but under one billion in assets, and with a long history of consecutive increases in earnings and dividends. Companies such as John H. Harland, Dun & Bradstreet, and Rubbermaid come to mind.

The problem with most so-called emerging growth stocks is that most of them never emerge. Most of them are characterized by the greater fool theory: one buys them with the expectation that a greater fool will take them off his hands at a higher price. Emerging growth stocks are often mere concepts, un-

19

derpinned with negligible assets, marginal earnings, and selling at prices that discount the future. To say that a stock has compounded earnings 35 percent annually for the past five years, when earnings have gone from 5¢ to 22¢, doesn't signify much. Therefore, the claims for substantial percentage earnings gains in emerging growth stocks, while they may be accurate, are not very meaningful. The fledgling investor, who can least afford to lose money, is usually the market for these issues.

The best opportunities in growth stocks arise when the market is temporarily depressed. Fear and greed are the greatest obstacles to market success. While one should not put all his eggs in one basket, it is also a mistake to put them in too many baskets. Diversification is good up to a point. While wide diversification protects the investor against staggering losses, it also insulates him from dramatic gains. Try to invest when you believe the long-term market is turning upward. Search for stocks that are about to have explosive earnings growth, but whose prices have not yet discounted it. Investigate and then invest—do not do as so many do, invest and then investigate. Condition your emotions to make mistakes and take losses. Many investors cling to the falling stock as an inexperienced parachute jumper clings to a falling airplane.

It is often stated that America's enormous industrial complex was built with risk dollars. While the statement is true, it is certainly not a justification for risk-taking when the risk-reward ratio is not realistic. Trying to find the next superstock should be reserved for the investor with extensive market experience, and even then it is an extremely difficult task.

Many brokerage firms and mutual funds hire electronic engineers to evaluate high-tech firms; but while the engineers are usually long on technical expertise, they are more often short on market expertise.

Unfortunately, many neophyte investors begin their investment career trying to pick the next Microsoft. This inevitably leads to unmitigated investment disaster. An intelligent approach to picking the next superstock would be to review securities selected by analysts, who specialize in this pursuit. Investors seeking maximum long-term capital appreciation might take a look at ALLTEL Corporation, Diagnostic Products Corporation, First Financial Management Corporation, and Thermo Electron Corporation, all highlighted in this book.

Predicting the future direction of the market is fraught with danger. There are dozens, even hundreds of financial variables that fluctuate daily and have an influence on the market direction. There is a tendency for the market to overreach itself, going too high on the upside and too low on the downside. The longer a bull market extends, the more it discounts the possibility of picking up sound values and ultimate capital gains. Many investors buy too early and sell to late.

Traditionally, there is a three-point spread between interest rates and inflation. When there is a divergence, either one or the other will eventually give way. When interest rates are high and inflation is low, it means that inflationary expectation is high. When interest rates rise, investors capitalize earnings at a lower multiple; conversely, when interest rates fall, investors capitalize earnings at a higher multiple. What usually aborts a recovery is excess build-up in inventory and capital spending.

A rising (bull) market raises all ships; conversely, a falling (bear) market lowers all ships. Every bull market creates a raft of new so-called market experts but only a handful of them, such as John Marks Templeton, Warren Buffett, Peter Lynch, the late T. Rowe Price, and the late Ralph Coleman, withstand the test of time. When such men retire or pass on, they are usually succeeded by technocrats with accounting, computer, and assorted MBA degrees. These successors rarely can continue in the footsteps of their mentors, many of whom had little or no formal business education.

No two bull or bear markets are exactly alike. The various indicators in a bull market top or a bear market bottom yield different and diverse weightings in the historical pattern of market movements. This is the principle reason why it is almost impossible to objectively pinpoint exact market tops and bottoms. Tops and bottoms are a composite of numerous indicators, evidencing a variety of quantitative strengths and weaknesses at market turns. Experienced investors can reasonably identify market highs and lows, when such a composite of indicators are in evidence. Investing in growth stocks, in a down market, when price-earnings ratios are low, should provide a minimum of portfolio turnover.

The market is basically manic-depressive, fluctuating between moods of euphoria and gloom. A market high is generally discernible when the number of Big Board stocks hitting new highs has dried up, price-earnings ratios by historical standards are high, institutional cash reserves (including those of mutual funds) are low, Big Board short-interest ratio is low, market sentiment is euphoric with economists predicting the millennium has arrived, and a surging number of new issues and concept stocks are coming to market, many being underwritten by brokerage firms with repeated regulatory problems.

The characteristics of a bear-market low are discernible when the market is hitting new lows, yet the number of new lows on the Big Board has dried up, the market fails to yield much on the downside to gloomy economic news; institutional cash reserves (including those of mutual funds) are surging; the Big Board short-interest ratio is high; negative sentiment is extremely high; and there is a dearth of new issue and concept stocks.

While individual stocks should be bought on the basis of track record and value rather than chart formations, certain technical indicators are excellent for following market trends. When the price-earnings ratio for the Dow Jones Industrials is below 9, the market is on the low side; and when it is above 19, it is getting high. At market highs, the Dow Industrials tend to have a dividend yield below 3.2 percent; and at market lows a dividend yield of 5 percent or above. Over the years the market has generally seen its highs when the Dow Industrials have sold above 1.9 times book value, and its lows when the same average has sold at 1.2 times book value. The cash position of mutual funds usually hovers around 3 percent to 4 percent at market tops and around 9 percent to 10 percent at market bottoms. The Big Board short-sales ratio is a major technical factor: when it reaches 8.5 percent of all transactions on the Big Board, it is reasonably safe to buy, and when it falls below 6.5 percent the market is ready for a sale. A high short-interest ratio means that eventually the shorts will have to cover, thus creating buying power. The cash position of brokerage accounts tends to rise rapidly toward the termination of a bear market.

Much of the selling on the downside of a market is caused not only by disillusionment but also by the technical factor of margin calls, which adds to the cascade. The value of institutional cash holdings as a predictor of future market moves has been blunted by the fact that most large institutional investors now tend to convert cash to money-market funds and other short-term instruments. The advent of options trading and extensive arbitrage have also diminished the reliability of the short-interest indicator. The problem with many market indicators is that there is often a time lag between when they occur and when they are published. While statistics don't lie, inferences drawn from them often do. In short, it is much easier to ferret out undervalued equities than it is to predict future market trends.

Mutual funds

The advantage of mutual funds are said to be diversification of risk, low start-up costs, professional management, freedom from bookkeeping, little emotional involvement, automatic reinvestment of dividends, and readily available information on fund records. Yet aside from a few outstanding funds such as the Templeton Growth Fund and the Magellan Fund, most funds have a lackluster long-term performance.

The rating of a fund's performance can vary widely depending upon the time periods used. Any comparative rating of a fund's performance is influenced by the time frame used. For example, the comparative rating of funds on an annual, five-year, or ten-year span will yield quite divergent results.

A number of mutual funds are specialized and will perform in accordance with their specialty. For example, the performance of a fund which specializes in medical equities or life insurance issues will parallel the performance of those industries. While having a large family of funds will enhance a management's chance for a winner, it will be a negative in management's overall performance, because mass phenomena tend toward stability, or average performance.

Mutual funds have a number of inbuilt problems. Their funds tend to be bought in small amounts by the masses of people (the public). These small investors usually buy funds in good times, when they are flush with money, and cash them in during a recession, when they need cash. The result is that mutual funds must purchase shares on a surging market and sell them on a falling market. A way to partially negate this problem is to invest in a fund which requires an initial high down payment.

Another problem is that in both mutual fund and institutional investing, safety is often sacrificed on the high altar of performance. Money moves toward performance; so many fund managers, while they may be aware of market euphoria, cannot afford to lose that final 1 percent or 2 percent rise, and get caught in the downturn.

Also, fund managers are often motivated to buy and sell stocks for a variety of reasons other than the prospects for an individual company. They might want to dress up the portfolio at the end of a quarter by selling a loser and buying a winner. They might want to increase or decrease capital gains distributions, or they might be motivated to sell a stock because an executive officer of a company refused to take phone calls or ignored their visit. It is also very difficult for a fund manager to stick with an undervalued stock that is not moving. In short, professional investment managers are often caught between the chasm of sound investment practices and a greedy, get-rich-quick constituency.

UNDERSTANDING THE FINANCIAL LISTINGS IN A NEWSPAPER

The accompanying chart shows a New York Stock Exchange Listing from *The Wall Street Journal* on August 3, 1993.

Note that the companies are listed alphabetically. All stock prices are quoted in dollars and multiples of one-eighth of a dollar (12½¢). Find AFLAC

Quotations as of 5 p.m. Eastern Time

Monday, August 2, 1993

	52 Weeks Hi	Lo	Stock	Sym	Div	Yld %	PE	Vol 100s	Hi	Lo	Close	Net Chg
				-A-A-A-								
s	32⅛	23	AFLAC	AFL	.40	1.3	15	629	29⅞	29½	29⅞	+ ¼
	29⅜	**13¾**	**AL Labs A**	**BMD**	**.18**	**1.1**	**22**	**6738**	**16**	**15⅛**	**15¾**	**+1⅛**
	65⅞	52¾	AMP	AMP	1.60	2.5	23	1992	64⅞	63⅞	64¾	+ ¾
	72⅞	54⅜	AMR	AMR		...	dd	3059	66⅜	65	65	− ½

Incorporated (AFLAC), which is the first company profiled in this book. The small "s" to the extreme left of AFLAC indicates that AFLAC has paid a stock dividend at some time during the past 52 weeks. To the left of AFLAC, under the columns "Hi" and "Lo," are two share prices. The number on the left, $32\frac{1}{8}$, represents the high per share price for AFLAC during the past 52 weeks, while the number on the right, 23, represents the low per share price for AFLAC during the past 52 weeks.

Immediately to the right of AFLAC is the symbol AFL. This is the symbol under which AFLAC shares trade on the New York Stock Exchange.

To the right of AFL, under the column "Div" is .40, which means that AFLAC currently pays a dividend of 40¢ per share on its common stock per year.

To the right of the dividend column is the "Yld" column, which indicates 1.3. This means that, based on the present per share price of AFLAC ($29\frac{7}{8}$) and a dividend of 40¢, the shareholder receives a cash return of 1.3 percent on his investment in AFLAC.

To the right of the "Yld" column is a column headed "PE," which indicates the number 15. This is the price-earnings ratio, a popular yardstick for evaluating market prices. It is derived by dividing the current price per share by the earnings per share for the past 52 weeks. Earnings-per-share figures are not available in daily *Wall Street Journal* listings, but are available in *Barron's Weekly* and a number of Standard & Poor's and Moody's publications. Growth stocks traditionally have higher price earnings per share than income stocks.

The next column to the right is headed "Vol 100s" and furnishes the volume, or total number of shares (in hundreds), traded the previous day. In AFLAC's case, the 629 means that 629,000 shares were traded the previous day.

The next three columns headed "Hi," "Lo," and "Close" report the prices for the previous day's trading. In the AFLAC transactions some investors paid a high of $29\frac{7}{8}$ per share, a low of $29\frac{1}{2}$ per share, and the last or closing sale of $29\frac{7}{8}$ per share. Thus, AFLAC closed at its high for the day.

The last column headed "Net Chg" represents the net change in price from the closing price of the preceding day. In this case the price per share of AFLAC increased $\frac{1}{4}$ (25¢) from the preceding day.

KEY TO STATISTICAL DATA ON COMPANY PROFILES

Assets and liabilities

Assets represent the total amount of property belonging to a corporation, whereas liabilities represents the total amount of indebtedness or obligations of a corporation. Total assets consist of both current and long-term assets; likewise, total liabilities consist of both current and long-term liabilities.

Current assets are quick assets such as cash, raw materials, inventory, accounts receivable, and other items, which can be readily turned into cash, as opposed to long-term assets such as plant, equipment, and other assets, which cannot readily be turned into cash.

Current liabilities represent short-term indebtedness such as accounts payable, expenses, taxes payable, and other debts owed within a year, as opposed to long-term debt, bonding issues, preferred stock, and common stock.

The total assets of a company are indicative not only the total value of a corporation but also the size of a corporation. A corporation with over $1 billion in total assets is a large corporation. A corporation with total assets between $100 million and $1 billion is medium-sized. A corporation with under $100 million in total assets is considered small.

Current ratio

The current ratio is the mathematical ratio of current assets to current liabilities. It strikes the balance between what a corporation owns and owes on a short-term basis. It determines the credit risk of a corporation. It is determined by dividing current assets by current liabilities. For example, if a corporation has $150 million in current assets and $100 million in current liabilities, it has a current ratio of 1.5. The higher the ratio, the stronger the corporation is financially. If a current ratio is below 1.00, the corporation has a negative net worth.

Common shares outstanding

Shares of common stock represent that portion of a corporation's capitalization which is not preferred, such as debt, bonding issues, and preferred stock. In the default of a corporation, the common stockholders receive payment only after the indebtedness of all senior or preferred obligations have been met.

Revenues

Revenues represent the income or cash receipts of a company.

Net income

Net income is synonymous with net earnings. It is that amount which may be applied to surplus and dividends after deducting the cost of goods sold, including all overhead, administrative, and selling expenses.

Earnings per share

The per share earnings are calculated by dividing net income by the total number of common shares outstanding.

Dividends

The common stock dividend is that amount of per share earnings paid to the stockholder. The remaining goes into the coffers of the corporation for further expansion and investment.

A stock dividend is payable in shares of stock to the common stockholder. For example, a 10 percent stock dividend means that a common shareholder will receive ten additional shares of common stock for each one hundred shares held. Since stock dividends merely subdivide the total pie, they are nontaxable.

Stock dividends are paid usually by rapidly growing companies, which wish to preserve capital for expansion.

Note

It is important to note that all per share earnings, dividends, and yearly Hi and Lo prices have been adjusted to reflect stock splits and dividends.

Abbott Laborato⟩

One Abbott Park Road
Abbott Park, Illinois 60064-3500
Tel. (708) 937-6100
Listed: NYSE
Investor contact: V.P. Investor Relations, Ellen M. Walvᴏ
Ticker symbol: ABT
S&P rating: A+

From humble beginnings in the home laboratory of Dr. Wallace G. Abbott in 1888, Abbott laboratories has grown into one of American's largest health care companies. "The company's principal business is the discovery, development, manufacture

and sale of a broad and diversified line of health care products and services. With sales in 130 countries worldwide, Abbott benefits from a global business-mix with positions across a continuum of health care—from prevention to diagnosis, and acute care to therapy.

"Pharmaceutical and nutritional products represented 51 percent of the company's worldwide sales in 1992. This segment includes a broad line of adult and pediatric pharmaceuticals and nutritionals. These products are sold primarily on the prescription or recommendation of physicians and other health care professionals. The segment also includes agricultural and chemical products, bulk pharmaceuticals, and consumer products.

"The company's key pharmaceutical products include clarithromycin (a broad-spectrum antibiotic), which is marketed in the United States as Biaxin; and other pharmaceutical products such as Hytrin (a once-a-day alpha blocker), Depakote (an anti-convulsant agent), and Abbokinase (a clot dissolving drug).

"The primary role of Abbott's chemical business is to supply bulk pharmaceuticals to internal divisions and external customers. Abbott is the world's leading producer of biorational, or environmentally compatible, insecticides and plant-growth regulators.

"Abbott's nutritional business includes total and supplemental nutritional products for infants, children, and adults.

"Hospital and laboratory products represented 49 percent of Abbott's worldwide sales in 1992. Products in this segment include intravenous and irrigation fluids, and equipment for administration; drugs and drug delivery sys-

anesthetics; critical care and other medical specialty products for hospitals, and alternate-care sites; and diagnostic systems for blood banks, hospitals, commercial laboratories, and alternate-care testing sites.

"Abbott continues to hold a leadership position in the global market for anesthetics. Abbott recently began marketing the leading inhalation anesthetics isoflurane and enflurane in the United States."

In 1992, pharmaceutical and nutritional products accounted for 51.3 percent of revenues and 55.6 percent of operating profits; hospital and laboratory products accounted for 48.7 percent of revenues and 44.4 percent of operating profits.

During 1993, Abbott attained its twenty-second consecutive year of increased sales and earnings. Abbott has paid consecutive cash dividends since 1926. Institutions control about 50 percent of the outstanding shares. Abbott paid a 100 percent stock dividend in 1981, a 100 percent stock dividend in 1986, a 100 percent stock dividend in 1990, and another 100 percent stock dividend in 1992.

Total assets: $7.7 billion
Current ratio: 1.1
Common shares outstanding: 821.1 million

	1984	1985	1986	1987	1988	1989	1990	1991	1992	1993
Revenues (Mil.)	3,104	3,360	3,808	4,388	4,937	5,380	6,159	6,877	7,852	8,408
Net Income (Mil.)	403	465	541	633	752	860	966	1,089	1,239	1,399
Earnings per share	.42	.48	.58	.69	.83	.96	1.11	1.27	1.47	1.69
Dividends per share	.15	.18	.21	.25	.30	.35	.42	.50	.60	.66
Prices Hi	6.1	9.0	13.8	16.8	13.1	17.6	23.1	34.8	34.1	30.9
Lo	4.6	5.0	7.9	10.0	10.8	11.5	15.6	19.6	26.1	22.6

AFLAC Incorporated
1932 Wynnton Road
Columbus, Georgia 31999
Tel. (706) 323-3431
Listed: NYSE
Investor relations: Vice Pres. Kenneth S. Janke, Jr.
Ticker symbol: AFT
S&P rating: A

As profiled in its 1993 Annual Report, "AFLAC Incorporated is a Georgia-based holding company whose primary subsidiary is American Family Life Assurance Company of Columbus (AFLAC), the world's leading supplemental health insurance. AFLAC sells its specialty insurance products in six countries, with major markets in the United States and Japan. AFLAC also owns seven network-affiliated television stations.

AFLAC Incorporated

"Thirty-five million policyholders worldwide depend on AFLAC for their supplemental health insurance needs, and AFLAC takes its commitment to honor their trust very seriously. Our fast, fair processing of claims is perhaps the best example of our commitment to policyholders. In 1992 alone, the company paid approximately $1.3 billion in claims worldwide.

"AFLAC was primarily a one-product company selling cancer expense insurance until the mid-1980's, when we broadened our product line to meet the expanding needs of American consumers. Today, AFLAC is a true supplemental health insurer offering policies to meet the needs of customers of all ages and income levels. Cancer insurance remains our primary product, and we still dominate that market. However, we now also provide accident and disability, hospital indemnity, Medicare supplement, intensive care, long-term care, and home health care policies for our customers. These and other supplemental health products accounted for 62 percent of annualized new premium sales in 1993.

"AFLAC Japan, a branch of AFLAC and the principal contributor to the company's earnings, continues to be one of the greatest success stories among American-based companies conducting business in Japan. By adopting the Japanese style of business and offering products that are attractive to Japanese consumers, AFLAC Japan has become the only foreign life insurance company that ranks among the top five of the thirty life insurance companies in Japan in terms of policies in force.

"AFLAC U.S. has shown considerable improvement in its business performance during the last several years. AFLAC U.S. has worked to develop a wide range of supplemental health insurance products that meet the needs of today's consumers. The marketing knowledge and management expertise we have gained through our U.S. business experience provides a bank of information which we share with our insurance operations around the world.

"The company's other operations consist of seven network-affiliated television stations located in mid-size U.S. markets and insurance operations in four foreign countries (other than Japan), operated as branches and subsidiaries."

29

AFLAC has paid consecutive cash dividends since 1975. Institutions control about 45 percent of the outstanding common shares. AFLAC paid a 20 percent stock dividend in 1983, a 10 percent stock dividend in 1984, a 50 percent stock dividend in 1985, a 33-1/3 percent stock dividend in 1986, a 100 percent stock dividend in 1987, and a 25 percent stock dividend in 1993.

Total assets: $15.4 billion
Common shares outstanding: 103.5 million

	1984	1985	1986	1987	1988	1989	1990	1991	1992	1993
Revenues (Mil.)	824	954	1,431	1,893	2,328	2,438	2,678	3,283	3,986	5,001
Net Income (Mil.)	55	55	101	102	109	81	117	149	183	244
Earnings per share	.44	.54	1.00	1.02	1.08	.80	1.15	1.46	1.79	2.32
Dividends per share	.11	.14	.17	.18	.20	.23	.26	.30	.34	.39
Prices Hi	5.0	9.4	15.0	14.8	13.6	18.0	15.4	24.9	27.9	34.0
Lo	2.7	4.6	8.3	7.9	9.2	10.7	9.7	14.3	19.3	24.8

Albertson's, Inc.
250 Parkcenter Boulevard (P.O. Box 20)
Boise, Idaho 83726
Tel. (208) 385-6200
Listed: NYSE
Investor contact: Vice Pres. & Treasurer, David I. Connolly
Ticker symbol: ABS
S&P rating: A+

As profiled in its 1993 Annual Report, "Albertson's, Inc. is the fourth largest retail food-drug chain in the United States. The company operates 676 stores located in 19 western, midwestern and southern states. Retail operations are supported by eleven company-operated distribution centers. Albertson's is headquartered in Boise, Idaho, and employs 75,000 people.

"We believe the ideal store size ranges from 35,000 to 60,000 square feet. These stores provide one-stop shopping convenience and can couple the basics–grocery, general merchandise, meat, and produce–with quality service departments like pharmacy, video rental, floral, bakery, service delicatessen, and service seafood and meat.

"Combination stores carry all the merchandise offered by a full-line super drugstore and supermarket. They offer prescription drugs, cosmetics, and non-foods in addition to specialty service departments. We have 234 of these stores, ranging in size from 48,000 to 67,000 square feet.

"Superstores, smaller versions of the combination store, carry few non-food items. These 272 stores require less retail size and are sized from 35,000 to 48,000 square feet.

"Conventional stores are full-line supermarkets under 35,000 square feet. They carry groceries, fresh meat, produce, dairy products, and limited nonfood lines. Some also have an in-store bakery and a service delicatessen. Many of our 106 conventional stores will be expanded or replaced with superstores.

"Warehouse stores offer limited service but significant savings to customers who like to buy in quantity. We currently operate 44 of them.

"In April 1992, we purchased seventy-four Jewel Osco combination food-drug stores from American Stores Company. This important acquisition included stores in Texas, Oklahoma, Florida, and Arkansas, as well as a general merchandise warehouse in Ponca City, Oklahoma, and related assets, including potential store locations.

"Automated systems fully integrate data collection and analysis for every aspect of our operation. During 1992, we installed our new Direct Store Delivery (DSD) system in 185 stores to automate the receiving process for items delivered directly to vendors. DSD uses a unique hand-held computer that "scans" items as they are delivered and transmits data to an in-store processor. The computer calculates total payment based on the price previously agreed upon between Albertson's and the vendor, and then electronically sends a receiving document to the corporate office for payment."

Albertson's has increased revenues and earnings for 24 consecutive years and has increased dividends for 23 consecutive years. It has paid consecutive cash dividends since 1960. Institutions control about 35 percent of the outstanding common shares. Albertson's paid a 100 percent stock dividend in 1980, a 100 percent stock dividend in 1983, a 100 percent stock dividend in 1987, a 100 percent stock dividend in 1990, and a 100 percent stock dividend in 1993.

> Total assets: $3.3 billion
> Current ratio: 1.2
> Common shares outstanding: 253.4 million

	1984	1985	1986	1987	1988	1989	1990	1991	1992	1993
Revenues (Mil.)	4,297	4,736	5,060	5,380	5,869	6,773	7,423	8,219	8,680	10,174
Net Income (Mil.)	70	80	85	100	125	163	197	234	258	269
Earnings per share	.27	.31	.33	.38	.47	.61	.74	.88	.97	1.02
Dividends per share	.075	.085	.095	.11	.12	.14	.20	.24	.28	.32
Prices Hi	3.7	4.2	6.2	8.5	9.7	15.1	18.9	25.7	26.7	29.6
Lo	2.9	3.3	3.4	5.1	6.0	9.2	12.2	16.3	18.4	23.4

ALLTEL Corporation

One Allied Drive
Little Rock, Arkansas 72202
Tel. (501) 661-8000
Listed: NYSE
Investor contact: Vice President Corporation Communication,
Ronald D. Payne
Ticker symbol: AT
S&P rating: A

ALLTEL
Corporation

As profiled in its 1993 Annual Report, "ALLTEL Corporation is a leading telecommunications and information services company. In addition to providing local telephone service, ALLTEL subsidiaries provide cellular telephone service and communications products.

"ALLTEL provides local telephone service to 1.6 million customers in twenty-two states. With the majority of its service areas located in rural or suburban markets, ALLTEL not only enjoys steady line growth, but is less vulnerable to competitive pressures. ALLTEL's customer base increased 4 percent in 1992. That increase was due to solid internal growth. In addition, approximately 42,000 lines came from the company's acquisition of SLT Communications of Sugar Land, Texas.

"ALLTEL serves more than 276,000 cellular telephone customers. The company's markets include 7.7 million pops–an industry term for one gauge of potential customers–in 19 states. With cellular operating income and customers nearly doubling each year, Cellular Operations is becoming an increasingly larger factor in the Company's earnings growth.

"The company participates in the fast-growing information services area through its Systematics and Computer Power, Inc. (CPI) subsidiaries. Systematics is a leading provider of information processing management, software, and services to the financial, telecommunications and health care industries. CPI is the nation's largest provider of software and processing services to the mortgage industry.

"ALLTEL's product distribution area consists of ALLTEL Supply, a provider of communications and data products, and HWC Distribution Corp., the nation's largest master distributor of specialty wire and cable products selling exclusively to electrical distributors.

"ALLTEL's Mobile provides cellular mobile telephone service in various U.S. markets.

"ALLTEL Mobile also operates wide-area, computer-driven paging networks as a complementary service to cellular telephones.

"ALLTEL owns a 13.4 percent interest in LDDS Communications, Inc., a publicly-held company, which is one of the largest regional long-distance companies in the United States, and provides long-distance services to customers located in 41 states."

During 1992, revenues and operating income were apportioned as follows: telephone 45.3 percent of revenues and 68.8 percent of income, information services 27.7 percent of revenues and 20.6 percent of income, product distribution 18 percent of revenues and 4 percent of income, cellular 6 percent of revenues and 4.6 percent of income and finally other operations 3 percent of revenues and 2 percent of income.

ALLTEL has paid consecutive cash dividends since 1961. It paid a 6 percent stock dividend in 1983, a 50 percent stock dividend in 1987, and a 100 percent stock dividend in 1993.

Total assets: $4.3 billion
Current ratio: 1.3
Common shares outstanding: 187.5 million

	1984	1985	1986	1987	1988	1989	1990	1991	1992	1993
Revenues (Mil.)	640	672	697	1,244	1,362	1,557	1,691	1,884	2,082	2,342
Net Income (Mil.)	63	70	56	134	146	179	200	199	229	262
Earnings per share	.59	.67	.70	.77	.84	1.01	1.09	1.10	1.22	1.39
Dividends per share	.41	.42	.44	.47	.52	.59	.66	.71	.76	.82
Prices Hi	5.7	6.7	10.0	11.4	12.6	21.0	19.6	21.7	25.0	31.3
Lo	4.5	5.3	6.5	7.7	8.6	11.7	12.4	15.9	17.4	22.9

American Business Products, Inc.

2100 River Edge Parkway, Suite 1200
P.O. Box 105684
Atlanta, Georgia 30329
Tel. (404) 953-8300
Listed: NYSE
Investor contact: President, Thomas R. Carmody
Ticker symbol: ABP
S&P rating: A-

American Business Products, Inc.

As profiled in its 1993 Annual Report, "American Business Products, Inc. manufactures and markets business forms, envelope products, and other supplies for business and industry; manufactures and distributes hardcover and softcover books for the publishing industry; and produces and markets extrusion coating and laminating of papers, films, and nonwoven fabrics for use in medical, industrial, and consumer packaging of products. The company has forty-one production facilities located throughout the continental United States and Hawaii. Products are marketed and distributed in all fifty states through ABP's operating companies, principally by a combined direct sales force of approximately 700 people. A joint venture company based in Germany, with facilities in four countries, produces and distributes envelope products in Europe.

"Curtis 1000 Inc. supplies a wide array of products for businesses, and these include four-color brochures, matching letterheads and envelopes, labels for every business need, and specialty envelopes by Tyvek.

"Forms produced by Vanier Business Forms & Services are the lifeblood of business office functions requiring such items as continuous forms for accounting, the multipart continuous mailer, and single-sheet laser forms.

"A leader in high-quality books for publishers, BookCrafters prints, binds, and distributes popular hardcover books as well as a variety of products from spiral-bound cookbooks to softcover books in short and medium runs.

"Protective jackets for critical x-ray documents are produced by American Fiber-Velope Mfg. Co. for the medical profession. Other AFV products include color-coded medical filing systems, Tyvek envelopes and computer diskette jackets, and sturdy Kraft envelopes.

"Jen-Coat, Inc.'s extrusion coating products provide the sanitary disposable gown and cap for the surgeon, pressure-release line for such items as postage stamps, and packaging for consumer products such as sugar substitutes.

"A major expansion of its product line and entry into Poland marked the progress of Curtis 1000 Europe GmbH in 1992. The company, based in Andernach, Germany, is the leading producer and distributor of Tyvek envelopes in Europe, but broadened its product line to include all types of envelopes by acquiring Neuwieder Couvert Fabrik of Neuwied, Germany."

During 1992, revenues and operating profits were apportioned as follows: business supplies and printing 73.6 percent of revenues and 49.9 percent of profits, book manufacturing 9.4 percent of revenues and 18.3 percent of profits, and extrusion coating and laminating 17 percent of revenues and 31.8 percent of profits.

1993 marked the fifty-fifth consecutive year of increased sales and the thirty-sixth consecutive year of increased dividends. The Curtis family controls about 28 percent, and institutions about 25 percent, of the outstanding common shares. American Business Products paid a 50 percent stock dividend in 1983, a 25 percent stock dividend in 1989, and a 50 percent stock dividend in 1991.

Total assets: $382.2 million
Current ratio: 2.6
Common shares outstanding: 10.7 million

	1984	1985	1986	1987	1988	1989	1990	1991	1992	1993
Revenues (Mil.)	275	296	312	326	358	387	399	447	463	486
Net Income (Mil.)	11	12	11	11	13	14	14	16	30	17
Earnings per share	1.01	1.16	1.05	1.04	1.21	1.27	1.33	1.55	1.83	1.56
Dividends per share	.30	.34	.41	.43	.47	.52	.59	.63	.70	.75
Prices Hi	12.6	18.2	19.6	16.8	14.2	18.0	15.9	28.0	31.3	31.0
Lo	9.5	10.9	12.4	8.2	9.6	13.0	12.1	12.5	22.8	21.1

American Home Products Corporation

685 Third Avenue
New York, New York 10017-4085
Tel. (212) 878-5000
Listed: NYSE
Investor contact: Vice Pres.-Finance, John R. Considine
Ticker symbol: AHP
S&P rating: A+

As profiled in its 1992 Annual Report, "American Home Products Corporation makes a significant contribution to health care worldwide as a leader in researching, developing, manufacturing, and marketing products that meet important health needs.

"Our prescription drugs, nutritionals, over-the-counter medications, and medical devices, supplies, and instrumentation benefit millions of people. We also produce and market well-known quality food brands in the United States and Canada.

"Wyeth-Ayerst Laboratories currently is the number-one prescription drug company in the United States. Wyeth-Ayerst is relatively less dependent on single products than many other pharmaceutical companies. It is the leader in female health care, having the world's largest-selling hormonal contraceptive franchise (Norplant System, Triphasil, Lo/Ovral, and Nordette) in addition to the leading estrogen, Premarin, in the United States. Wyeth-Ayerst also has a significant presence in anti-inflammatories (Lodine, Lodine SR, and Orudis), cardiovascular therapies (Cordarone Injection, Quinidex Extentabs, Inderal LA, Verelan, ISMO, and Tenex), psychotropic drugs (Ativan and Effexor), anti-infectives (Maxaquin), vaccines, immunomodulators, and infant nutritionals (Nursoy).

"Whitehall Laboratories and A.H. Robbins continued to strengthen their leadership in some of the largest consumer health care categories such as analgesics and cough/cold/allergy remedies. Their top-selling brands include Advil, Anacin, Dristan, Robitussin, and Dimetapp.

"Sherwood Medical Company has made headway in developing strong franchises in growing specialty fields, such as enteral feeding and wound care dressings. Corometrics Medical Systems continues to be the leader in the U.S.

obstetrical monitoring and diagnostic ultrasound markets, and Quinton Instrument Company is a leader in high-technology medical and fitness products.

"Fort Dodge Laboratories is in the forefront of veterinary research and development, and has an expanding number of leading pharmaceuticals and biologicals. In 1992, our new Lyme disease vaccine, LymeVax, became the single-largest, dollar-volume, canine biological in the history of the company.

"The leadership of American Home Products' Chef Boyardee prepared pasta line and its pioneering expertise in shelf-stable microwave foods enabled us to capitalize on the important trend toward convenience foods. American Home Foods made a strong initial entry into the fast-growing Mexican food category by acquiring Ro Tel, the leading brand of canned tomatoes and green chilies in its segment.

"On January 16, 1992, American Home Products acquired a majority interest in Genetics Institute, Inc., a biopharmaceutical company engaged in the discovery, development, and licensing of therapeutic products, principally in the hematologic, oncologic, and bone growth areas."

During 1992, revenues and operating income were apportioned as follows: health care products 89 percent of revenues and 92.3 percent of income, and food products 11 percent of revenues and 7.7 percent of income.

Geographically, the United States provided 68.4 percent of revenues and 72.3 percent of operating income, Canada and Latin American 9.6 percent of revenues and 9.2 percent of income, Europe and Africa 15.8 percent of revenue and 13.5 percent of income, and Asia and Australia 6.2 percent of revenue and 5 percent of income.

American Home Products has paid consecutive cash dividends since 1919 and has increased cash dividends for forty-one consecutive years. Institutions control about 65 percent of the outstanding common shares. American Home Products split two-for-one effective April 19, 1990.

Total assets: $7.7 billion
Current ratio: 3.0
Common shares outstanding: 310.1 million

	1984	1985	1986	1987	1988	1989	1990	1991	1992	1993
Revenues (Mil.)	5,089	5,385	5,684	5,850	6,401	6,747	6,775	7,079	7,874	8,305
Net Income (Mil.)	695	818	866	928	995	1,102	1,231	1,375	1,461	1,469
Earnings per share	2.14	2.54	2.73	2.98	3.22	3.54	3.92	4.36	4.65	4.73
Dividends per share	1.32	1.45	1.55	1.67	1.80	1.95	2.15	2.38	2.66	2.86
Prices Hi	27.9	33.4	47.4	48.4	42.1	54.6	54.9	86.3	84.3	69.0
Lo	23.4	25.1	30.6	31.0	35.2	40.1	44.0	47.1	62.3	55.5

American International Group, Inc.

70 Pine Street
New York, New York 10270
Tel. (212) 770-7000
Listed: NYSE
Investor contact: Director of Investor Relations, Charlene Hamral
Ticker symbol: AIG
S&P rating: A+

American International Group, Inc.

As profiled in its 1993 Annual Report, "American International Group, Inc. (AIG) is the leading U.S.-based international insurance organization and the nation's largest underwriter of commercial and industrial coverages. Its member companies write property, casualty, marine, life, and financial services insurance in approximately 130 countries and jurisdictions, and are engaged in a range of financial services businesses.

"AIG's general insurance operations are the largest underwriters of commercial and industrial insurance in the United States, and our overseas network is the most extensive of any insurance organization. The major components of the Group are Domestic General-Brokerage, United Guaranty Corporation, and Foreign General.

"The Domestic General-Brokerage Group (DBG) markets its products through the brokerage community to large corporate buyers and other commercial customers. DBG companies are market leaders in many specialty and difficult-to-place classes of business. Five principal companies comprise the Group: National Union Fire Insurance Company of Pittsburgh, PA, American Home Assurance Company, Lexington Insurance Company, Commerce and Industry Insurance Company, and New Hampshire Insurance Company.

"AIG's Domestic General-Agency Group now consists of the Audobon Insurance Group, which conducts agency marketing of personal and small commercial coverage in southern and western states.

"United Guaranty Corporation (UGC), whose subsidiaries write mortgage guaranty insurance for financial institutions nationwide, is the fourth largest company in the U.S. mortgage guaranty market.

"The Foreign General Group comprises AIG's overseas property-casualty operations, the largest foreign network of any U.S. insurance organization. Foreign General produces a steady, growing, and diversified stream for AIG. Its client base includes local businesses, individuals and national and multinational accounts.

"AIG's life operations, located largely overseas, comprise the largest and most extensive worldwide life insurance network of any company, and are a major source of earnings growth, stability, and diversification for AIG.

"AIG's Specialty and Agency Companies engage in fee-based services as agent and managers, provide technical and support service activities, conduct mass marketing of personal insurance products, and earn commission income from premiums generated for AIG's insurance companies.

"AIG has a 45 percent ownership interest in Transatlantic Holdings, Inc., a holding company whose subsidiaries, Transatlantic Reinsurance Company and Putnam Reinsurance Company, provide worldwide reinsurance capacity on both a treaty and facultative basis through regional offices in North America and overseas offices in London, Tokyo, and Hong Kong. Transatlantic is the third largest publicly traded U.S.-based reinsurance organization, and a leader in the specialty casualty area, including medical malpractice and other professional liability, directors and officers liability, environmental impairment liability, and asbestos abatement liability.

"The Financial Services Group consists of AIG's diversified and targeted businesses in financial services, domestically and overseas. They provide a steady and growing income stream for AIG. Our strategy for financial services is to focus on businesses where we can add value and achieve a competitive advantage by capitalizing on our Triple-A rating, international network and entrepreneurial culture. The major components of the Group are, International Lease Finance Corporation, AIG Financial Products Corp., and AIG Trading Corporation."

During 1993, income by major business segment was derived as follows: Domestic General 38.3 percent, Foreign General 15.9 percent, Life 29.2 percent, Financial Services 15.6 percent and Other 1 percent.

Likewise, during 1992, revenues and operating income were apportioned as follows: General Insurance 57.4 percent of revenues and 51.6 percent of operating income, Life Insurance 33.8 percent of revenues and 30.7 percent of operating income, Agency and Service Fee 1.2 percent of revenues and 2.4 percent of operating income, and Financial Services 7.6 percent of revenues and 15.3 percent of operating income.

American International Group, Inc. has paid consecutive cash dividends since 1969. Institutions control over 50 percent of the outstanding common shares, and an additional 30 percent are closely held. American International Group paid a 50 percent stock dividend in 1981, a 25 percent stock dividend in 1983, a 100 percent stock dividend in 1986, a 25 percent stock dividend, and a 50 percent stock dividend in 1993.

Total assets: $79.8 billion
Common shares outstanding: 317.4 million

	1984	1985	1986	1987	1988	1989	1990	1991	1992	1993
Revenues (Mil.)	4,300	5,895	8,776	11,027	12,844	14,150	15,702	16,884	18,389	20,135
Net Income (Mil.)	302	420	791	1,033	1,209	1,367	1,442	1,553	1,657	1,929
Earnings per share	1.08	1.47	2.59	3.35	3.92	4.43	4.61	4.85	5.20	6.11
Dividends per share	.12	.12	.12	.14	.19	.23	.27	.31	.35	.39
Prices Hi	19.5	29.3	38.3	44.7	36.7	59.7	56.0	67.9	80.9	100.3
Lo	13.6	17.3	27.7	28.6	26.1	35.3	39.1	48.0	54.7	73.4

Anheuser-Busch Companies, Inc.

One Busch Place
St. Louis, Missouri 63118-1852
Tel. (314) 577-2000
Listed: NYSE
Investor contact: Gerald C. Thayer, Investor Relations
Ticker symbol: BUD
S&P rating: A+

As profiled in its 1993 Annual Report, "Anheuser-Busch Companies, Inc. is a diversified corporation whose subsidiaries include the world's largest brewing organization, the country's second-largest producer of fresh-baked goods, and the country's second-largest theme park operator. The company also has interest in container manufacturing and recycling, malt and rice production, international brewing and beer marketing, snack foods, international baking, refrigerated and frozen foods, real estate development, major league baseball, stadium ownership, creative services, railcar repair and transportation services, and metalized-label printing.

"Anheuser-Busch, Inc.'s naturally brewed brands include fourteen beer brands, a nonalcohol brew, and three high-quality imports. Budweiser remains the "King of Beers" and continues to dominate across all demographic segments in the U.S. beer market. Busch Light is among the fastest-growing major brands in the U.S. Bud Dry remains the best-selling dry beer in the country with more than 50 percent share of category. Anheuser-Busch's Michelob family—Michelob, Michelob Light, Michelob Dry and Michelob Classic Dark—marked a new direction in beer marketing by appealing to both male and female adult beer drinkers. Michelob's two premium test market brands—Michelob Gold Draft and Michelob Gold Draft Light—continue to perform well, especially in the northwest and upper midwest. O'Doul's, Anheuser-Busch's nonalcohol brew, became the number-one selling nonalcohol brew in 1992. The company imports three brands from Denmark: Carlsberg, Carlsberg Light, and Elephant Malt Liquor. Today, Anheuser-Busch brands are exported to more than fifty countries and brewed under Anheuser-Busch's supervision in five countries.

"In 1992, Busch Entertainment Corporation acquired Water Country USA in Williamsburg, Virginia. Other Anheuser-Busch theme parks include, Busch Gardens in Tampa, Florida, and Williamsburg, Virginia; Cypress Gardens in Winter Haven, Florida; Adventure Island in Tampa, Florida; Sea World marine-life parks in Orlando, Florida, San Antonio, Texas, Aurora, Ohio, and San Diego, California; and Sesame Place in Langhorne, Pennsylvania. Together, the ten parks offer visitors a variety of entertaining and education experiences.

"Busch Properties, Inc. manages Anheuser-Busch's real estate holdings, including development properties, land for potential expansion, leased facilities, and dispositions.

"More than 2.7 million fans visited Busch Stadium in 1992 to watch the St. Louis Cardinals—the company's major league baseball subsidiary—during its centennial season in the National League. For the eleventh consecutive year, the Redbirds drew more than two million fans, making the Cardinals one of the most popular teams in professional baseball.

"Campbell Taggart, Inc. is a highly diversified, Dallas-based food products company with operations in about 35 percent of the United States and in certain European markets, and is involved in the production and distribution of baked goods, refrigerated dough products, frozen foods, refrigerated salad dressings, snack dips, and toppings to retail and food service customers.

"Eagle Snacks continued to expand its product line in 1992 with the introduction of El Grande Style tortilla chips, an expanded line of pretzel products, and new flavor offerings in its potato chip line."

During 1992, revenues and operating income were apportioned as follows: beer and beer-related products 75.4 percent of revenues and 92.7 percent of income, food products 18.6 percent of revenues and 4.2 percent of income, and entertainment 6 percent of revenues and 3.1 percent of income.

1993 marked Anheuser's seventeenth consecutive year of earnings and dividend increases. Boatmen's Bancshares, Inc. owns about 7.4 percent, and institutions control about 55 percent, of the outstanding common shares. "The company has paid dividends in each of the past sixty years. During that time, the company's stock has split on seven different occasions and stock dividends were paid three times." Anheuser-Busch paid a 200 percent stock dividend in 1985 and a 100 percent stock dividend in 1986.

Total assets: $10.9 billion
Current ratio: 1.0
Common shares outstanding: 267 million

	1984	1985	1986	1987	1988	1989	1990	1991	1992	1993
Revenues (Mil.)	6,501	7,000	7,677	8,258	8,924	9,481	10,744	10,996	11,394	11,505
Net Income (Mil.)	392	444	518	615	716	767	842	940	918	595
Earnings per share	1.24	1.42	1.69	2.04	2.45	2.68	2.96	3.26	3.48	2.17
Dividends per share	.32	.37	.44	.54	.66	.80	.94	1.06	1.20	1.36
Prices Hi	12.5	22.9	29.1	40.1	34.4	46.0	45.3	62.0	60.8	60.3
Lo	9.0	11.9	19.8	25.8	29.0	30.6	34.0	39.3	51.8	43.0

Automatic Data Processing, Inc.

One ADP Boulevard
Roseland, New Jersey 07068-1728
Tel. (201) 994-5000
Listed: NYSE
Investor contact Senior Vice Pres., Fred D. Anderson, Jr.
Ticker symbol: AUD
S&P rating: A+

As profiled in its fiscal 1993 Annual Report, "Automatic Data Processing, Inc. (ADP) is one of the largest companies in the world dedicated to providing computerized transaction processing, data communications, and information services.

"ADP's services, which help 300,000 clients improve their business performance, include: payroll, payroll tax, and human resource information management; brokerage, industry-specific services to auto and truck dealers; and computerized auto repair and replacement estimating for auto insurance companies and body repair shops.

"Employer Services, Brokerage Services, Dealer Services, and Automotive Claims Services are the company's largest businesses. Together, they represent over 90 percent of ADP's revenue and are the key strategic elements of the company's future growth."

"ADP's oldest and largest business is Employer Services. It contributes about 60 percent of company revenue. Employer Services provides payroll and related human resource information services to more than 275,000 clients of all sizes in virtually every business sector. These services include: payroll processing, payroll tax filing, job costing and labor distribution, management reports, unemployment compensation management, human resource information, and benefits administration support.

"Brokerage Services represents over 20 percent of ADP's revenue, and provides record-keeping, market data, order entry, proxy services, and relevant services to the brokerage and financial communities.

"ADP's third largest business is Dealer Services. It contributes 12 percent of ADP revenue by providing more than twenty industry-specific applications to over 7,500 auto and truck dealers in North America, and separate product sets to over 1,000 auto dealers in Germany and the United Kingdom.

"Auto dealerships use ADP's on-site systems to manage their accounting inventory, leasing, sales, and service activities. ADP also links clients to other dealers for parts and vehicle locating, and connects dealers with manufacturers for warranty processing, price updates, and vehicle and parts ordering.

"Other operations include Automotive Claims Services (ACS), Network, Wholesale Distribution, and European payroll services. Automotive Claims Services, ADP's fourth largest business, provides computer-based collision repair estimating and total loss valuation to auto insurance companies, claims adjusters, repair shops, and salvage yards."

ADP has been noted for its consistency in earnings and dividends. Fiscal 1993 marked ADP's forty-fourth consecutive year of record revenues and earnings. As of June 1993, ADP completed its 128th consecutive quarter of "double digit" earnings per share growth. This uninterrupted string of record quarters is the best such performance of any publicly-held company in America. Institutions control about 70 percent of the outstanding common shares. ADP has paid consecutive increased cash dividends for the past nineteen years, since initiation in 1974. ADP paid a 100 percent stock dividend in 1981, a 100 percent stock dividend in 1986, and a 100 percent stock dividend in 1991.

Total assets: $2.4 billion
Current ratio: 1.9
Common shares outstanding: 141.1 million

	1984	1985	1986	1987	1988	1989	1990	1991	1992	1993
Revenues (Mil.)	889	1,030	1,204	1,384	1,549	1,678	1,714	1,772	1,941	2,223
Net Income (Mil.)	75	88	106	132	170	188	212	228	256	294
Earnings per share	.54	.62	.73	.88	1.10	1.26	1.44	1.63	1.84	2.08
Dividends per share	.15	.16	.18	.20	.23	.27	.31	.36	.42	.48
Prices Hi	10.1	15.0	19.5	27.3	23.7	25.4	30.2	46.4	55.6	56.9
Lo	7.4	9.7	14.0	13.9	17.3	17.9	22.7	25.0	38.8	46.9

BANC ONE CORPORATION

100 East Broad Street
Columbus, Ohio 43271-0261
Tel. (614) 248-5944
Listed: NYSE
Investor contact: Treasurer, George R. Melling
Ticker symbol: ONE
S&P rating: A+

As profiled in its 1993 Annual Report, "BANC ONE CORPORATION is a bank holding company, incorporated in Ohio. The corporation operates 81 affiliate banking organizations in Arizona, California, Colorado, Illinois, Indiana, Kentucky, Michigan, Ohio, Texas, Utah, West Virginia, and Wisconsin. BANC ONE also operates several additional corporations that engage in data processing, venture capital, investment and merchant banking, consumer finance, and insurance.

"BANC ONE is fortunate to have not only a sound base from which to operate, but also the promise of additional new markets in some of the fastest growing areas of the country.

"Our long-term perspective shows growth in size, expansion in markets served, improved profitability, increased capital strength, and a record of performance consistency. All these reflect adherence to our basic strategies which are unchanged. We view them as including:

1. Serving retail and middle-market customers through community banks, which operate with significant local autonomy, coupled with strong, central financial and credit controls.

2. Investing in and implementing technologies which enhance retail products, create competitive advantages, provide operating efficiencies, and generate non-traditional bank revenue sources.

3. Treating bank acquisitions as an ongoing line of business, requiring rigorous pricing and management disciplines, which permit market expansion and provide economic diversification.

"Our objective is to continue to concentrate on retail and on small- and middle-market business lending into the natural market areas served by our banks. We do not actively seek large national credit relationships.

"While we added seven banking organizations, eighteen banks, and nearly more assets and banking offices during the year than at any time in our history, the basic structure of the company expanded but did not change much. This structure centers around our bank and non-bank affiliates, and all activities are designed to support their individual efforts. This philosophy is based on decentralization of the people side of the business, centralization of the paper and electronic transaction sides of the business, and dependence on a superb financial management system to measure and report results continually.

"We've been experimenting with a concept called Personal Investment Centers (PICs) in a handful of our existing banking offices. PICs offer non-traditional banking services, including mutual funds, brokerage services, and some insurance products. The PICs are staffed with licensed professionals who can offer an expanded product line to branch banking customers. Results of the experimentation have been so successful that we plan to open up to 400 PICs throughout our branch network during 1993."

During 1993, loans of $53.8 billion were apportioned as follows: commercial, financial, and agricultural 26 percent; real estate commercial 8.2 percent, real estate construction 3 percent, and real estate residential 20 percent; installment 29.6 percent, credit card 11.2 percent, and leases 2 percent.

BANC ONE has paid consecutive cash dividends since 1933. In 1993 BANC ONE posted its twenty-fifth straight year of increased earnings per share. Institutions control about 55 percent of the outstanding common shares. BANC ONE paid stock dividends of 10 percent in 1980, 10 percent in January 1982, 50 percent in December 1982, 50 percent in 1983, 10 percent in 1984, 50 percent in 1985, 10 percent in 1986, 10 percent in 1988, 10 percent in 1990, 10 percent in 1992, 25 percent in 1993, and 10 percent in 1994.

Total assets: $79.9 billion
Common shares outstanding: 380.7 million

	1984	1985	1986	1987	1988	1989	1990	1991	1992	1993
Net Income (Mil.)	108	130	200	209	340	348	423	529	877	1,140
Earnings per share	.96	1.02	1.16	1.19	1.56	1.66	1.83	2.12	2.29	2.98
Dividends per share	.32	.38	.45	.49	.55	.62	.69	.77	.89	1.07
Prices Hi	8.7	13.8	18.1	16.1	16.6	22.2	21.9	34.9	38.9	44.8
Lo	7.0	8.3	12.9	9.7	12.6	13.4	12.6	16.4	30.6	32.3

Bandag, Incorporated

Bandag Center
2905 N. Highway 61
Muscatine, Iowa 52761-5886
Tel. (319) 262-1400
Listed NYSE
Investor contact: Senior Vice President & Chief Financial Officer,
Thomas E. Dvorchak
Ticker symbol: BDG
S&P rating: A+

As profiled in its 1992 Annual Report, "Bandag has long been the leader in tire retreading research and development. Working hand-in-hand with other Bandag departments, such as marketing and manufacturing, as well as with our dealers and end users for trial testing and evaluation, Bandag's research and development consistently establishes new standards in the retreading industry.

"In past years, we've introduced commercially unprecedented process improvements, such as the pressure curing chamber, single-ply cushion gum, the rubber curing envelope, the first-ever nondestructive (NDI) tire casing analyzer, and the Eclipse System. These and scores of other developments revolutionized the precured retreading process.

"Every minute, hundreds of pounds of Bandag tread rubber roll off the presses of our rubber manufacturing plants ready for finishing, packaging, and delivery to Bandag dealers.

"It is a monumental challenge to provide over 1,200 dealers worldwide with this continuous stream of quality rubber in over 475 different design and size combinations."

"The typical Bandag dealer is a hands-on manager, keeping a close eye on the overall business while remaining deeply involved in the day-to-day operations. Employing eight to ten people, he produces approximately 66 Bandag retreads a day, as well as offer a new line of tires. He thrives on both commercial and retail business, and may operate several sales locations.

"Although a few large fleets number among his clientele, his 'bread and butter' comes from the local trucking operation down the street.

"Our long-term goal includes gradually increasing the Eclipse System product line to more effectively fit the needs of our target market. Our primary focus remains on offering it as a new tire alternative to major long-haul or pick-up-and-delivery operators, who are currently using new tires only on drive positions, or who are 100 percent new tire buyers. The Eclipse System retread appeals to fleets who place a premium on wear performance and superior appearance."

During 1992, revenues and operating income were geographically apportioned as follows: the United States 61.5 percent of revenues and 83.2 percent of income, Western Europe 19.1 percent of revenues and 3.5 percent of income, and other 19.4 percent of revenues and 13.3 percent of income.

The founding Carver family owns about 35 percent of all outstanding shares and, through a Class B weighted common share issue, controls about 72 percent of the voting power. Bandag's dividends have increased each year since initiation in 1976. It paid a 50 percent stock dividend in 1982, a 100 percent stock dividend in 1986, a 50 percent stock dividend in 1987, and a 100 percent stock dividend in 1992.

Total assets: $550.7 million
Current ratio: 3.1
Common shares outstanding: 11.2 million
Class A 13.6 million
Class B 24 million

	1984	1985	1986	1987	1988	1989	1990	1991	1992	1993
Revenues (Mil.)	319	330	370	423	491	525	586	583	591	590
Net Income (Mil.)	44	43	49	63	70	76	79	80	83	79
Earnings per share	1.21	1.26	1.43	1.95	2.34	2.61	2.75	2.86	2.99	2.98
Dividends per share	.28	.30	.33	.37	.41	.46	.51	.56	.61	.66
Prices Hi	13.5	15.5	22.9	34.5	33.7	44.7	45.5	60.0	71.0	60.3
Lo	9.5	12.2	14.3	21.0	26.5	32.2	33.0	40.8	55.0	44.8

Bausch & Lomb Incorporated

One Chase Square
Rochester, New York 14601-0054
Tel. (716) 338-6000
Listed: NYSE
Investor contact: Manager of Investor Relations, Efrain Rivera
Ticker symbol: BOL
S&P rating: A

**BAUSCH
& LOMB**

As profiled in its 1992 Annual Report, "Bausch & Lomb is one of America's oldest and most successful companies, with a heritage of technical achievement and product excellence dating from 1853. The company markets its products on the basis of quality, differentiated benefits, and, in many cases, the recommendation of health care professionals. Its strategic focus is one of selected segments of global health care and optics markets where it is competitively advantaged with superior technology, low product costs, and established brand names. Indicative of Bausch & Lomb's global span, regions outside the United States represent 48 percent of corporate revenues. Manufacturing or marketing organizations have been established in thirty-three countries, and the company's products are distributed in more than seventy other nations.

"The Health Care Segment consists of three strategic sectors:

1. The Personal Health Sector (52 percent of segment revenues) is comprised of branded products purchased directly by consumers in health and beauty aid sections of pharmacies, food stores, and mass merchandise outlets. Products include contact lens solutions (ReNu Multi-Purpose Solution and Boston Advance Conditioning Solution for rigid gas-permeable lenses), oral care products (Interplak plaque removal, Interject Water Pik, and Clear Choice Mouth Wash), eye care products (Bausch & Lomb Moisture Drops, Bausch & Lomb Allergy Drops, and Bereril Moisturizing Eye Drops), and non-prescription medications (analgesics, sleep aids, hay fever remedies such as Dr. Mann Pharma's Vividrin, nasal moisturizers, and optic products).

2. The Medical Sector (33 percent of segment revenues) consists of contact lenses (the Quantum 2 and Boston lines of rigid gas-permeable lenses, and the SeeQuence 2 and Medalist soft contact lenses), ophthalmic pharmaceutical (Normoglaucon beta-blocker used to treat glaucoma, OptiPranolol, a proprietary antiglaucoma medication, Pilostat 4 percent an anti-glaucoma pharmaceu-

tical, Floxal and Dexamytrex ophthalmic antibiotics, and Artelac Dry eye treatment), periodontal diagnostic equipment, hearing aids, dental implants, and other products sold to health care professionals, or which are obtainable by consumers only through a prescription.

3. The Biomedical Sector (15 percent of segment revenues) provides researchers throughout the world with purpose-bred, highly-defined, live animal models essential to the discovery and validation of new pharmaceuticals. Its products are marketed through the company's Charles River Laboratories subsidiary and are assisting in the fight against AIDS, cancer, hypertension, and other life-threatening illnesses.

"The Optics Segment consists primarily of products used by consumers for the protection or enhancement of vision, such as sunglasses (Ray-Ban, Outlook's licensed Liz Claiborne sunglass line, Outlook's Suncloud line, Balorama sunglasses, Wayfarer, Cats, and Killer Loop), binoculars, and telescopes. This segment also includes specialized optical thin coating services and products provided to customers in the display and medical lighting industries."

During 1992, health care products represented 60.5 percent of revenues and 56.4 percent of operating earnings, and optical products represented 39.5 percent of revenues and 43.6 percent of operating earnings.

Geographically, during 1992, the United States represented 52 percent of revenues and 57.6 percent of operating earnings, and foreign operations represented 48 percent of revenues and 42.4 percent of operating earnings.

Bausch & Lomb has paid consecutive cash dividends since 1952. Institutions control over 70 percent of the outstanding common shares. Bausch & Lomb paid a 100 percent stock dividend in 1983 and another 100 percent stock dividend in 1991.

Total assets: $2.5 billion
Current ratio: 2.0
Common shares outstanding: 60.2 million
Class B 936 thousand

	1984	1985	1986	1987	1988	1989	1990	1991	1992	1993
Revenues (Mil.)	534	596	699	840	978	1,220	1,369	1,520	1,709	1,872
Net Income (Mil.)	59	67	75	85	98	114	131	149	171	157
Earnings per share	.99	1.11	1.23	1.40	1.63	1.89	2.19	2.47	2.84	2.60
Dividends per share	.39	.39	.39	.43	.50	.58	.66	.72	.80	.98
Prices Hi	13.9	17.8	22.0	24.8	24.0	32.9	36.5	57.5	60.5	57.5
Lo	8.8	12.4	15.9	15.4	17.2	20.4	26.4	31.8	44.5	43.0

Becton, Dickinson and Company

One Becton Drive
Franklin Lakes, New Jersey 07417-1880
Tel. (201) 847-6800
Listed: NYSE
Investor contact: Ronald Jaspar
Ticker symbol: BDX
S&P symbol: A+

As profiled in its fiscal 1993 Annual Report, "Becton, Dickinson and Company manufactures and sells a broad range of medical supplies and devices and diagnostic systems for use by health care professionals, medical research institutions, and the general public.

"The company's operations are comprised of two worldwide business segments: Medical Supplies and Devices, and Diagnostic Systems.

"The major products in the Medical Supplies and Devices segment are hypodermic products, specially designed devices for diabetes care, prefillable syringe systems, vascular access products, and surgical devices (including disposable scrubs, surgical gloves, specialty and surgical blades, and pre-surgery patient prep kits).

"This segment also includes infusion systems, elastic support products, thermometers, examination gloves, and contract packaging services. The company's contract packaging services are provided to pharmaceutical, cosmetic, and toiletries companies.

"The major products in the Diagnostic Systems segment are blood collection products, tissue culture labware, classical and instrumented microbiology products, instrumentation systems for cellular analysis, hematology instruments, and other diagnostic systems, including immunodiagnostic test kits.

"The company's Vacutainer brand blood collection products are needles, evacuated tubes, and microcollection devices used to obtain blood samples for laboratory analysis as an aid in the diagnosis of disease.

"The company's tissue culture labware products include petri dishes, pipettes and tubes, plastic labware used in tissue culture, as well as extracellular matrix products, cytokines and serum substitutes used by medical researchers.

"The company's microbiology products are designed to facilitate the detection and characterization of bacteria for diagnostic purposes. These products include dehydrated growth media, prefilled media products, anti-microbial susceptibility testing systems, anaerobic growth and detection systems, and instrumentation for the detection of bacteria. During fiscal 1992, the company acquired the worldwide microbiology business of Hoffman-LaRoche, which produces a variety of manual and instrumented microbiology products.

"The company produces radioimmunoassay and non-isotopic immunodiagnostic manual and instrumented test systems. Immunodiagnostics is the application of the very sensitive and rapid antibody-antigen reaction in diagnostics.

"The company manufactures and sells several types of hematology instruments, including a microprocessor-based, centrifugal hematology system useful in primary care clinical diagnosis for analysis of blood counts.

"The company's Fluorescence Activated Cell Sorter (FACS) brand cell sorter and analyzer systems make possible the clinical analysis and multi-parameter measurement of individual cells, and provide basic functional information about blood and bone marrow cell populations. FACS brand systems are used in major research laboratories throughout the world for basic and applied research in a variety of disciplines, including immunology, genetics, oncology, and biotechnology. FACS brand systems also are used increasingly in clinical laboratories to help diagnose and monitor various immune system diseases and disorders.

"The company currently offers more than 260 different monoclonal antibody reagents. Monoclonal antibodies are an important factor in biological research, and are the consumables for the company's FACS brand systems."

During fiscal 1993, revenues and operating income were apportioned as follows: Medical Supplies and Devices provided 55.1 percent of revenues and 67.2 percent of operating income, and Diagnostic Systems provided 44.9 percent of revenues and 32.8 percent of operating income.

Geographically, during fiscal 1993, the United States provided 55.6 percent of revenues and 68.5 percent of operating income, Europe 28.4 percent of revenues and 23.4 percent of operating income, and other nations provided 16 percent of revenues and 8.1 percent of operating income.

Becton, Dickinson and Company has paid consecutive cash dividends since 1926. Institutions control approximately 80 percent of the outstanding common shares. Becton, Dickinson paid a 100 percent stock dividend in 1986, and another 100 percent stock dividend in 1993.

Total assets: $3.1 billion
Current ratio: 1.8
Common shares outstanding: 74.7 million

	1984	1985	1986	1987	1988	1989	1990	1991	1992	1993
Revenues (Mil.)	1,127	1,144	1,312	1,463	1,709	1,811	2,013	2,172	2,365	2,465
Net Income (Mil.)	63	88	112	148	149	158	182	190	201	213
Earnings per share	.76	1.05	1.18	1.65	1.84	2.00	2.33	2.43	2.57	2.71
Dividends per share	.29	.30	.33	.37	.43	.50	.54	.58	.60	.66
Prices Hi	10.3	16.5	30.7	34.5	31.1	31.2	38.4	40.9	42.1	40.8
Lo	7.8	9.9	15.4	21.1	23.8	24.2	27.9	29.0	32.2	32.6

Bemis Company, Inc.

222 South Ninth Street Suite 2300
Minneapolis, Minnesota 55402-4099
Tel. (612) 376-3000
Listed: NYSE
Investor contact: Asst. Secy., Lisa D. Locken
Ticker symbol: BMS
S&P rating: A

As profiled in its 1993 Annual Report, "Bemis is a principal manufacturer of flexible packaging, and specialty coated and graphics products. More than 75 percent of the Company's sales are packaging related.

"The flexible packaging business is a leading supplier of lightweight flexible packaging to the food industry and other markets. Flexible packaging products include coated and laminated films, and polyethylene packaging; packaging machinery; multiwall paper bags, consumer-size paper packaging, and flexible liquid packaging.

"The company's pressure-sensitive materials business is the principal operation of specialty coated and graphics products, with major operations in North America and Europe. It is a large supplier of a wide range of pressure-processing and laser printing applications, industrial bonding, and graphics signage. Smaller business segments include the manufacture of label applicating machinery, pressure-sensitive labels, and rotogravure cylinders.

"The primary market for the company's products is the food industry, which accounts for approximately 70 percent of sales. Other markets include chemicals, agribusiness, pharmaceutical, medical, printing and graphic arts, and a variety of other industrial end uses. The company holds a strong or dominant position in many markets it serves, and seeks out special market segments where the company's technological and other capabilities give it a competitive advantage.

"The company has a strong technical base in polymer chemistry, film extrusion, coating and laminating, printing and converting, packaging machinery systems, and pressure-sensitive adhesive technology. These capabilities are being brought together to provide an expanding level of innovation and growth in the company's major businesses.

"The company's more technically-oriented, higher-margin, flexible packaging and pressure-sensitive material businesses are being actively expanded through a strong capital program in North America and Europe."

During 1993, flexible packaging products provided 75.2 percent of revenues and 72.3 percent of operating profits, and specialty coated and graphics products provided 24.8 percent of revenues and 27.8 percent of operating profits. Geographically, revenues and operating profits were apportioned as follows: The United States 84.4 percent of revenues and 92.1 percent of profits, Canada 3.5 percent of revenues and 2.6 percent of profits, and finally, Europe 12.1 percent of revenues and 5.3 percent of profits.

The Bemis Company has paid consecutive cash dividends since 1922. Officers and directors control about 10 percent and institutions about 45 percent of the outstanding common shares. Bemis paid a 100 percent stock dividend in 1984, a 100 percent dividend in 1986, a 100 percent dividend in 1988, and a 100 percent stock dividend in 1992.

Total assets: $789.8 million
Current ratio: 1.8
Common shares outstanding: 51.2 million

	1984	1985	1986	1987	1988	1989	1990	1991	1992	1993
Revenues (Mil.)	779	787	865	930	1,069	1,077	1,128	1,142	1,181	1,203
Net Income (Mil.)	18	23	26	32	40	47	51	53	57	44
Earnings per share	.32	.41	.47	.59	.74	.90	.99	1.03	1.11	.86
Dividends per share	.11	.13	.15	.18	.22	.30	.36	.42	.46	.50
Prices Hi	3.4	5.8	7.8	10.5	12.8	18.8	18.8	20.8	29.6	27.4
Lo	2.6	3.1	4.9	6.4	8.0	11.3	12.9	13.5	19.8	19.9

Betz Laboratories, Inc.

4636 Somerton Road
Trevose, Pennsylvania 19053-6783
Tel. (215) 355-3300
Listed: NYSE
Investor contact: V.P. Finance & Treas., R. Dale Voncanon
Ticker symbol: BTL
S&P rating: A

Betz
Laboratories,
Inc.

As profiled in its 1993 Annual Report, "Our business is the engineered chemical treatment of water, wastewater, and process systems operating in a wide variety of industrial and commercial applications, with particular emphasis on the chemical, petroleum refining, paper, automotive, electrical utility, and steel industries.

"Betz produces and markets a wide range of specialty chemical products, including the technical and laboratory services necessary to utilize Betz products effectively. Chemical treatment programs are applied for use in boilers, cooling towers, heat exchangers, paper and petroleum process streams, and both influent and effluent systems.

"The company has thirteen production plants in the United States and eight in foreign countries, employing approximately 4,105 persons, of which 1,495 represent a highly technical sales force. With additional engineering and laboratory backup from product management and research functions, Betz monitors changing water, process, and plant operating conditions, so as to prescribe the appropriate treatment program to solve such customer problems as scale, corrosion, and deposit formation. The end value of such programs is the preservation or enhancement of productivity, reliability, and efficiency in customer plant operations.

"Betz PaperChem, Inc. markets the company's line of specialty process chemicals to the pulp and paper industry. Betz Process Chemicals, Inc. markets specialty process chemicals to the oil refining, petrochemical, and steel industries. Betz MetChem Division, which markets process chemicals used in metals finishing, evidences strong growth in its NORINSE II pretreatment programs to the coil industry. Betz Industrial, our largest operating unit, markets our tradition boiler water, cooling water, and wastewater treatment programs to large industry. During 1992, Betz Entec, Inc., which serves the commercial, institutional, and light industrial marketplace, introduced its OPTI-Series products, a new generation of boiler treatment technology that significantly improves boiler reliability and efficiency.

"The Betz Quality in Action (QIA) process puts the talent, creativity, spirit, and ideas of our employees to work in quality improvement programs. Our technical staffs provide specialized support in such areas as engineering, environmental regulations, analytical testing, microbiology, metallurgical analysis, and statistical process control."

During 1992, revenues of $706.9 million were apportioned as follows: the United States 78.8 percent, Europe 13.6 percent, and other (principally Canada, the Caribbean, and the Pacific) 7.6 percent.

Betz Laboratories has increased its cash dividend for the twenty-seventh consecutive year. Institutions control over 70 percent of the outstanding common shares. Betz paid a 100 percent stock dividend in 1981 and another 100 percent stock dividend in 1990.

Total assets: $521.1 million
Current ratio: 2.3
Common shares outstanding: 28.1 million

	1984	1985	1986	1987	1988	1989	1990	1991	1992	1993
Revenues (Mil.)	304	319	344	386	448	517	597	666	707	685
Net Income (Mil.)	37	37	36	41	48	56	65	76	82	63
Earnings per share	1.16	1.17	1.12	1.29	1.57	1.76	2.12	2.47	2.71	2.12
Dividends per share	.58	.65	.69	.75	.82	.92	1.05	1.20	1.33	1.38
Prices Hi	19.5	19.1	22.4	29.1	26.3	31.3	43.3	62.0	66.3	62.9
Lo	13.6	15.1	17.5	17.5	20.6	23.6	27.8	38.8	48.3	40.0

H&R Block, Inc.

4410 Main Street
Kansas City, Missouri 64111
Tel. (816) 753-6900
Listed: NYSE
Investor contact: Vice Pres. & Treas., Donald W. Ayers
Ticker symbol: HRB
S&P rating: A+

As profiled in its fiscal 1993 Annual Report, "H&R Block, Inc., is a diversified personal services company, providing services to its customers in three industry areas.

"H&R Block Tax Services, Inc., a wholly-owned subsidiary, provides service to the tax-paying public. These services include tax return preparation and electronic filing, provided to taxpayers in the United States and Australia, and tax return preparation and refund discounting to the public in Canada. The company also provides tax preparation services to U.S. taxpayers at military installations outside the U.S.

"Executive Tax Service (ETS) experienced continued growth in 1993. The ETS environment is an attractive alternative to the service offered by higher priced accounting firms, and we remain committed to its further development.

"Taxpayer preparation volume has increased in each of the thirty-eight years in the company's history. Our market share of taxpayers served in the U.S. increased to 14.7 percent, up from 14.5 percent in the prior year. The company's share of Canadian returns filed was approximately 12.4 percent in fiscal 1993, up from 12.3 percent in the preceding year.

"CompuServe Incorporated, a wholly-owned subsidiary, provides communications and information services to personal computer owners worldwide through the CompuService Information Service. Compuserve also provides electronic mail, database access, software, systems integration, frame relay, and wide and local network services.

"Besides the CompuServe Information Service, the Information Services Division offers a number of private applications to corporate markets. The CompuServe Mail Hub enables users of certain local area network (LAN)-based e-mail systems to communicate with each other. CompuServe continued as the industry leader in providing PC-based scheduling services for airline pilots and flight attendants, and was a major player in automating the system used by health maintenance organizations to determine patient eligibility for Medicare benefits. The CompuService Financial Systems Group, which serves Wall Street institutional investment firms, developed two new products to help money managers effectively utilize data key to their day-to-day decision making.

"Interim Services, Inc., a wholly-owned subsidiary, provides temporary personnel, healthcare workers, and other employment services throughout North America, Hawaii and Puerto Rico. Interim provides personnel with skills which include clerical, secretarial, paralegal support, accounting, technical, industrial, nursing, physician, therapist, and home health aide and companion. Interim is represented by 669 offices spread across two divisions: the Commercial Division, made up of 353 offices, and the HealthCare Division, made up of 316 offices."

During fiscal 1993, tax return preparation provided 48.1 percent of revenues and 64.7 percent of operating profits, computer services provided 20.7 percent of revenues and 25.2 percent of operating profits, temporary helps services provided 29.5 percent of revenues and 6.6 percent of operating profits, and other operations provided 1.7 percent of revenues and 3.5 percent of operating profits.

In January 1994, H&R Block offered 100 percent (8 million shares) of its Interim Services, Inc., temporary help agency to the public in an initial public offering valued at $160 million. The fourth largest temporary help agency in the United States. Interim Services, Inc., is in a highly competitive low margined business. H&R Block, Inc. will use the proceeds of the sale to focus on its two largest highly profitable businesses H&R Block Tax Services and CompuServe. In a separate development H&R Block, Inc. acquired MECA Software (personal financial software) in a friendly $4.2 million cash tender offer.

The H.W. Bloch family controls about 6 percent, and institutions about 65 percent, of the outstanding common shares. H&R Block has paid consecutive cash dividends since 1962. Block paid a 100 percent stock dividend in 1985, a 100 percent stock dividend in 1987, and a 100 percent stock dividend in 1991.

Total assets: $1.1 billion
Current ratio: 1.4
Common shares outstanding: 106.8 million

	1984	1985	1986	1987	1988	1989	1990	1991	1992	1993
Revenues (Mil.)	419	497	615	722	813	900	1,053	1,191	1,371	1,526
Net Income (Mil.)	48	55	62	75	90	100	124	140	162	181
Earnings per share	.47	.54	.60	.71	.86	.95	1.15	1.31	1.49	1.68
Dividends per share	.26	.29	.33	.37	.42	.50	.61	.75	.86	.97
Prices Hi	6.3	10.0	13.3	16.7	17.2	18.7	22.8	38.3	41.1	42.8
Lo	4.8	5.5	9.0	10.0	11.4	13.1	15.0	19.9	30.1	31.9

Carter-Wallace, Inc.

1345 Avenue of the America's
New York, New York 10105
Tel. (212) 339-5000
Listed: NYSE
Investor contact: Vice Pres., Secretary and General Counsel, Ralph Levine
Ticker symbol: CAR
S&P rating: A

As profiled in its fiscal 1993 Annual Report, "Carter-Wallace, Inc. is engaged in the manufacture and sale of a diversified line of products in the Consumer Products and Health Care segments. The company markets toiletries, pharmaceuticals, diagnostic specialties, proprietary drugs, and pet products.

"In the Carter Products Division, Arrid continued as one of the nation's leading anti-perspirant/deodorant brands. Arrid will enter a new segment of the anti-perspirant/deodorant category with the introduction of Arrid Teen Image, developed expressly to appeal to the young female user.

"Trojan continued to dominate the condom market. Two new product introductions, Trojan Very Sensitive and Trojan Very Thin, were introduced into the fastest growing segment of the condom market.

"Nair continued as the leading depilatory brand by a significant margin. A new Nair Cream Gentle Formula was introduced for the 1993 summer.

"The importance to the division of the pregnancy test business was enhanced by the completion of the successful introduction of First Response One-Step pregnancy test. Division brands represented one-quarter of total pregnancy test category sales.

"Pearl Drops continued as a leading brand in the fast-growing whitening toothpaste segment by introducing a new Baking Soda whitening toothpaste in February 1993.

"The Wallace Laboratories Division's Soma 350 brand of muscle relaxants posted a new sales high. The division's cough and cold products group, including Organidin expectorant and mucolytic, Tussi-Organidin and Tussi-Organidin DM cough preparations, and Rynatan antihistamines containing decongestants, sustained its number-one position in prescriptions written for cough/cold products. Targeted promotion to selected physicians resulted in significant growth and an all time high sales level for Doral tablets.

"The division is preparing to launch Felbatol (felbamate), a new anti-epilepsy drug, awaiting approval by the FDA.

"The Wampole Laboratories Division's Clearview line of diagnostic tests for chlamydia, group A streptococcus, and hCG as an aid in the determination of pregnancy, was a major contributor to the division's sales increase.

"The Isostat product line for the rapid detection of micro-organisms in the blood continued to be a significant contributor to the microbiology product line.

"The division maintained its leadership position in the increasingly competitive serological testing market where Streptozyme, a test for streptococcal antibodies, Rheumaton, a test to detect rheumatoid factors, and Mono-Test and Mono-Latex, products for the diagnosis of infectious mononucleosis, all retained dominant market positions.

"The Zeus Scientific line of immunofluorescent and enzyme immunoassay tests again reached record sales with particularly strong growth recorded among products used for the detection of autoimmune diseases and of antibodies to Epstein-Barr virus and mycoplasma.

"The Stat-Crit system for the rapid measurement of hematocrit levels in the blood continued to be a strong performer.

"Sales of the Lambert Kay line to pet shops increased substantially. These sales gains were due, in large part, to the introduction of new products including Fine Idea Flea Comb, Teflon Coated Easy Glider Flea Comb, Color Guard Flea Collar for Large Dogs, large size Fresh 'N Clean Housebreaking Pads, and Chew Toys.

"The division also launched two new X-O-Trol insecticide products, X-O-Trol Flea and Tick Spray for Dogs, and X-O-Trol Flea and Tick Household Spray. X-O-Trol's IGR provides the longest lasting effectiveness of any product of this type.

"Seven new products were introduced into the Lassie line: grooming combs, flea combs, puppy slicker brushes, puppy shampoo, tea-tree oil shampoo, dog cologne, and insecticidal ear wash for dogs. The Lassie line is especially designed for mass merchandisers, as is the Tiny Tiger line of cat products."

During fiscal 1993, revenues and operating profits were apportioned as follows: Health care 43 percent of revenues and 45 percent of operating profits, and consumer products 57 percent of revenues and 55 percent of operating profits.

Geographically, the United States provided 74.1 percent of revenues and 85.1 percent of operating profits, other North America 10.5 percent of revenues and 7.2 percent of operating profits, and other countries 15.4 percent of revenues and 7.7 percent of operating profits.

Carter-Wallace, Inc. has paid consecutive cash dividends since 1883. The CPI Development Corporation, controlled by the Hoyt family, controls about 35 percent of the outstanding common shares and 90 percent of the Class B shares (ten votes per share). Carter-Wallace paid a 100 percent stock dividend in 1987 and a 200 percent stock dividend in 1992.

Total assets: $600.6 million
Current ratio: 2.4
Common shares outstanding: 33.1 million
Class: B 12.7 million

	1984	1985	1986	1987	1988	1989	1990	1991	1992	1993
Revenues (Mil.)	323	349	400	451	483	515	555	635	673	654
Net Income (Mil.)	18	21	28	32	38	45	50	52	46	47
Earnings per share	.40	.44	.61	.71	.83	.99	1.10	1.12	1.00	1.03
Dividends per share	.077	.082	.097	.13	.17	.21	.26	.30	.33	.33
Prices Hi	4.6	8.6	14.4	25.2	14.4	20.2	19.6	41.9	45.9	36.6
Lo	3.3	4.2	8.0	8.0	10.6	13.1	14.9	17.5	22.6	20.1

Central Fidelity Banks, Inc.

1021 East Cary Street, P.O. Box 27602
Richmond, Virginia 23261
Tel. (804) 782-4000
Listed: NASDAQ
Investor contact: President, William F. Shumadine, Jr.
Ticker symbol: CFBS
S&P rating: A+

Central Fidelity Banks, Inc.

As profiled in its 1993 Annual Report, "Central Fidelity is an $9.7 billion asset bank holding company headquartered in Richmond, Virginia with banking offices throughout the Commonwealth of Virginia.

"The company serves only Virginia markets, primarily through its wholly-owned subsidiary Central Fidelity Bank. At year-end 1992, the Bank operated 230 branch offices, including 29 full-service supermarket locations and 192 automated teller machines throughout the Commonwealth of Virginia. The company, through the Bank and its other subsidiaries, provides a wide range of financial services to a broad customer base of individuals, corporations, institutions, and governments, primarily located in Virginia.

"The Bank is an issuer of MasterCard and VISA credit cards. Through the use of reciprocally shared automated teller machines, the company can deliver service through its membership in the Internet/MOST regional and PLUS national networks of automated teller machines.

"The company also engages in limited international banking activities, primarily in connection with foreign trade financing for Virginia-based companies.

"In addition to commercial activities, through its Financial Services Group, the company generates noninterest income by sales of trust and fiduciary services, annuities, private label mutual funds, and other investment services.

"In April 1992, the Bank formed a mortgage banking subsidiary, Central Fidelity Mortgage Corporation, to increase mortgage origination and servicing fee income, and to expand the Bank's residential mortgage loan portfolio.

"The company's national bank subsidiary, Central Fidelity Bank, N.A., organized in 1986, is supervised and examined by the Comptroller of the Currency.

"Bank-related subsidiaries, all of which are wholly-owned, are engaged in insurance and other bank-related services. Such subsidiaries, of which there are six, have made only a nominal contribution to revenues for each of the past five years."

In 1993, loans of $4.8 billion were apportioned as follows: commercial and commercial real estate 35.6 percent, construction 6.6 percent, residential real estate 24.4 percent, consumer second mortgage 9.5 percent, installment 13.9 percent, and bank card 10.6 percent.

Central Fidelity has paid consecutive cash dividends since 1911. Earnings have increased for 19 consecutive years. Institutions control about 25 percent of the outstanding common shares. Central Fidelity paid a 50 percent stock dividend in 1983, a 50 percent stock dividend in 1985, a 50 percent stock dividend in 1991, and a 50 percent stock dividend in 1983.

Total assets: $9.6 billion
Common shares outstanding: 39 million

	1984	1985	1986	1987	1988	1989	1990	1991	1992	1993
Net Income (Mil.)	29	33	42	47	49	54	55	60	78	103
Earnings per share	1.01	1.09	1.23	1.34	1.42	1.57	1.65	1.87	2.25	2.66
Dividends per share	.32	.36	.41	.47	.51	.54	.63	.74	.82	1.00
Prices Hi	8.6	13.8	16.2	13.3	13.1	15.3	14.5	26.3	28.3	35.3
Lo	5.6	8.5	11.0	10.2	11.1	11.8	8.0	8.9	22.3	25.8

Circuit City Stores, Inc.

9950 Mayland Drive
Richmond, Virginia 23233-1464
Tel. (804) 527-4000
Listed: NYSE
Investor contact: Director of Financial Relations, Ann M. Collier
Ticker symbol: CC
S&P rating: A

Circuit City Stores, Inc.

As profiled in its fiscal 1993 Annual Report, "Circuit City Stores, Inc.'s retail operations consist of Circuit City Superstores, Circuit City Stores and mall stores. The company has a wholly-owned credit card bank subsidiary, First North American National Bank, that extends consumer credit. In fiscal 1994, the Company will begin a limited test of a retail concept selling previously owned automobiles.

"The company is the nation's largest specialty retailer of brand-name consumer electronics and major appliances. It sells video equipment, including televisions, video cassette recorders, and camcorders; audio equipment, including home and car stereo systems, tape recorders, tape players, and compact disc players; other consumer products, including telephones, portable radios, home computers, and facsimile machines; and microwave ovens. Most stores sell major appliances, including washers, dryers, refrigerators, and ranges. In Fiscal 1993, music software was introduced in Superstores in three markets.

"The company's seven Circuit City stores (4,000 to 15,000 square feet) offer the company's full line of merchandise, excluding major appliances. The company's 214 Circuit City Superstores (15,000 to 47,000 square feet) sell a broader selection of the same lines of merchandise sold in the Circuit City Stores and, in addition, sell major appliances. The company's thirty-nine mall stores (2,000 to 4,000 square feet) are located in shopping malls and primarily carry small gift-oriented consumer electronic products. The mall stores operate under the names of Impulse and Circuit City Express.

"The company's expansion strategy is based on two principles: regional concentration and clear market leadership. The company attempts to minimize the expense and effort of growth by concentrating its resources in compact areas of substantial opportunity. Its policy is, emphatically, to favor depth over breadth.

"The company plans to continue growing within its Central, Southern and Western regions. The company has entered the Boston, Massachusetts, market and has planned entries into the Chicago, Illinois, market. The company plans to open approximately forty Supermarkets in fiscal 1994 in new and existing markets."

During fiscal 1993, sales by merchandise categories were as follows: Television 23 percent, VCR/Camcorders 19 percent, Audio 20 percent, Home Office 7 percent, Other Electronics 12 percent and Appliances 19 percent.

Circuit City has paid consecutive cash dividends since 1979. Institutions control about 85 percent of the outstanding common shares. Circuit City Stores paid a 100 percent stock dividend in 1981, a 50 percent stock dividend in March 1983, a 200 percent stock dividend in November 1983, a 100 percent stock dividend in 1986, a 100 percent stock dividend in 1989, and a 100 percent stock dividend in 1993.

Total assets: $1.6 billion
Current ratio: 2.1
Common shares outstanding: 96.1 million

	1984	1985	1986	1987	1988	1989	1990	1991	1992	1993
Revenues (Mil.)	351	511	694	995	1,334	1,701	2,078	2,367	2,790	3,270
Net Income (Mil.)	9	17	17	28	43	60	69	57	78	110
Earnings per share	.12	.21	.19	.31	.48	.65	.76	.61	.82	1.15
Dividends per share	.01	.02	.02	.01	.02	.03	.04	.05	.05	.07
Prices Hi	3.8	3.9	8.6	10.5	11.3	13.5	14.5	13.0	26.1	33.9
Lo	1.5	2.4	3.0	4.3	4.7	8.9	4.5	5.6	11.1	19.8

Citizens Utilities Company

High Ridge Park (P.O. Box 3801)
Stamford, Connecticut 06905-1390
Tel. (203) 329-8800
Listed: NYSE
Investor contact: Arthur D. Dague, Investor Relations
Ticker symbol: CZNA CZNAB
S&P rating: A+

CITIZENS
☎ ✂ ⚴ 🔥 〰
UTILITIES

As profiled in its 1992 Annual Report, "Citizens Utilities Company, incorporated in 1935, is a diversified public utility providing telecommunications, natural gas, electric, water, or wastewater services in 13 states: Arizona, California, Colorado, Hawaii, Idaho, Illinois, Indiana, Louisiana, Ohio, Oregon, Pennsylvania, Vermont and Washington. Citizens also holds a significant ownership interest in a cellular telephone company, serving markets with a population of approximately 4.2 million.

"The company provides telecommunications services in Arizona, Oregon, Pennsylvania and Washington to approximately 142,000 customer connections as of December 31, 1992. The California telephone subsidiary represents 19 percent of the company's 1992 operating revenues. In addition to the contract with Pacific Bell, the California telephone subsidiary was restructured and has designed and implemented efficiency standards and employee attitude surveys to ensure that services provided exceed customer expectations.

"Operating divisions of the company provide electric services to approximately 92,000 residential, commercial, and industrial customers in Arizona, Hawaii, and Vermont as of December 31, 1992. The company purchases over 80 percent of needed electric supplies; this is believed to be adequate to meet current demands and to provide for additional sales to new customers. As a whole, the company's electric segment does not experience material seasonal fluctuations.

"Operating divisions of the company provide gas transmission and distribution services to residential, commercial, and industrial customers in Arizona, Colorado, and Louisiana. Total number of gas customers served as of December 31, 1992, was approximately 328,000.

"The company provides water and/or wastewater services to approximately 249,000 customer connections in Arizona, California, Idaho, Illinois, Indiana, Ohio, and Pennsylvania as of December 31, 1992.

"We are addressing competition in the local telephone market through Electric Lightwave, Inc. Its network allows commercial users to bypass local exchange carriers, and connect direct with their long-distance company.

"Citizens is active in the cellular telephone market through its significant ownership in Centennial Cellular Corp., which serves markets with an estimated population of 4.2 million, and through Citizens Mohave Cellular Company, located in Arizona's fast-growing Mohave County."

Citizens Utilities Company has both Series A and Series B common shares. Series A shares are convertible, share for share, into Series B shares. Both Series A and Series B shares pay stock dividends. However, Series B shareholders can opt to have their stock dividends sold and the net cash proceeds distributed to them. Cost of the sale is 5 cents per share and the cash distribution is taxed at the capital gain rate. Citizens Utilities paid a 50 percent dividend in 1992, a 1.2 percent stock dividend in February 1993, a 1 percent stock dividend in May 1993, a two-for-one split August 4, 1993, a 1.1 percent stock dividend August 24, 1993, and a 1 percent stock dividend in December 1993.

Total assets: $2.6 billion
Current ratio: 0.4
Common shares outstanding: Series A 129.8 million
Series B 52.5 million

	1984	1985	1986	1987	1988	1989	1990	1991	1992	1993
Revenues (Mil.)	251	267	422	434	460	484	528	548	580	619
Net Income (Mil.)	44	51	56	75	84	85	106	112	115	126
Earnings per share	.31	.33	.36	.41	.47	.53	.58	.65	.66	.71
Dividends per share	.24	.26	.28	.32	.35	.41	—	—	—	—
Prices Hi	4.0	5.6	8.0	8.6	8.9	11.4	10.5	11.4	14.6	19.6
Lo	2.8	3.6	5.1	5.8	6.5	7.6	5.8	6.4	10.5	13.1

The Coca-Cola Company

One Coca-Cola Plaza, N.W.
Atlanta, Georgia 30313
Tel. (404) 676-2121
Listed: NYSE
Investor contact: Juan D. Johnson, Investor Relations
Ticker symbol: KO
S&P rating: A+

The Coca-Cola Company

As profiled in its 1993 Annual Report, "The Coca-Cola Company is the largest manufacturer, marketer, and distributor of soft drink concentrates and syrups in the world. It manufactures soft drink concentrates and syrups, which it sells to bottling and canning operations, and manufactures fountain/postmix soft drink syrups, which it sells to authorized fountain wholesalers and fountain retailers. The company has substantial equity investments in numerous soft drink bottling and canning operations, and it owns and operates certain bottling and canning operations outside the United States.

"The foods business sector's principal business is processing and marketing citrus, and other juice and juice-drink products, primarily orange juice. It is the world's largest marketer of packaged citrus products.

"Coca-Cola, the world's most recognized trademark and the best-selling soft drink, is now available in more than 195 countries. Diet Coca-Cola/Coca-Cola Light, the number-one diet soft drink in the world and the third best-selling carbonated soft drink of any kind, was introduced in several new markets in 1992, expanding its availability to 117 markets worldwide. Fanta, the world's fourth best-selling carbonated soft drink is sold in 164 countries, making it the only true global brand in the orange segment. Sprite, the world's best-selling lemon-lime soft drink, which is sold in 164 countries, is also the world's fifth best-selling carbonated soft drink of any kind.

"Emerging brands led by TAB Clear, PowerAde, Nestea, and Nordic Mist represent a tiny portion of our current business, but are raising in overall volume and represent solid growth potential.

"Our market leadership has not only been built on the cachet of our brands, but also through the massive distribution capabilities of our global Coca-Cola bottling system—a distribution network unmatched by any other company.

"Coca-Cola Foods maintained its leading share of the juice and juice-drink industry. The availability of Minute Maid juices packaged in single-serve bottles and cans doubled to include 86 percent of the U.S. market."

During 1993, soft drinks represented 87 percent of revenues and 96 percent of income, and foods represented 13 percent of revenues and 4 percent of income. Geographically, the United States represented 33 percent of revenues and 21 percent of income, Latin America 12 percent of revenues and 16 percent of income, the European Community 27 percent of revenues and 25 percent of income, Northeast Europe/Africa 7 percent of revenues and 9 percent of income, and the Pacific and Canada 21 percent of revenues and 29 percent of income.

Berkshire Hathaway—that is Warren Buffet—controls about 7 percent and has Federal approval to purchase up to 15 percent of the common shares. Institutions control about 55 percent of the common shares. Coca-Cola has paid consecutive cash dividends since 1893. It paid a 200 percent stock dividend in 1986, a 100 percent stock dividend in 1990, and a 100 percent stock dividend in 1992.

Total assets: $12.0 billion
Current ratio: 0.9
Common shares outstanding: 1.2 billion

	1984	1985	1986	1987	1988	1989	1990	1991	1992	1993
Revenues (Mil.)	5,442	5,879	6,977	7,658	8,065	8,622	10,236	11,572	13,074	13,957
Net Income (Mil.)	629	722	934	916	1,045	1,537	1,382	1,618	1,664	2,176
Earnings per share	.40	.46	.60	.61	.71	1.10	1.02	1.21	1.43	1.68
Dividends per share	.23	.25	.26	.28	.30	.34	.40	.48	.56	.68
Prices Hi	5.5	7.4	11.2	13.3	11.3	20.2	24.5	40.9	45.4	45.1
Lo	4.1	4.9	6.4	7.0	8.7	10.8	16.3	21.3	35.6	37.5

Commerce Bancshares, Inc.

1000 Walnut (P.O. Box 13686)
Kansas City, Missouri 64199-3686
Tel. (816) 234-2000
Listed: NASDAQ
Investor contact: Treasurer & Comptroller, Charles E. Templer
Ticker symbol: CBSH
S&P rating: A

As profiled in its 1993 Annual Report, "Commerce Bancshares, Inc. is a registered, multi-bank holding company organized as a Missouri corporation in 1966. With $8.0 billion in total assets at December 31, 1993, the company is the third largest bank holding company in Missouri. The company, through its subsidiary banks, conducts a general banking business in over 160 locations. These banks provide a comprehensive range of financial services, including investment management, trust, retail, commercial, brokerage, and correspondent banking services. The

Commerce

company also has non-banking subsidiaries involved in small business investment, credit and related insurance, mortgage banking, and real estate activities."

"Commerce Bancshares, Inc. presently owns, or controls substantially, all of the outstanding capital stock of eleven national banking associations located in Missouri, three national banking associations located in Illinois, one state bank and three national banking associations in Kansas, and a credit card bank which is located in Nebraska and is limited in its activities to the issuance of credit cards.

"The banking subsidiaries which are located in Missouri comprise 92.7 percent of the banking assets of the company, and compete with over 600 Missouri banks, together with savings and loans, and other financial institutions.

"We specialize in providing sophisticated banking services with the hands-on involvement of senior management and an understanding on the community level of the needs of our customers. While we emphasize services to middle-market companies and the core consumer market, we have developed products for customers of every size.

"We aim to develop long-term relationships with our customers by providing them with distinctive value, convenience, dependability, and security. We have the advantages of knowing our communities and the needs of our customers, combined with the resources of a large-scale financial institution.

"Our Corporate Services Division continues to expand. The Cash Management Department has long been recognized as an innovative leader in the area. A full range of options are offered to corporations, designed to allow them to make the most efficient use of their funds based on their specific needs."

During 1993 loans of $4 billion were apportioned as follows: business 34.3 percent, real estate-construction 2.2 percent, real estate-business 13.3 percent, real estate-personal 18.3 percent, consumer 22.8 percent, and credit card 9.1 percent.

Commerce Bancshares, Inc. has paid consecutive cash dividends since 1936. Institutions control about 55 percent of the outstanding common shares. Commerce paid a 100 percent stock dividend in 1986, a 100 percent stock dividend in 1989, and a 50 percent stock dividend in 1993.

Total assets: $8.0 billion
Common shares outstanding: 31.8 million

	1984	1985	1986	1987	1988	1989	19%		
Net Income (Mil.)	31	38	39	40	49	59	58		
Earnings per share	.99	1.21	1.25	1.30	1.64	2.08	2.01		
Dividends per share	.33	.35	.36	.37	.39	.42	.47		
Prices Hi	7.9	10.7	14.1	12.9	14.1	19.7	18.3	2.	
Lo	6.7	7.5	10.3	8.9	9.5	13.1	12.3	14..	

ConAgra, Inc.

One ConAgra Drive
Omaha, Nebraska 68102-5001
Tel. (402) 595-4000
Listed: NYSE
Investor contact: Vice Pres. Corporate Communications, Walter H. Casey
Ticker symbol: CAG
S&P rating: A+

As profiled in its fiscal 1993 Annual Report, "ConAgra is a diversified, international food company. We operate across the food chain around the world. Our profits range from convenient prepared foods for today's busy consumers to supplies farmers need to grow their crops.

"We have major businesses in branded grocery products—shelf-stable and frozen foods, processed meats, chicken and turkey products, and cheeses—as well as in specialty retailing, potato products, private label grocery products, beef, pork, seafood, grain and pulse merchandising, worldwide trading, grain processing, crop protection chemicals, fertilizer, and animal feed.

"ConAgra is a family of independent operating companies. These companies operate in three industry segments of the food chain: Prepared Foods, Trading & Processing, and Agri-Products.

"Prepared Foods' products and services for consumer and food service markets include branded shelf-stable food items such as Hunt's, Wesson, Orville Redenbacher's, Healthy Choice, Swiss Miss, Peter Pan, and La Choy; branded frozen foods such as Healthy Choice, Banquet, Chun King, Morton, and Armour Classics; branded processed meats such as Armour, Swift Premium, Healthy Choice, and Hebrew National; branded chicken and turkey ucts such as Butterball, Country Pride, Country Skillet, and Armour Falls Poultry; beef, pork, and lamb products such as Healthy Choice, Monfort, and Blue Ribbon Beef; seafood products such as Singleton, Taste O'Sea, and Country Skillet; cheeses and refrigerated dessert toppings such as County Line, Healthy Choice, Armour, Miss Wisconsin, Swiss Miss, and Reddi Wip." Other prepared food products include french fries, frozen potato products, delicatessen and food service products, private label consumer products, premium food products marketed by direct mail, pet accessories, and home sewing accessories.

"Trading & Processing includes flour milling, dry corn milling, barley processing, natural spices, seasonings, spray-dried food ingredients, feed ingredient merchandising, worldwide commodity trading (grains, beans, peas, wool, fishmeal, etc.), commodity futures brokerage, and food processing and distribution in Asia, Australia, Europe and Latin America.

"Agri-Products include the marketing and distribution of crop protection chemicals, fertilizer products, animal feeds and animal health care products, high quality lactic acid, and 208 retail stores principally in rural U.S. areas."

During fiscal 1993, Prepared Foods accounted for 76.7 percent of revenues and 78.8 percent of operating profits, Trading & Processing for 10.9 percent of revenues and 11.6 percent of profits, and Agri-Products for 12.4 percent of revenues and 9.6 percent of profits.

ConAgra has paid consecutive cash dividends since 1976. Institutions control about 30 percent of the outstanding common shares. ConAgra paid a 100 percent stock dividend in 1980, a 50 percent stock dividend in 1984, a 100 percent stock dividend in 1986, a 50 percent stock dividend in 1989, and a 50 percent stock dividend in 1991.

Total assets: $10.0 billion
Current ratio: 1.1
Common shares outstanding: 251.7 million

	1984	1985	1986	1987	1988	1989	1990	1991	1992	1993
Revenues (Mil.)	3,302	5,498	5,911	9,002	9,475	11,340	15,501	19,505	21,219	21,519
Net Income (Mil.)	63	92	105	149	155	198	232	311	372	401
Earnings per share	.46	.59	.68	.82	.86	1.09	1.25	1.42	1.50	1.58
Dividends per share	.16	.19	.22	.25	.29	.33	.39	.45	.52	.60
Prices Hi	6.1	10.5	14.3	16.9	15.1	20.1	25.5	36.5	35.8	33.6
Lo	4.4	5.8	8.6	9.3	10.5	12.9	15.1	22.4	24.5	22.8

Crawford & Company

5620 Glenridge Drive, N.E. (P.O. Box 5047)
Atlanta, Georgia 30342-5047
Tel. (404) 256-0830
Listed: NYSE
Investor contact: Exec. Vice Pres., D.R. Chapman
Ticker symbols: CRD.B CRD.A
S&P rating: A

As profiled in its 1992 Annual Report, "Crawford & Company is a diversified service firm that provides claims services, risk management services, healthcare management, and risk control services, as well as risk management systems, to insurance companies, corporations, and self-insured entities. Skilled professionals deliver high-quality services from more than 800 offices in forty-two countries.

Crawford &
Company

"Claims Services provide complete investigation, evaluation, disposition, and management of claims for the insurance industry, including areas such as catastrophe, environmental pollution, property, casualty, and workers compensation.

"Graham Miller International is an international claims services provider with expertise in specialty areas such as oil and energy, banking, fine art, jewelry, the entertainment industry, reinsurance, construction, and property.

"HealthCare Management offers a full range of managed care services designed to reduce medical and disability costs for both the workers compensation and group health markets.

"Risk Control Services provides a broad range of pre-loss services to help corporations control or reduce their risk and also for underwriting purposes.

"Risk Sciences Group is a software applications and consulting firm providing computer-based information systems and analytical forecasting services to the risk management and insurance industry.

"Risk Management Services (RMS)—new in 1992—provides its clients with integrated risk management services, including claims services, medical case management and cost containment, risk control consulting, and state-of-the-art information systems. Working closely with Graham Miller International, RMS also is expanding into the global marketplace to serve the unique needs of our multi-national clients.

"RMS's SISDAT risk management information system provides the link that connects all of Crawford's risk management services together into a meaningful whole. We continue to improve SISDAT capabilities and flexibility with on-line access to claims files for our clients, six new standard loss data reports, expanded data fields, and enhanced systems supporting year-end IRS From 1099 reporting."

During 1992 revenues were apportioned as follows: claims services 73.1 percent, health and rehabilitation services 22.7 percent, and other risk management services 4.2 percent.

Crawford has both Class A and Class B shares of common stock. The Crawford family controls about 60 percent of both Class A and Class B shares. Consecutive cash dividends have been paid since 1968. Crawford paid a 50 percent stock dividend in 1986, a 50 percent stock dividend in 1989, and a 100 percent stock dividend in 1990.

Total assets: $316.8 million
Current ratio: 2.6
Common shares outstanding: Class A 18 million
Class B 18 million

	1984	1985	1986	1987	1988	1989	1990	1991	1992	1993
Revenues (Mil.)	186	214	244	265	294	374	449	538	598	576
Net Income (Mil.)	12	13	15	16	19	28	32	37	40	38
Earnings per share	.35	.39	.44	.47	.54	.79	.91	1.05	1.13	1.06
Dividends per share	.15	.16	.17	.19	.21	.26	.32	.35	.40	.44
Prices Hi	4.3	6.4	8.8	9.5	7.8	18.1	18.3	28.5	30.0	24.3
Lo	2.9	4.0	6.0	4.9	5.6	7.4	10.1	15.1	17.6	15.0

Crompton & Knowles Corporation

One Station Place, Metro Center
Stamford, Connecticut 06902
Tel. (203) 353-5400
Listed: NYSE
Investor contact: Yanis Ribelneiks
Ticker symbol: CNK
S&P rating: A+

As profiled in its 1992 Annual Report, "Crompton & Knowles produces and markets specialty chemicals and equipment in North America, Europe, Latin America and Asia. The corporation's businesses are grouped into two segments: Specialty Chemicals and Specialty Process Equipment and Controls.

"Crompton & Knowles is a major producer and marketer of dyes worldwide, and a major producer and marketer of specialty food and pharmaceutical ingredients in the United States.

"Specialty Chemicals includes dyes and auxiliary chemicals, flavors, specialty sweeteners, seasoning blends, food colors, fragrances, pharmaceutical coatings, and organic intermediates.

"Specialty ingredients produced by Crompton & Knowles are used by (1) the pharmaceutical industry to coat oral dosage medicines, as well as to provide color and flavor; (2) food producers to enhance the taste of products such as microwavable rice; (3) beverage producers to provide flavor, stability, and color in sports drinks; (4) condiment makers to improve the taste of barbecue sauces; (5) bakeries to produce fresh and delicious ready-to-eat cookies.

"Markets for specialty chemicals and ingredients include apparel, home furnishings, paper, automotive fabrics, leather, food, pharmaceuticals, beverages, cosmetics, toiletries, and tobacco.

"Crompton & Knowles is a recognized world leader in extrusion systems and related electronic controls for the plastics industry.

"Specialty Process Equipment and Controls include plastics extruders, industrial blow molding equipment, electronic process controls, process system design, engineering, installation, maintenance, and modernization.

"Markets for Specialty Process Equipment and Controls include producers of plastic packaging for food and consumer goods; manufacturers of plastic parts for appliances, automobiles, housing, and health care; and manufacturers of wire and cable, and plastic recyclers."

During 1992, revenues and operating profit were apportioned as follows: Specialty Chemicals 76.3 percent of revenues and 76 percent of operating profit, and Specialty Process Equipment and Control 23.7 percent of revenues and 24 percent of operating profit.

Crompton & Knowles has paid cash dividends for 240 consecutive quarters and has increased its cash dividend in each of the past sixteen years. S. Knowles de Cuizart owns about 7.5 percent, and institutions control about 50 percent, of the outstanding common shares. Crompton & Knowles paid a 100 percent stock dividend in 1987, a 100 percent stock dividend in 1989, a 100 percent stock dividend in 1990, and a 100 percent stock dividend in 1992.

Total assets: $363.2 million
Current ratio: 2.3
Common shares outstanding: 52.2 million

	1984	1985	1986	1987	1988	1989	1990	1991	1992	1993
Revenues (Mil.)	155	163	178	199	290	356	390	450	518	558
Net Income (Mil.)	7.9	7.6	1.0	12	15	25	30	36	34	52
Earnings per share	.14	.15	.17	.25	.36	.50	.61	.73	.87	1.00
Dividends per share	.07	.08	.08	.08	.11	.15	.20	.25	.31	.38
Prices Hi	1.5	1.8	2.5	3.9	4.5	7.9	11.6	20.3	23.9	24.3
Lo	1.3	1.3	1.6	2.3	2.5	3.8	6.8	8.4	16.0	15.0

Crown Cork & Seal Company, Inc.

9300 Ashton Road
Philadelphia, Pennsylvania 19136
Tel. (215) 698-5100
Listed: NYSE
Investor contact: Vice Pres. & Treas., Craig R.L. Calle
Ticker symbol: CCK
S&P rating: B+

Rescued by the late John F. Connelly from near financial collapse in 1957, Crown Cork & Seal has grown consistently over the years, both through increased volume of business and acquisitions.

As profiled in its 1993 Annual Report, "The company's business is the manufacture and sale of metal and plastic containers and crowns, of aluminum and plastic closures, and the building of filling, packaging and handling machinery. These products are manufactured in eighty-four plants within the United States and seventy plants outside the United States and are sold through our own sales organization to the food, citrus, brewing, soft drink, oil, paint, toiletry, drug, antifreeze, chemical, and pet food industries.

"Fabricated products include aerosol cans, beer and beverage cans, food cans, crowns, closures, cone top cans, "F" style rectangular cans, motor oil cans (steel and composite), and paint cans.

"Machinery products include bottle washers and rinsers; bottle and can warmers; bottle fillers for beer, beverages, and juices; can fillers for beer, beverages, and juices; casers and decasers, crowners, and conveyors for bottles, cans and case goods; process equipment for carbonated beverages; palletizers for cans and case goods; depalletizers for cans and case goods; can end presses; crown dust removal equipment, ironers for D&I can making, liners, rotary printers for D&I can making, spray machines for can making, trimmers for D&I can making, and ultra mark date coding machines.

"Plastic products include P.E.T. beverage containers, water containers, food containers, personal care containers, and dish detergent containers; HDPE containers, Polypropylene medical disposal devices, PVC containers, and P.E.T. Preforms and Closures.

"In October 1992, the Company acquired CONSTAR International, Inc. CONSTAR, with 1991 sales of $548 million, is one of the world's leading manufacturers of plastic containers for the beverage, food, household, chemical, and other industries. CONSTAR, also maintains a 44 percent interest in Wellstar Holding, which services the European market from five plants located in the Netherlands, England, France, and Hungary."

During 1992, metal packaging and machinery products provided 94.5 percent of revenues and 92.6 percent of operating profits, and plastic packaging provided 5.5 percent of revenues and 7.4 percent of operating profits. Geographically, the United States provided 63.8 percent of revenues and 79 percent of operating profits, Europe 15.3 percent of revenues and 8.9 percent of operating profits, North and Central America 13.2 percent of revenues and 2.8 percent of operating profits, and other foreign countries 7.7 percent of revenues and 9.3 percent of operating profits.

Crown Cork & Seal has not paid a cash dividend in over thirty years. Institutions control over 50 percent of the common shares. Crown Cork paid a 200 percent stock dividend in 1988, a 200 percent stock dividend in 1988, and a 200 percent stock dividend in 1992.

Total assets: $4.2 billion
Current ratio: 1.0
Common shares outstanding: 88.8 million

	1984	1985	1986	1987	1988	1989	1990	1991	1992	1993
Revenues (Mil.)	1,370	1,487	1,619	1,718	1,834	1,910	3,072	3,807	3,781	4,163
Net Income (Mil.)	60	72	79	88	93	94	107	128	155	99
Earnings per share	.53	.72	.83	.95	1.12	1.19	1.24	1.48	1.79	2.08
Dividends per share	—	—	—	—	—	—	—	—	—	—
Prices Hi	5.3	10.0	12.7	15.5	15.8	19.0	22.3	30.9	41.1	41.9
Lo	3.9	4.9	8.6	9.5	10.0	14.6	16.5	18.1	27.4	33.3

Dauphin Deposit Corporation

213 Market Street (P.O. Box 2961)
Harrisburg, Pennsylvania 17105
Tel. (717) 255-2121
Listed: NASDAQ
Investor contact: Senior Vice Pres. & Secy., Claire D. Flemming
Ticker symbol: DAPN
S&P rating: A

Dauphin Deposit
Corporation

As profiled in its 1992 Annual Report, "Dauphin Deposit Corporations, headquartered in Harrisburg, Pennsylvania, is the parent company of Dauphin Deposit Bank and Trust Company, which includes the Bank of Pennsylvania Division, and Farmers Bank and Trust Company of Hanover. The Banks operate ninety-nine branch offices in Pennsylvania."

"Dauphin has a 158-year history of solid performance and consistent growth while serving both consumers and the business sector. As recently as ten years ago, management began to clearly identify major market segments, their characteristics and expectations for financial services. The objective has been to continually evolve product as well as delivery in response to market changes. Although each line function is responsible for certain core business sectors in the marketplace–the Community Banking Division for the consumer; the Corporate Division serving business clients; and the Financial Services Division providing trust and investment services—each contributes to the common purpose of creating an interdisciplinary delivery system.

"On July 1, 1992, the merger of FB&T Corporation became effective, and this strong, $650,000,000, Hanover, Pennsylvania, based banking company became part of corporation. A market extending merger, the linkage of Dauphin and FB&T, positions the corporation for future growth and expansion in the very attractive south-central Pennsylvania and northern Maryland markets.

"Hopper Soliday & Co., Inc., our Lancaster based securities broker/dealer subsidiary, underwrote $1.6 billion in general obligation and revenue bonds in 1992, and was once again one of the top underwriters of general obligation bonds in the State.

"Several new consumer products and product enhancements were released in 1992. The first is our new Combined Statement. At the customer's discretion, deposit accounts, including certificates of deposit and lines of credit, can be assigned to one monthly statement reporting all monthly account and transaction details.

"Shortly thereafter, the new Personal Choice package account was made available. Personal Choice incorporates the Combined Statement in its menu of standard benefits and also includes one other major 1992 product development—our MagiCard/VISA Debit card."

During 1992, loans of $2.2 billion were apportioned as follows: commercial, financial and agricultural 46.8 percent, real estate construction 6 percent, real estate residential 31.5 percent, consumer 15.2 percent, lease financing .7 percent and unamortized net loan fees -.2 percent.

Dauphin Deposit has increased earning, for the twenty-second consecutive year and cash dividends for the seventeenth consecutive year. It has paid consecutive cash dividends since 1910. Institutions control about 25 percent of the common shares. Dauphin paid a 10 percent stock dividend in 1981, a 100 percent stock dividend in 1983, a 100 percent stock dividend in 1985, a 5 percent stock dividend in 1989, and a 100 percent stock dividend in 1992.

Total assets: $4.6 billion
Common shares outstanding: 29.9 million

	1984	1985	1986	1987	1988	1989	1990	1991	1992	1993
Net Income (Mil.)	21	24	33	37	41	44	45	53	57	64
Earnings per share	1.06	1.22	1.27	1.42	1.57	1.71	1.78	1.84	1.93	2.15
Dividends per share	.44	.48	.53	.58	.62	.69	.72	.75	.77	.83
Prices Hi	7.9	13.6	18.7	17.0	16.3	18.8	17.6	18.6	25.3	28.0
Lo	6.0	7.9	13.4	12.3	13.6	14.2	12.0	12.5	17.6	22.5

Deluxe Corporation

1080 West County Road F (P.O. Box 64399)
St. Paul, Minnesota 55126-8201
Tel. (612) 483-7111
Listed: NYSE
Investor contact: Vice Pres. Corporate Public Relations, Stuart Alexander
Ticker symbol: DLX
S&P rating: A

As profiled in its 1993 Annual Report, "Deluxe Corporation began business in 1915, printing checks for financial institutions and their customers. Throughout its seventy-nine year history, Deluxe's reputation for providing quality products and excellent service has helped it become the nation's largest supplier of checks, deposit tickets, and other magnetic-ink encoded transaction forms.

"In recent years, Deluxe has expanded the line of products and services it offers to the payment systems industry. In addition to printing checks and related documents, Deluxe provides electronic funds transfer processing services and software, ATM card services, and account verification services to financial institutions. The company also provides check authorization services to retailers.

"Deluxe has also expanded into new markets. Its Business Systems Division has become a major supplier of short-run computer forms, business forms, and related office products to small businesses and professional practices. In addition, Business Systems provides forms and electronic tax filing services to independent tax professionals. The company's Consumer Specialty Products Division markets greeting cards, gift wrap, stationery, and a variety of related products to the nation's households.

"Payment Systems (Deluxe Check Printers, Deluxe Data Systems, Inc., ChexSystems, Inc., Electronic Transaction Corp., Deluxe Card Services, and Deluxe Financial Forms) accounting for 71.5 percent of Deluxe's 1992 revenues, is our largest business group. Deluxe Check Printers, the largest business within this division, is the nation's leading printer of checks and deposit tickets for consumers and small businesses. Deluxe has also established leading positions in segments of the emerging electronic payment systems market. We are a major provider of transaction processing services and software for regional ATM networks. We are also involved in electronic benefit transfer, retail point-of-sale, and automated clearinghouse services. Account verification for financial institutions and check authorization for retailers are two other rapidly growing businesses for Deluxe in the payment systems market.

"Deluxe Business Systems (General Business Forms Market Group, Healthcare Forms Market Group and Nelco, Inc.), accounting for 12.7 percent of Deluxe's 1992 revenues, established in 1988, is one of the nation's largest suppliers of short-run forms and related products to small businesses. Given Deluxe's expertise in short-run customized printing, Deluxe Business Systems represents a logical extension of our printing operations. With revenues increasing at a 14 percent annual compound rate over the past five years, Deluxe Business Systems has become Deluxe's fastest growing division.

"Consumer Specialty Products accounting for 15.8 percent of Deluxe's 1992 revenues was greatly expanded by our 1987 acquisitions of Current, Inc. Current is the nation's largest direct-mail marketer of greeting cards, gift wrap, small gifts, and related products. As a specialty printer and technologically advanced direct mailer, Current is an excellent extension of Deluxe's core capabilities. Current has grown at an 11 percent compounded annual rate since 1988."

The ability to generate high levels of profitable growth year in and year out has been one of the hallmarks of the company. In 1993, Deluxe Corporation increased sales of the fifty-fifth consecutive year and dividends for the thirty-second consecutive year. Among Fortune 500 companies, Deluxe has recorded above-average profitability for more than five decades. It has paid consecutive cash dividends since 1921. Institutions control about 60 percent of the outstanding common shares. Deluxe paid a 100 percent stock dividend in 1981, a 100 percent stock dividend in 1985, and a 100 percent stock dividend in 1986.

Total assets: $1.3 billion
Current ratio: 1.8
Common shares outstanding: 82.3 million

	1984	1985	1986	1987	1988	1989	1990	1991	1992	1993
Revenues (Mil.)	683	764	867	948	1,196	1,316	1,414	1,474	1,534	1,582
Net Income (Mil.)	88	104	121	149	143	153	172	183	203	142
Earnings per share	1.00	1.22	1.42	1.74	1.68	1.79	2.03	2.18	2.42	1.71
Dividends per share	.39	.49	.58	.76	.86	.98	1.10	1.22	1.34	1.42
Prices Hi	14.5	24.9	38.0	42.3	28.4	35.8	35.9	48.5	49.0	47.9
Lo	8.9	13.6	21.5	20.0	21.0	24.0	26.6	32.8	38.1	31.8

Diagnostics Products Corporation

5700 West 96th Street
Los Angeles, California 90045-5597
Tel. (213) 776-0180
Listed: NYSE
Investor contact: Vice Pres. Finance, Julian R. Bockserman
Ticker symbol: DP
S&P rating: B+

Diagnostics Products Corporation

As profiled in its 1993 Annual Report, "Diagnostic Products Corporation (DPC) is the world's leading independent manufacturer of immunodiagnostic kits and instrumentation. The kits measure hormones, drugs and other medically important substances present in body fluids and tissues at infinitesimal concentrations. They provide information vital to the diagnosis and management of thyroid disorders, diabetes, allergy, drugs of abuse, and certain forms of cancer. DPC's diagnostic instrumentation systems fulfill increasing demands by the marketplace for more fully automated labor-saving devices. DPC uses molecular biology techniques–including monoclonal anti-bodies, recombinant DNA, and genetic engineering–to bring about significant advances in diagnostics and therapeutics. Facilities include corporate headquarters in Los Angeles, California; affiliated R&D and manufacturing at Cirrus Diagnostics Inc. in New Jersey; EURO/DPC in Wales; De Pu (DPC) in China; and Nippon DPC, a joint venture in Japan; plus partially or wholly owned interests in several of its key distributors.

"IMMULITE, DPC's new totally automated random access immunoassay system, coupled with DPC's strong resources for producing quality reagents at competitive prices, provides a significant platform for expansion within the next decade. Ten assays were on board as of the end of 1992, with an additional twenty tests to be released in 1993.

"DPC's allergy development made significant gains in 1992 with the release of the ALASTAT MICROPLATE-BASED ALLERGY System, which includes automated instrumentation, such as the MARK 5 ROBOTIC PIPETTOR and MILENIA MAX AUTOPROCESSOR.

"Maxsoftware interfaces with a variety of automated and manual instruments to make DPC's allergy system compatible with laboratories of all sizes.

"DPC's cancer-related kits encompass a broad spectrum of tissue types and diseases.

"The 1992 acquisition of Cirrus Diagnostics Inc. provides the company with a unique opportunity to enter the field of fully automated, random-access immunodiagnostic systems. The key challenges for the company during 1993 are to continue the rapid development of kits for the IMMULITE System, to respond effectively to the significant demand for IMMULITE instruments, and to enhance DPC's service and training capabilities, consistent with the needs of the IMMULITE System."

During 1992, the United States provided 57 percent of revenues and Europe 45 percent of revenues.

DPC has no long-term debt. Cash dividends were initiated in 1988. Chairman Sigi Ziering and Vice President Marilyn Ziering control over 20 percent of the outstanding common shares. Institutions control about 25 percent of the common stock. Diagnostic Products paid a 900 percent stock dividend in 1982, a 50 percent stock dividend in 1983, and a 100 percent stock dividend in 1989.

Total assets: $137.1 million
Current ratio: 5.0
Common shares outstanding: 13.1 million

	1984	1985	1986	1987	1988	1989	1990	1991	1992	1993
Revenues (Mil.)	18	23	29	37	47	60	76	90	103	107
Net income (Mil.)	2.9	3.9	6.3	9.3	12	14	15	16	17	14
Earnings per share	.27	.37	.54	.75	.97	1.13	1.17	1.20	1.26	1.04
Dividends per share	—	—	—	—	.12	.20	.24	.32	.32	.40
Prices Hi	6.9	7.9	13.6	20.3	22.8	38.0	44.0	53.8	44.0	30.8
Lo	3.5	4.4	7.4	10.3	14.0	19.3	22.3	28.5	20.1	17.1

Dillard Department Stores, Inc.

1600 Cantrell Road (P.O. Box 486)
Little Rock, Arkansas 72201
Tel. (501) 376-5200
Listed: NYSE
Investor contact: Vice President–Chief Financial Officer, James I. Freeman
Ticker symbol: DDS
S&P rating: A+

As profiled in its 1993 Annual Report, "Dillard Department Stores, Inc. operates a regional group of 227 retail traditional department stores, 60 in Texas, 28 in

DILLARD DEPARTMENT STORES, INC.

Florida, 17 in Louisiana, 16 in Missouri, 14 in Ohio, 14 in Oklahoma, 14 in Arizona, 13 in North Carolina, nine in Kansas, eleven in Tennessee, seven in Arkansas, six in Nebraska, four in New Mexico, four in South Carolina, three in Nevada, two in Illinois, two in Mississippi, one in Alabama, and one in Iowa. The stores vary in size from 48,000 square feet to 409,000 square feet and feature fashion brands catering to middle to upper-middle income consumers, with special emphasis upon fashion apparel and home furnishings. Price points are based upon an everyday pricing strategy that replaces storewide sales events. In many cases, these everyday prices offer the consumer a better value than competitor's sale prices.

"An often-overlooked but fundamental measure of success in the company's growth throughout the last decade is our aggressive expansion and remodeling of stores in key areas. All our remodels and expansions are of the highest caliber, and receive a great deal of local publicity through both advertising and word of mouth. We have expanded and remodeled over forty existing stores in the last ten years, with twelve remodels in the last year alone. This is one of the best ways to boost our market dominance, and one we will continue to pursue in the years ahead. In 1993, we plan to remodel and expand two stores, one in New Mexico and on in Ohio.

"If someone were to ask what the one secret to Dillard's success in the last decade, the phrase 'timely acquisitions of prime real estate' would surely spring to mind. It would be an understatement to say that such acquisitions have played an important role in the company's expansion into new, fertile market areas. The fact is, when we acquire a store, we're often more interested in the real estate it sits on than in the store itself. We believe that putting a Dillard's sign on the front of someone else's store is not enough to make it one of our own. So when we acquire a store, we generally use the existing site as the foundation for a completely new store—a Dillard's store from the ground up."

During 1992, sales were allocated as follows: women's clothing 26 percent, men's clothing and accessories 17.7 percent, cosmetics 12.2 percent, lingerie and accessories 10.3 percent, shoes 7.7 percent, children's clothing 6.8 percent, juniors' clothing 5.5 percent, decorative home fashion 5.2 percent, and other 8.6 percent.

There are both Class A and Class B shares. The Class A common shares are 25 percent owned by a Dutch company; but the Class B controlling shares, which elect two-thirds of the directors, are owned by the Dillard family, which is active both in the control and day-to-day operation of the company.

Dillard has paid consecutive cash dividends since 1969. It paid a 100 percent stock dividend in 1983, a 100 percent stock dividend in 1984, a 100 percent stock dividend in 1985, and a 200 percent stock dividend in 1992.

Total assets: $4.4 billion
Current ratio: 3.1
Common shares outstanding: Class A 108.9 million
Class B 4.0 million

	1984	1985	1986	1987	1988	1989	1990	1991	1992	1993
Revenues (Mil.)	1,277	1,601	1,851	2,206	2,558	3,049	3,606	4,036	4,714	5,131
Net income (Mil.)	50	67	74	91	114	148	183	206	236	241
Earnings per share	.61	.76	.78	.94	1.18	1.45	1.67	1.84	2.11	2.14
Dividends per share	.029	.035	.040	.047	.053	.060	.067	.073	.080	.080
Prices Hi	7.0	12.8	15.3	19.2	15.5	24.8	32.0	45.6	51.5	52.9
Lo	3.6	6.0	10.7	8.0	8.4	13.7	20.6	27.5	30.0	33.1

Dun & Bradstreet Corporation

200 Myala Farms
Westport, Connecticut 06880
Tel. (203) 222-4200
Listed: NYSE
Investor contact: V.P. Investor Services, Frank L. Alexander
Ticker symbol: DNB
S&P rating: A+

As profiled in its 1993 Annual Report, "The Dun & Bradstreet (D&B) Corporation is the world's leading marketer of information, software and services for business decision making. D&B's products and services help customers manage their businesses more efficiently by strengthening their information resources and systems, and by enhancing their ability to make timely decisions and take actions that increase revenue and profitability. D&B's global capabilities include offices in more than sixty countries.

"Marketing Information Services include IMS International, the leading supplier of information and decision-support services for the worldwide pharmaceutical industry, and A.C. Nielsen, the worldwide leader in the marketing research industry and the leading provider of television audience research information services in the U.S.

"Risk Management and Business Marketing Information Services include Dun & Bradstreet Information Services (DBIS), which is the world's leading supplier of business commercial-credit and business marketing information services, with operations in more than thirty countries and a worldwide database covering more than twenty-five million businesses; Moody's Investors Service, which issues ratings on corporate and government obligations and issuers of commercial paper in the U.S., Canada, Europe, and Asia-Pacific, and publishes business and financial information; and Interactive Data, which provides securities-related information and software to the North American Investment community.

"Software Services include Dun & Bradstreet Software, which is the world's leading provider of financial, human-resource, distribution and manufacturing software and related services; Sales Technologies, which provides sales-force-management software in the U.S. and Europe; and Erisco, which provides software and services for employee-benefits administration.

"Directory Information Services includes Reuben H. Donnelley, which compiles, publishes, and serves as sales and marketing representative for more than 400 directories in seventeen states and the District of Columbia. Donnelley serves markets in various regions of the country in association with Nynex, Cincinnati Bell, Centel Corporation, and Sprint, and is a proprietary publisher in the mid-Atlantic area and California. DonTech, a partnership with Ameritech Publishing, serves Illinois and northwestern Indiana. Thomson Directories, Ltd., a partnership with The Thomson Corporation, serves markets in the United Kingdom.

"Other Business Services include Dun & Bradstreet Plan Services, which provides group health-insurance marketing and administration services to insurance companies, agents, and businesses. Dun & Bradstreet Pension Services supplies small-business pension and profit-sharing services; NCH Promotional Services provides cents-off-coupon redemption, processing, and management services to retailers and manufacturers; and Data quest, which provides market-research information to the high-technology and heavy-industry sectors worldwide."

During 1992, revenues and operating income were apportioned as follows: Marketing Information Services 39.9 percent of revenues and 28.2 percent of income, Risk Management and Business Marketing Information Services 32 percent of revenues and 40.6 percent of income, Software Services 11.2 percent of revenues and -2.1 percent of income. Directory Information Services 08.8 percent of revenues and 16.9 percent of income, and Other Business Services 8.1 percent of revenues and 16.4 percent of income.

Dun & Bradstreet Corporation is exceptionally strong financially and has no long-term debt. It has paid consecutive cash dividends since 1934. Institutions control about 75 percent of the outstanding shares. Dun & Bradstreet paid a 100 percent stock dividend in 1983, and another 100 percent stock dividend in 1987.

Total assets: $5.2 billion
Current ratio: 1.0
Common shares outstanding: 170.3 million

	1984	1985	1986	1987	1988	1989	1990	1991	1992	1993
Revenues (Mil.)	2,625	3,022	3,463	3,789	4,267	4,319	4,837	4,651	4,751	4,710
Net income (Mil.)	281	325	379	439	499	552	507	507	554	(N/A)
Earnings per share	1.51	1.75	2.04	2.36	2.67	3.13	2.79	2.84	3.10	2.42
Dividends per share	.91	1.06	1.24	1.45	1.68	1.94	2.09	2.15	2.25	2.40
Prices Hi	33.9	43.9	60.3	71.8	57.5	60.3	48.6	58.0	59.1	68.5
Lo	25.6	31.5	40.5	44.5	45.9	41.3	36.1	39.1	50.6	55.8

Emerson Electric Co.

8000 West Florissant Avenue (P.O. Box 4100)
St. Louis, Missouri 63136-8506
Tel. (314) 553-2000
Listed: NYSE
Investor contact: Assistant Treasurer, John E. Kaiser
Ticker symbol: EMR
S&P rating: A+

As profiled in its fiscal 1993 Annual Report, "Emerson was incorporated in Missouri in 1890. Originally engaged in the manufacture and sale of electric motors and fans prior to World War II and aircraft armament items during the war, Emerson's product lines were subsequently expanded through internal growth and acquisitions. The company is now en-

gaged principally in the design, manufacture, and sale of a broad range of electrical and electronic products and systems.

"The products manufactured by the Company are classified into the following industry segments: Commercial and Industrial Components and Systems, and Appliance and Construction-Related Components.

"The Commercial and Industrial segment includes process control instrumentation and systems; industrial motors and drives; industrial machinery, equipment, and components; and computer support products. These products are generally highly engineered, both in product design and manufacturing process. Products of this segment are sold to commercial and industrial distributors and end-users for manufacturing and heavy commercial applications.

"The Appliance and Construction-Related Components segment consists of fractional horsepower motors; appliance components; heating, ventilating, and air conditioning components; and tools. This segment includes components sold to distributors and original equipment manufacturers for inclusion in end-products and systems (ultimately sold through commercial and residential building construction channels); and construction-related products, which retain their identity and are sold through distributors to consumers and professional tradesmen.

"Emerson utilizes various production operations and methods. The principal production operations are metal stamping, forming, casting, machining, welding, plating, heat treating, painting, and assembly.

"On October 1, 1992, Emerson acquired Fisher Controls International, Inc., and its subsidiaries and other related operations. Fisher is a worldwide manufacturer of control valves and control systems for major process industries including chemical, oil and gas, and pulp and paper. On September 30, 1992, Emerson and Robert Bosch GmbH established a fifty-fifty joint venture for the development, manufacture, and distribution of power tools. Emerson contributed its Skil business and Bosch contributed its U.S. power tool operations for form S-B Power Tool Company."

During fiscal 1993, revenues and operating income were apportioned as follows: Commercial and Industrial 59.8 percent of revenues and 52.7 percent of operating income, and Appliance and Construction-Related 40.2 percent of revenues and 47.3 percent of operating income.

Geographically, during fiscal 1993, revenues and operating income were distributed as follows: the United States 68.1 percent of revenues and 78.5 percent of operating income, Europe 23.8 percent of revenues and 15.2 percent of operating income, and other areas 8.1 percent of revenues and 6.3 percent of operating income.

Emerson Electric Co. has had thirty-six consecutive years of earnings and thirty-seven consecutive years of dividend increases. Emerson has paid consecutive cash dividends since 1947. Institutions control about 65 percent of the outstanding common shares. Emerson split its common shares 3 for 1 in 1987.

Total assets: $7.8 billion
Current ratio: 1.1
Common shares outstanding: 224.8 million

	1984	1985	1986	1987	1988	1989	1990	1991	1992	1993
Revenues (Mil.)	4,587	4,921	5,242	6,170	6,652	7,071	7,573	7,427	7,706	8,174
Net income (Mil.)	383	416	427	467	529	588	613	632	663	708
Earnings per share	1.62	1.76	1.83	2.00	2.31	2.63	2.75	2.83	2.96	3.15
Dividends per share	.77	.87	.92	.97	1.00	1.12	1.26	1.32	1.38	1.44
Prices Hi	23.9	27.5	30.9	42.4	36.0	39.9	44.4	55.5	58.0	62.4
Lo	18.4	19.5	22.3	26.8	27.3	29.5	30.8	36.9	46.8	52.8

Ethyl Corporation

330 South Fourth Street (P.O. Box 2189)
Richmond, Virginia 23217
Tel. (804) 788-5000
Listed: NYSE
Investor contact: Director–Investor Relations, John S. Patton
Ticker symbol: EY
S&P rating: A

As profiled in its 1993 Annual Report, "Ethyl Corporation makes and markets value-added performance chemicals worldwide for the petroleum and plastics industries. Ethyl also produces high-technology chemical intermediates for detergents, polymers, electronics, agricultural chemicals, and pharmaceuticals.

"Ethyl produces a diversified line of performance chemicals and specialty intermediates that enhance the quality of life each day for people around the world. More than half of Ethyl's chemical sales are to customers outside the U.S. The company's position is either first or second in a large majority of the markets it serves. Though hardly household items, Ethyl intermediates, catalysts, and additives are essential building blocks that help create consumer products and improve their performance in a broad range of end-use applications. These include detergents, plastic polymers, rubber modifiers, agricultural chemicals, drilling compounds, electronics, pharmaceuticals, fuels, and lubricants. Ethyl's Industrial Chemicals, Electronic Materials, Performance Products and Petroleum Additives divisions operate ten plants in the U.S., Canada and Europe.

"Intermediates and additives from the Industrial Chemical Division include plastic products, ranging from molded parts to films; household detergents and disinfectants; fabric softeners; personal-care products, such as cosmetics and shampoos; printing papers; and synthetic lubricants.

"The Electronics Materials Division manufactures the granular form of ultra-high-purity polysilicon, produced by a marriage of Ethyl's organometallic chemistry and breakthroughs in fluidized-bed process engineering and design.

"The Performance Products Division produces flame retardants, pharmaceutical intermediates, and SOLIMIDE polyamide insulating foam."

"Ethyl Petroleum Additives develops, makes, and markets performance-enhancing fuel and lubricant additives and services to refiners and marketers of petroleum products around the world.

"Ethyl conducts its ethical and over-the-counter pharmaceutical business through a wholly-owned subsidiary, Whitby, Inc., including Whitby Research, Inc. and Whitby Pharmaceuticals, Inc."

During 1992 revenues and operating profits were apportioned as follows: chemicals 56.9 percent of revenues and 47.6 percent of profits, and insurance 43.1 percent of revenues and 52.4 percent of profits.

Geographically, domestic sales of chemicals represented 71.3 percent of revenues and 79.2 percent of profits, and foreign sales of chemicals represented 28.7 percent of sales and 20.8 percent of profits.

Ethyl Corporation has paid consecutive cash dividends since 1957. The Gottwald family interests control about 18 percent of the outstanding shares, and institutions about 40 percent. Ethyl paid a 100 percent stock dividend in 1983, a 100 percent stock dividend in 1985, and a 100 percent stock dividend in 1986.

Total assets: $2.0 billion
Current ratio: 2.2
Common shares outstanding: 118.4 million

	1984	1985	1986	1987	1988	1989	1990	1991	1992	1993
Revenues (Mil.)	1,675	1,547	1,579	1,720	2,012	1,520	1,591	1,535	1,693	1,938
Net income (Mil.)	126	131	165	178	231	220	224	210	255	176
Earnings per share	.81	1.02	1.25	1.44	1.91	1.83	1.88	1.78	2.15	1.48
Dividends per share	.21	.29	.33	.40	.43	.51	.60	.60	.60	.60
Prices Hi	8.4	15.4	23.4	32.3	24.1	29.0	33.0	33.0	30.5	30.9
Lo	5.0	7.9	13.5	15.0	17.3	21.0	20.5	22.3	23.8	16.8

Fifth Third Bancorp

38 Fountain Square Plaza
Cincinnati, Ohio 45263
Tel. (513) 579-5300
Listed: NASDAQ
Investor contact: Senior Vice President, P. Michael Brumm
Ticker symbol: FITB
S&P rating: A+

As profiled in its 1993 Annual Report, "First Third Bancorp is a bank holding company that has thirteen wholly-owned subsidiaries. The company continues to concentrate on four businesses—Retail Banking, Commercial Banking, Trust and Investment Services, and Data Processing—focused primarily in Ohio, Kentucky, and Indiana.

"Retail Banking expanded its delivery system in 1993, with the addition of thirty-six new banking centers and the closing of thirteen, bringing the total to 289. Fifty-three banking centers are open seven days a week in select Kroger, FINAST, and Marsh Supermarkets and Retirement centers. Retail Banking services include personal checking accounts and savings programs, certificates of deposit, money market accounts, individual retirement accounts, and Keough plans.

"The Consumer Banking Division services individual as well as corporate customers, offering a broad range of credit programs for all retail customers including credit card banking under the VISA and Mastercard designation, as well as private label cards, installment loans, student loans, and secured and unsecured personal loans. The Residential Mortgage Loan Department provides

FHA, VA, and conventional as well as adjustable rate mortgage loans to individuals, and is active in originating mortgages for sale in the secondary market.

"The Commercial Banking Division provides a variety of services to meet the needs of the Bank's corporate customers. Available are all types of commercial loans, including lines of credit, revolving credits, term loans, real estate mortgage loans, and other specialized loans, including asset-based financing as well as various types of commercial leases.

"The Trust & Investment Division offers a full-range of trust and investment services for individuals, corporations, and not-for-profit organizations. The company's trust assets under care totalled $36.4 billion at year-end 1992.

"Data Processing, the fourth line of business, is a significant fee income generator. Midwest Payment Systems (MPS), our data processing subsidiary, is one of the nation's leading providers of electronic funds transfer (EFT) services. MPS offers an online automated teller machine (ATM) network, known as the JEANIE network."

In 1993, leans and leases of $7.5 billion were apportioned as follows: commercial, financial, and agricultural 30.3 percent; commercial mortgage 7.2 percent; construction 3.7 percent; commercial leases 3.4 percent; consumer installment 20.3 percent; consumer mortgage 24.5 percent; credit card 2.4 percent; and consumer loans 8.2 percent.

Fifth Third Bancorp has increased earnings for the nineteenth consecutive year. It has paid consecutive cash dividends since 1952. In 1992, it paid the twenty-fourth cash dividend increase since the formation of Fifth Third Bancorp seventeen years ago. It paid a 100 percent stock dividend in 1983, and 50 percent stock dividends in 1985, 1986, 1987, 1990, and 1992.

Total assets: $12.0 billion
Common shares outstanding: 61.4 million

	1984	1985	1986	1987	1988	1989	1990	1991	1992	1993
Net income (Mil.)	35	44	55	83	91	108	120	138	164	(N/A)
Earnings per share	.96	1.14	1.34	1.48	1.61	1.86	2.05	2.33	2.75	3.28
Dividends per share	.28	.33	.37	.45	.52	.60	.68	.78	.90	.99
Prices Hi	7.7	12.9	19.3	18.7	20.3	26.6	24.7	45.4	54.0	59.0
Lo	6.3	7.6	12.6	13.5	14.1	19.7	15.5	20.1	40.1	49.5

First Alabama Bancshares, Inc.

417 North 20th Street (P.O. Box 10247)
Birmingham, Alabama 35202-0247
Tel. (205) 326-7100
Listed: NASDAQ
Investor contact: Exec. Vice Pres & Comptroller, Robert P. Houston
Ticker symbol: FAB
S&P rating: A+

As profiled in its 1993 Annual Report, "First Alabama's primary business is banking. In 1993, First Alabama's affiliate banks contributed approximately $108 million to consolidated net income. First Alabama Bank, the company's principal banking subsidiary, operates 166 full-service banking offices through-

> **First Alabama Bancshares, Inc.**

out Alabama. First Security Bank of Tennessee, acquired in December 1992, operates twenty full-service offices in middle Tennessee, and Sunshine Bank, the company's Florida banking affiliate, operates twenty-three full-service banking offices in northwest Florida. In 1991, the company established a Georgia bank, First Alabama Bank of Columbus, which operates three full-service banking offices in Columbus, Georgia.

"Supplementing the company's bank operations are a mortgage banking company, credit life insurance related companies, and a registered broker/dealer firm. First Alabama has no foreign operations, although it has an International Department to assist customers with their foreign transactions. The mortgage banking subsidiary has become more important in recent years due to excellent growth. It now services approximately $6.3 billion in mortgage loans, and in 1992 contributed approximately $7.6 million to net income.

"The company's principal marketing areas are all of Alabama, middle Tennessee, northwest Florida, and Columbus, Georgia. In addition, real estate mortgage loan origination offices are located in other areas of Georgia, Florida and Tennessee, and throughout Mississippi and South Carolina.

"First Alabama's real estate mortgage portfolio includes $530 million of mortgage loans secured by owner-occupied, single family residences that were originated by First Alabama's mortgage company. The majority of these loans are secured by homes in Alabama, Georgia, and Florida, and most of the rest are secured by homes in other southeastern states.

"A sound credit policy and careful, consistent credit review are vital to a successful lending program. All affiliates of First Alabama operate under written loan policies which attempt to maintain a consistent lending philosophy, provide sound traditional credit decisions, provide an adequate return, and render service to the communities in which the banks are located. First Alabama's lending policy generally confines loans to local customers or to national and international firms doing business locally. Credit reviews and loan examinations help confirm that affiliates are adhering to these loan policies."

During 1993, loans of $6.8 billion were apportioned as follows: commercial industrial and agricultural 21.8 percent, real estate-construction 3.9 percent, real estate-mortgage 48.4 percent and installment 25.9 percent.

First Alabama Bancshares has paid consecutive cash dividends since 1968. Institutions control about 40 percent of the outstanding common shares. First Alabama paid a 100 percent stock dividend in 1984, a 100 percent stock dividend in 1986, and a 10 percent stock dividend in 1993.

Total assets: $10.5 billion
Common shares outstanding: 41.0 million

	1984	1985	1986	1987	1988	1989	1990	1991	1992	1993
Net income (Mil.)	46	54	55	56	58	63	69	78	95	112
Earnings per share	1.28	1.49	1.52	1.55	1.61	1.72	1.91	2.16	2.60	3.01
Dividends per share	.45	.51	.58	.69	.73	.76	.84	.87	.91	1.04
Prices Hi	11.2	16.9	24.1	21.9	15.3	17.6	16.8	27.1	33.9	38.4
Lo	7.7	9.8	14.9	12.1	12.2	13.7	13.3	15.9	23.8	29.6

First Empire State Corporation

One M&T Plaza
Buffalo, New York 14240-0223
Tel. (716) 842-4200
Listed: AMEX
Investor contact: Senior Vice President, Gary S. Paul
Ticker symbol FES
S&P rating: A+

As profiled in its 1993 Annual Report, "First Empire State Corporation is a bank holding company headquartered in Buffalo, New York, which had assets of $10.4 billion at December 31, 1993. Its subsidiaries include Manufacturers and Traders Trust Company (M&T Bank), with 106 offices throughout Western New York State and New York's Southern Tier (principally in Buffalo and Rochester), thirteen offices in the Hudson Valley of New York State, one in New York City, plus a branch in Nassau, The Bahamas, and loan production offices in Albany and Syracuse; and The East New York Savings Bank, with nineteen offices in metropolitan New York City.

First Empire State Corporation

"M&T Bank operates under a charter granted by the State of New York in 1892, and the continuity of its banking business is traced to the organization of the Manufacturers and Traders Bank in 1856. As of December 31, 1992, M&T Bank had consolidated total assets of $8.1 billion and deposits of $6.7 billion. As a commercial bank, M&T offers a broad range of financial services to a diverse base of consumers, businesses, professional clients, governmental entities, and financial institutions located in its markets. Lending is focused on consumers residing in New York State, and on New York-based small and medium-sized businesses.

"East New York, originally organized in 1868, was acquired by First Empire in 1987. Its principal executive offices are located at 2644 Atlantic Avenue, Brooklyn, New York 11207. As of December 31, 1992, East New York had total assets of $1.7 billion and deposits of $1.4 billion. East New York takes deposits from, and offers other banking services to, a diverse base of customers located in its markets. East New York concentrates on making commercial mortgage loans which are secured by income producing properties that are primarily located throughout the metropolitan New York City area, especially apartment buildings and cooperative apartments.

"M&T Capital Corporation (M&T Capital) provides equity capital and long-term credit to 'small-business concerns,' as defined by the SBIA.

"M&T Mortgage Corporation (M&T Mortgage) is the mortgage banking subsidiary of M&T Bank. M&T Mortgage's principal activities are comprised of the origination of residential mortgages from loan production offices currently located in Columbus, Ohio, and Pittsburgh, Pennsylvania, and providing mortgage servicing to M&T Bank and others.

"M&T Financial Corporation (M&T Financial) specializes in capital-equipment leasing.

"M&T Discount Brokerage Services, Inc. (M&T Discount Brokerage) provides securities brokerage services on a discounted-fee basis.

During 1992, loans and leases of $7.1 billion were apportioned as follows: commercial, financial and agricultural 19.7 percent, real estate-construction .5 percent, real estate-mortgage 62.6 percent, and consumer 17.2 percent.

First Empire State has paid consecutive cash dividends since 1979. Institutions control about 50 percent, and officers and directors about 20 percent of the outstanding common shares. First Empire State paid a 100 percent stock dividend in 1987.

Total assets: $10.4 billion
Common shares outstanding: 6.9 million

	1984	1985	1986	1987	1988	1989	1990	1991	1992	1993
Net income (Mil.)	17	22	26	40	44	51	54	67	98	102
Earnings per share	3.04	4.13	4.80	4.78	6.02	7.04	7.91	9.32	13.41	13.87
Dividends per share	.53	.63	.70	.80	.95	1.10	1.25	1.40	1.60	1.90
Prices Hi	23.3	35.8	49.5	59.0	56.3	72.5	67.5	99.8	142.0	159.0
Lo	15.6	22.1	34.6	35.0	39.0	51.4	47.0	52.5	99.0	130.3

First Financial Management Corporation

3 Corporate Square Suite 700
Atlanta, Georgia 30329
Tel. (404) 321-0120
Listed: NYSE
Investor contact: Senior Vice President, Donald Y. Sharp
Ticker symbol: FFM
S&P rating: B+

As profiled in its 1992 Annual Report, "First Financial Management Corporation (FFMC) is a national leader in information services, offering a vertically integrated set of data processing, storage, and management products for the capture, manipulation, and distribution of data. Services include merchant credit card authorization, processing, and settlement; check verification; debt collection and accounts receivable management; data imaging, micrographics, and electronic data base management; integrated health care management services, and the development and marketing of data communications and information processing systems.

"FFMC serves a large and diverse institutional customer base that services the consumer: merchants, restaurants, hotels, manufacturers, wholesalers, financial institutions, insurance companies, hospitals and physicians, utilities, and various national, state and local government agencies. The company provides services to 220,000 customers through a distribution network of 410,000 on-line devices and 180 business units throughout the United States, Canada. and the Caribbean.

"FFMC has brought together a full array of information processing services, particularly as related to the payments system. Our largest business area, Merchant Services, is composed of four companies: NaBANCO, the nation's largest merchant credit card authorization and settlement business; TeleCheck, a leading provider of check verification and guarantee services; Nationwide Credit, a leader in credit collections; and MicroBuilt, which develops and markets data communication and information processing systems. These four companies offer a full-service solution for merchants at the point-of-sale.

"The largest player in Merchant Services is NaBANCO with a customer base of over 129,000 merchants. During 1992, NaBANCO processed over $42 billion in total merchant credit transactions. Major emphasis was placed on expanding further into the regional and local account marketplace.

"The second business area is Health Care Services. There are two components to our health care business: FIRST HEALTH Services, a leading provider of health care processing for the government; and FIRST HEALTH Strategies, a key provider of third party administration of health claims for corporate America.

"The final business area, Data Imaging Services, is represented by First Image Management Company. First Image is comprised of four distinct operations, including print and mail services, demand publishing, data input, and the largest provider of computer output micrographics in the nation.

"During the past twenty years, FFMC has integrated well over seventy acquisitions."

First Financial Management initiated cash dividends in 1987. Institutions control over 70 percent of the outstanding common shares. The company paid a 50 percent stock dividend in 1985, a 50 percent stock dividend in 1987, a 5 percent stock dividend in 1989, and a 50 percent stock dividend in 1992.

> Total assets: $1.6 billion
> Current ratio: 2.0
> Common shares outstanding: 59.9 million

	1984	1985	1986	1987	1988	1989	1990	1991	1992	1993
Revenues (Mil.)	35	52	68	189	447	607	816	1,057	1,425	1,670
Net income (Mil.)	2.6	3.4	5.5	24	57	69	79	105	145	216
Earnings per share	.25	.32	.44	.72	1.13	1.01	1.10	1.23	1.42	2.10
Dividends per share	—	—	—	—	—	.07	.07	.07	.10	.10
Prices Hi	5.1	10.3	11.7	20.2	21.3	26.0	22.5	31.9	44.6	58.5
Lo	3.7	4.9	7.8	10.0	15.4	15.6	9.5	13.5	24.8	36.0

First Hawaiian, Inc.

1132 Bishop Street
Honolulu, Hawaii 96813
Tel. (808) 525-7000
Listed: NASDAQ
Investor contact: Executive Vice Pres. & Treasurer, Howard H. Karr
Ticker symbol: FHWN
S&P rating: A

As profiled in its 1992 Annual Report, "First Hawaiian, Inc. is a bank holding company with total assets of $6.6 billion. Its principal subsidiary, First Hawaiian Bank, was founded in 1858 and is the oldest financial institution on the islands. The Bank presently has sixty-two branches throughout Hawaii, two in Guam, an offshore branch in Grand Cayman, British West Indies, and a representative office in Tokyo, Japan. Other major subsidiaries include First Hawaiian Creditcorp, Inc., the State's largest locally-owned financial services loan company, with 10 branches statewide and a branch in Guam; and First Hawaiian Leasing, Inc., which is primarily engaged in commercial equipment and vehicle leasing.

"First Hawaiian Bank, the oldest institution in Hawaii, was established as Bishop & Co. in 1858 in Honolulu. The Bank is a full-service bank conducting general, commercial, and consumer banking business and offering trust services. Its banking activities include demand, savings, and time deposits for personal and commercial accounts; commercial, agricultural, real estate, and consumer loans; United States tax depository facility, money transfer, cash management, travelers checks, and bank money orders; letters of credit; domestic and foreign collections; safe deposit and night depository facilities; renting safe deposit boxes; providing data processing services to customers; lease financing; and investment in U.S. Treasury securities and securities of other U.S. government agencies and corporations, and state and municipal securities.

"The lending activities of First Hawaiian Creditcorp, Inc. are concentrated in both consumer and commercial financing, which are primarily collateralized by real estate. Creditcorp's primary source of funds is the issuance of investment certificates with various fixed terms and certificates of investment in which the funds are subject to withdrawal upon presentation of a passbook. Creditcorp has ten branch offices located throughout the four major islands, a commercial loan office in Honolulu, and a loan production office in Guam.

"First Hawaiian Leasing, Inc., a financial services loan company, finances and leases personal property and equipment, and acts as agent, broker or advisor in the leasing or financing of such property for affiliates as well as third parties."

During 1992, loans and leases of $4.4 billion were apportioned as follows: commercial, financial, and agricultural 26.7 percent; real estate-construction 9.9 percent, real estate-commercial 16.4 percent, real estate-residential 27.7 percent, consumer 10.8 percent, lease financing 3.9 percent, and foreign 4.6 percent.

First Hawaiian has paid consecutive cash dividends since 1929. It has had twenty-nine years of consecutive earnings growth. Institutions control approximately 30 percent of outstanding common shares. First Hawaiian paid a 10 percent stock dividend in 1981, a 100 percent stock dividend in 1984, a 100 percent stock dividend in 1986, and a 100 percent stock dividend in 1990.

Total assets: $7.3 billion
Common shares outstanding: 32.5 million

	1984	1985	1986	1987	1988	1989	1990	1991	1992	1993
Net income (Mil.)	24	27	31	35	43	57	71	82	87	82
Earnings per share	.91	1.02	1.15	1.33	1.62	2.14	2.45	2.55	2.70	2.52
Dividends per share	.33	.36	.43	.48	.58	.70	.83	.95	1.06	1.14
Prices Hi	6.3	8.9	13.5	15.4	16.5	26.8	25.8	31.3	29.8	30.8
Lo	5.1	6.3	8.3	8.9	11.3	14.9	14.5	17.8	23.5	23.8

First of America Bank Corporation

211 South Rose Street
Kalamazoo, Michigan 49007
Tel (616) 376-9000
Listed: NYSE
Investor contact: Exec. Vice Pres. & Chief Financial Officer,
Thomas W. Lambert
Ticker symbol: FOA
S&P rating: A

First of America Bank Corporation

As profiled in its 1932 Annual Report, "First of America Bank Corporation is a multi-bank holding company headquartered in Kalamazoo, Michigan. Its principal activity consists of owning and supervising twenty affiliate financial institutions which operate general, commercial banking, and thrift businesses from 572 banking offices and facilities located in Michigan, Indiana, and Illinois. First of America also has divisions and non-banking subsidiaries which provide mortgage, trust, data processing, pension consulting, revolving credit, discount securities brokerage, and investment advisory services.

"As of December 31, 1993, First of America had three wholly-owned subsidiaries: First of America Bank–Southeast Michigan, N.A., First of America Bank–Michigan, N.A., 2nd First of America Bank–Security.

"First of America is the third largest bank holding company in Michigan. It has the largest and most broadly based branch network, serving over 25 percent of the state's households. Since 1987, assets in the Michigan franchise have grown $4.9 billion, or 66 percent, on an originally reported basis, with $3.3 billion of the growth from acquisitions.

"First of America entered Indiana in late 1986 and, since then, has acquired fifty branches serving two of the state's more attractive markets–Indianapolis and LaPorte.

"During 1991 and 1992, to better serve the Indiana market, three affiliates were merged into the Indianapolis bank, and the Rensalaer bank was merged into the LaPorte bank.

"First of America's Illinois franchise has experienced the most rapid growth and continues to represent an excellent opportunity for further expansion. First of America's franchise today has 109 offices serving rural and suburban communities across the state. At the end of 1991, First of America acquired

Champion Federal Savings and Loan, a $2.3 billion thrift, with a thriving mortgage banking and consumer loan operation.

"Our strategic focus has always been community banking—serving local customers, gathering deposits locally, and reinvesting those deposits in the same communities in the form of loans. Community banking has paid off handsomely for First of America in a stable, low-cost source of deposits, strong net interest margins and superior asset quality."

During 1992, loans of $13.7 billion were apportioned as follows: residential real estate 32 percent, consumer 31.3 percent, commercial real estate 20.8 percent, and commercial, financial and agricultural 15.9 percent.

First of America Bank Corporation has paid consecutive cash dividends since 1964. Institutions control about 35 percent of the outstanding common shares. First of America Bank paid a 50 percent stock dividend in 1984 and a 100 percent stock dividend in 1990.

Total assets: $21.2 billion
Common shares outstanding: 59.5 million

	1984	1985	1986	1987	1988	1989	1990	1991	1992	1993
Revenues (Mil.)	20	24	40	64	90	117	150	184	248	296
Net Income (Mil.)	2.9	4.2	6.8	12	18	23	30	38	50	64
Earnings per share	.14	.19	.25	.39	.48	.60	.72	.90	1.13	1.42
Dividends per share	.55	.67	.75	.83	.93	1.05	1.13	1.22	1.31	1.55
Prices Hi	13.5	22.5	26.4	27.0	25.1	28.0	26.0	31.8	37.9	43.3
Lo	8.9	13.3	20.5	16.9	19.0	19.1	15.4	18.3	29.0	36.5

Forest Laboratories, Inc.

150 East 58th Street
New York, New York 10155-0015
Tel. (212) 421-7850
Listed: AMEX
Investor contact: Vice Pres.—Finance, Kenneth E. Goodman
Ticker symbol: FRX
S&P rating: B+

As profiled in its fiscal 1993 Annual Report, "Forest Laboratories, Inc. and its subsidiaries develop, manufacture, and sell both branded and generic forms of ethical drug products which require a physician's prescription, as well as non-

99

prescription pharmaceutical products sold over-the-counter. Forest's most important United States products consist of branded ethical drug specialties marketed directly, or 'detailed,' to physicians by the company's salesforce and its controlled release line of generic products sold to wholesalers, chain drug stores, and generic distributors. Forest's products include those developed by Forest and those acquired from other pharmaceutical companies and integrated into Forest's marketing and distribution systems.

"Forest products are marketed principally in the United States, Western and Eastern Europe, and Puerto Rico. Marketing is conducted by Forest and through independent distributors.

"Its leading product, Aerobid, continues to grow almost 50 percent per annum, and still the inhaled steroids have not achieved nearly the usage in asthma treatment their clinical importance requires. In the analgesic field, the company has several unique dosages and combinations which have been well received by physicians, with growth out of Lorcet and Esig Lines at 30 percent per annum. Sales of Tessalon, its non-narcotic cough suppressant, continue to increase, although it now has a generic competitor.

The company hopes to introduce Flumadine in the United States, probably next year but possibly this year depending on FDA action. Flumadine is an oral antiviral for the treatment and prophylaxis of Influenza A infection. The drug was acquired from DuPont Merck Pharmaceuticals, Inc.

"The most interesting development this year was the completion of three studies with Synapton, the company's controlled release physostigmine for the treatment of Alzheimer's Disease. If Synapton, after further testing is approved, it should be the first-choice drug because of its clear safety advantage.

"Forsest Laboratories expects to complete its studies this year with Monuril and Infasurf. Monuril, which is licensed from Zambon in Italy, is a one dose antibiotic for the treatment of uncomplicated urinary tract infection. Infasurf is a surfactant for premature babies licensed from Ony, Inc., an American company."

During fiscal 1993, revenues and operating profits were apportioned as follows: the United States 88.9 percent and 92.5 percent of operating profit, Europe 1.1 percent of revenues and 1.4 percent of operating profit, and The United Kingdom and Ireland 10 percent of revenues and 6.1 percent of operating profit.

Forest Laboratories, Inc. has never paid a cash dividend. Institutions control about 70 percent of the outstanding common shares. Forest Laboratories,

Inc. paid a 100 percent stock dividend in 1986 and another 100 percent stock dividend in 1991.

Total assets: $520.5 million
Current ratio: 7.6
Common shares outstanding: 43.0 million

	1984	1985	1986	1987	1988	1989	1990	1991	1992	1993
Revenues (Mil.)	20	24	40	64	90	117	150	184	248	296
Net income (Mil.)	2.9	4.2	6.8	12	18	23	30	38	50	64
Earnings per share	.14	.19	.25	.39	.48	.60	.72	.90	1.13	1.42
Dividends per share	—	—	—	—	—	—	—	—	—	—
Prices Hi	8.1	8.1	12.4	15.0	12.8	22.3	25.4	43.6	44.9	47.9
Lo	2.8	3.9	6.9	6.6	7.9	12.1	16.8	22.3	30.0	27.5

Franklin Resources, Inc.

777 Mariners Island Blvd. (P.O. Box 7777)
San Mateo, California 94404-7777
Tel. (415) 312-3000
Listed: NYSE
Investor contact: Senior Vice Pres. & Treas., Charles E. Johnson
Ticker symbol: BEN
S&P rating: A-

As profiled in its fiscal 1993 Annual Report, "Franklin Resources is one of the United States' largest investment management organizations whose expertise encompasses both domestic and international fixed-income and equity investment. Through its subsidiaries, the company manages over $100 billion for individuals and institutions in the 156 portfolios that make up the Franklin/Templeton Group of open and closed-end investment companies. The company privately manages over $7 billion for corporations, trusts, endowments and pension plans as well as limited individual accounts. With the acquisition of Templeton in October, 1992, Franklin Resources formed a global alliance, operating through twenty offices in ten countries worldwide.

Franklin Resources, Inc.

"Franklin Resources, Inc. and its majority-owned subsidiaries derives its revenue from its principal line of business which is providing investment management, administration, and related services to the Franklin and Templeton Groups of Mutual Funds, managed accounts and other investment products.

"The company continues to expand its range of investment products and services in the United States and abroad. The most significant development during the fiscal year ending September 30, 1993, was the company's acquisition on October 30, 1992, of the assets and liabilities of Templeton, Galbraith & Hansberger Ltd., a Cayman Island corporation, for approximately $786 million. The acquisition of the investment management, distribution, and related companies servicing the Templeton Group of Mutual Funds and managed accounts had the effect of increasing the company's net assets under management by over $20 billion, to $90.7 billion on the date of acquisition.

"The company has a diversified base of assets under management and a full range of investment management products and services to meet the needs of most individuals and institutions. The company's revenues are derived largely from the amount and composition of assets under management; consequently, fluctuations in financial markets impact revenues and the results of operations."

As of September 30th, 1993, The Franklin/Templeton Group, representing over three million mutual fund accounts worldwide, had $107.5 billion of fund assets under management. These funds were apportioned as follows: Franklin Tax-Free 37.8 percent, Franklin U.S. Government 18.3 percent, Franklin Equity/Income 14.4 percent, Franklin Money Funds 2.4 percent, Templeton Equity 19.6 percent, Templeton Fixed Income 1 percent and Managed Accounts 6.5 percent.

Cash dividends were initiated on the common stock in 1991. Officers and directors control about 55 percent of the outstanding common shares (including 39 percent by the Johnson family), and institutions control another 30 percent. Franklin Resources paid a 25 percent stock dividend in 1982, a 100 percent stock dividend in 1983, a 25 percent stock dividend in 1984, a 100 percent stock dividend in 1985, a 100 percent stock dividend in January 1986, a 50 percent stock dividend in October 1986, a 25 percent stock dividend in 1987, a 50 percent stock dividend in 1990, and a 100 percent stock dividend in 1992.

Total assets: $1.6 billion
Current ratio: 2.6
Common shares outstanding: 82.1 million

	1984	1985	1986	1987	1988	1989	1990	1991	1992	1993
Revenues (Mil.)	37	63	143	203	212	253	288	318	391	641
Net Income (Mil.)	6.1	14	32	59	66	79	89	98	124	176
Earnings per share	.08	.17	.41	.74	.84	1.00	1.14	1.26	1.59	2.12
Dividends per share	.010	.017	.032	.07	.14	.15	.20	.23	.26	.28
Prices Hi	1.1	5.8	9.9	14.3	7.9	15.1	17.9	28.3	39.0	51.9
Lo	0.6	1.1	5.3	4.0	5.7	7.5	11.3	14.7	22.8	32.0

General Electric Company

3135 Easton Turnpike
Fairfield, Connecticut 06431
Tel. (203) 373-2211
Listed: NYSE
Investor contact: Corporate Investor Communications, Pauline M. Berardi
Ticker symbol: GE
S&P rating: A+

General Electric Company (GE) is a large, diverse company; a description of industry segments and consolidated affiliates follows:

"Aircraft Engines includes jet engines, replacement parts, and repair services for all categories of commercial aircraft; a wide variety of military planes, including fighters, bombers, tankers, and helicopters; and executive and commuter aircraft. GE's 1992 combination with Martin Marietta will make us part of one of the world's largest aerospace electronics concerns.

"Appliances include major items such as refrigerators, freezers, electric and gas ranges, dishwashers, clothes washers and dryers, microwave ovens and room air conditioning equipment.

"Broadcasting includes primarily the National Broadcasting Company (NBC). Its principal businesses are furnishing U.S. network television services to more than 200 affiliated stations, production of television programs, operation of six VHF television broadcasting stations, and investment and programming activities in cable television.

"The Industrial Division includes lighting products such as lamps, wiring devices, and quartz products; electrical distribution and control equipment; transportation systems products; electric motors and related products; a broad range of electrical and electronic industrial automation products; and GE Supply, a U.S. network of electrical supply houses.

"The Materials division includes high-performance engineered plastics used in applications such as automobiles and housings for computers and other business equipment; ABS resins; silicons; superabrasives such as man-made diamonds; and laminates.

"Power Systems include products mainly for the generation, transmission and distribution of electricity, including related installation, engineering, and repair services. Market competition is global.

"Technical Products and Services include Medical systems such as magnetic resonance (MR) and computed tomography (CT) scanners, X-ray, nuclear imaging, ultrasound, and other diagnostic equipment sold worldwide to hospitals and medical facilities. This segment also includes a full range of computer-based information and data interchange services for commercial and industrial customers.

"General Electric Capital Services Financing operations include consumer services, specialized financing, equipment management, and mid-market financing. Very few of the products financed by GE Capital are manufactured by other GE segments.

"General Electric Capital Services Specialty Insurance includes U.S. and international multiple-line property and casualty reinsurance, and certain directly written specialty insurance; financial guaranty insurance, principally on municipal bonds and structured finance issues; private mortgage insurance; creditor insurance covering international customer loan repayments; and life reinsurance.

"General Electric Capital Services consists of broker-dealer Kidder, Peabody, a full-service international investment bank and securities broker, member of the principal stock and commodities exchanges, and a primary dealer in U.S. government securities."

During 1992, aircraft engines provided 12.5 percent of revenues and 13.9 percent of operating profits; appliances 9 percent of revenues and 4.2 percent of profits; broadcasting 5.7 percent of revenues and 2.2 percent of profits; industrial products 11.7 percent of revenues and 9.7 percent of profits; materials division 8.2 percent of revenues and 8 percent of profits; power systems 10.8 percent of revenues and 11.3 percent of profits; technical products and services 7.9 percent of revenues and 9.9 percent of profits; General Electric Capital Services 31.2 percent of revenues and 25.1 percent of profits; and other products 3 percent of revenues and 15.7 percent of profits. Geographically, the United States represented 81.9 percent of revenues and 89.4 percent of profits, and foreign nations 18.1 percent of revenues and 10.6 percent of profits.

General Electric has had only one year (1975) of down earnings since 1971. It has increased its cash dividend every year since 1899. Institutions control about 55 percent of the outstanding common shares. General Electric paid a 100 percent stock dividend in 1983, a 100 percent stock dividend in 1987, and a 100 percent stock dividend in 1994.

Total assets: $251.5 billion
Current ratio: 1.3
Common shares outstanding: 1.9 billion

	1984	1985	1986	1987	1988	1989	1990	1991	1992	1993
Revenues (Mil.)	27,947	28,285	35,211	39,315	49,414	53,884	57,662	59,379	56,274	60,562
Net Income (Mil.)	2,280	2,336	2,492	2,119	3,386	3,939	4,303	4,435	4,725	5,177
Earnings per share	1.26	1.29	1.37	1.60	1.88	2.18	2.43	2.55	2.76	3.03
Dividends per share	.51	.56	.59	.66	.73	.85	.96	1.04	1.16	1.44
Prices Hi	14.9	18.5	22.3	33.2	24.0	32.4	37.8	39.1	43.8	53.5
Lo	12.0	14.0	16.7	19.5	19.2	21.8	25.0	26.5	36.4	40.4

Genuine Parts Company

2999 Circle 75 Parkway
Atlanta, Georgia 30339
Tel. (404) 953-1700
Listed: NYSE
Investor contact: Senior Vice Pres. Finance, Jerry W. Nix
Ticker symbol: GPC
S&P rating: A+

As profiled in its 1993 Annual Report, "Genuine Parts Company is a service organization engaged in the distribution of automotive replacement parts, industrial replacement parts, and office products. In 1993, business was conducted throughout most of the United States and in western Canada from more than 1,100 operations.

"The Automotive Parts Group is engaged in the distribution of automotive replacement parts and related items. Genuine Parts Company, a member of the National Automotive Parts Association (NAPA), operates sixty-six NAPA Distribution Centers in the United States which serve approximately 5,900 stores, of which 691 are company-owned.

"Included in the Group is Balkamp, Inc., a majority-owned subsidiary, which purchases, packages, and distributes approximately 20,000 automotive service and supply items to NAPA Distribution Centers, as well as six plants where automotive parts are rebuilt and distributed under the name, Rayloc.

"In Canada, Genuine Parts Company Ltd., a wholly-owned subsidiary, owns a 49 percent interest in UAP/NAPA which operates eight automotive parts distribution centers and seventy-two jobbing stores located in the provinces of Alberta, British Columbia, and Saskatchewan, and in the Yukon Territories.

"Motion Industries, Inc., a wholly owned subsidiary, is headquartered in Birmingham, Alabama. Motion is engaged in the distribution of industrial replacement parts and related materials in the United States. Industrial replacement parts, and agricultural equipment and supplies, are distributed in Canada by Oliver Industrial Supply, Ltd., a wholly-owned subsidiary headquartered in Lethbridge, Alberta.

"A wide variety of industrial bearings, mechanical and fluid power transmission equipment, materials handling components, and other related parts and supplies are distributed. Oliver Industrial Supply also markets agricultural and irrigation equipment and supplies.

"Headquartered in Atlanta, Georgia, S.P. Richards Company distributes over 17,000 office products nationwide. A wholly-owned subsidiary of Genuine Parts, S.P. Richards is comprised of thirty-five distribution centers. Products ranging from furniture and desk accessories to business electronics and computer supplies are inventoried in each distribution center."

During 1992, automotive parts provided 63.2 percent of revenues and 70.5 percent of operating profits; industrial parts 20 percent of revenues and 15.8 percent of operating profits; and office products 16.8 percent of revenues and 13.7 percent of operating profits.

Genuine Parts has paid consecutive cash dividends since 1948. It has increased cash dividends for thirty-seven consecutive years. It has increased earnings for thirty-two consecutive years. Institutions control about 65 percent of the outstanding common shares. Genuine parts has paid nine stock dividends since 1959, the most recent being a 50 percent stock dividend paid in 1992.

Total assets: $1.9 billion
Current ratio: 4.3
Common shares outstanding: 124.3 million

	1984	1985	1986	1987	1988	1989	1990	1991	1992	1993
Revenues (Mil.)	2,304	2,333	2,394	2,606	2,942	3,161	3,319	3,764	4,017	4,384
Net Income (Mil.)	120	126	122	148	181	199	207	224	237	258
Earnings per share	.98	.99	1.01	1.25	1.57	1.72	1.79	1.81	1.91	2.08
Dividends per share	.45	.53	.67	.61	.69	.80	.92	.97	1.00	1.06
Prices Hi	15.0	17.0	21.5	29.6	27.3	28.9	28.5	32.9	34.8	39.0
Lo	10.7	13.4	15.7	18.2	21.7	24.0	22.1	23.2	29.0	32.9

The Gillette Company

Prudential Tower Building
Boston, Massachusetts 02199
Tel (617) 421-7000
Listed: NYSE
Investor contact: Robert E. DiCenso, Investor Relations
Ticker symbol: G
S&P rating: A

As profiled in its 1993 Annual Report, "The Gillette Company sells a wide array of products in over 200 countries and territories  through an experienced, efficient, and geographically far-reaching organization. Behind our record of success is a combination of factors that has placed the company in the leadership position it holds today.

"We believe that three principal factors account for these global achievements: world-class brands, products, and people. By world-class, we mean outstanding, superior, and achieving an international standard of excellence.

"Our major business areas—personal care products, stationery products and small electrical appliances—are worldwide in scope. Their success reflects solid and irreplaceable global franchises, innovative products that are technically driven, and experienced people at all levels of the organization.

"This focus on the worldwide marketplace, and the company's dramatic expansion within it, is most clearly illustrated by the blade and razor business.

"The worldwide blade market represents about 20 billion units in total. Historically, Gillette has had access to established markets representing some 12 billion blades. Since the mid-1980s, we have increased the availability of Gillette-branded products by expanding into a number of huge markets that previously had no significant Gillette presence. In less than a decade, we have added markets representing some 7 billion blades in India, the former Soviet Union, China, Turkey, and Eastern Europe. The Gillette Sensor shaving system has continued to gain strong acceptance in the United States and international markets.

"The company's other principal worldwide business, Braun (headquartered in Germany), also illustrates our global presence. A Gillette subsidiary since 1967, Braun produces electric shavers, and small household and personal care appliances renowned for their exceptional design and performance, including most recently the Flex Control rechargeable shaver.

"With its premium-quality, oral care products, Oral-B has been the toothbrush leader in the United States and several other countries for many years. Oral-B plaque remover showed exceptional gains in its second year.

"Within the stationery products line, Waterman has become one of the fastest growing brands in the prestige writing instruments category. The Flexgrip family of writing instruments continues to record substantial sales gains, and distribution was broadened from the North Atlantic markets to Latin America and the Far East.

"Jafra, whose quality skin care and cosmetic products are top performers in the toiletries and cosmetics line, is poised to carry out a program of geographic expansion. Acquired in 1973, Jafra operates companies in the United States, Europe, and Latin America, with entry into additional markets planned in 1993.

"The Gillette Series, a line of technologically advanced men's toiletries, was introduced at the year's-end. The line is being launched in the United States, Canada, and the United Kingdom, with major marketing support under the same theme that has been so successful for the Sensor system, 'Gillette, The Best a Man Can Get.' "

During 1992, revenues and profits were apportioned as follows: blades and razors 38.3 percent of revenues and 65.7 percent of profits, toiletries and cosmetics 18.8 percent of revenues and 8.8 percent of profits, stationary products 10.1 percent of revenues and 4.8 percent of profits, Braun products 25.7 percent of revenues and 16.1 percent of profits, and Oral-B products 7.1 percent of revenues and 4.6 percent of profits.

Geographically, the United States provided 30.9 percent of revenues and 29.8 percent of profits, Europe 42.3 percent of revenues and 41.4 percent of profits, Latin America 12.5 percent of revenues and 17.5 percent of profits, and Other 14.3 percent of revenues and 11.3 percent of profits.

Gillette has paid consecutive cash dividends since 1906. Institutions control over 70 percent of the outstanding common shares. Gillette paid a 100 percent stock dividend in 1986, a 100 percent stock dividend in 1987, and a 100 percent stock dividend in 1991.

Total assets: $5.1 billion
Current ratio: 1.1
Common shares outstanding: 221 million

	1984	1985	1986	1987	1988	1989	1990	1991	1992	1993
Revenues (Mil.)	2,289	2,400	2,818	3,167	3,581	3,819	4,345	4,684	5,163	5,411
Net Income (Mil.)	159	160	16	230	269	285	368	427	513	288
Earnings per share	.65	.65	.06	1.00	1.23	1.35	1.60	1.94	2.32	1.92
Dividends per share	.31	.33	.34	.39	.43	.48	.54	.62	.72	.81
Prices Hi	7.4	9.0	17.3	22.9	24.5	24.9	32.6	56.1	61.3	63.8
Lo	5.4	6.7	8.6	11.6	14.6	16.5	21.8	28.1	43.9	47.4

Great Lakes Chemical Corporation

Highway 52 Northwest (P.O. Box 2200)
West Lafayette, Indiana 47906
Tel. (317) 497-6100
Listed: NYSE
Investor contact: Associate Vice President, David R. Bouchard
Ticker symbol: GLK
S&P rating: A

As profiled in its 1993 Annual Report, "Great Lakes Chemical Corporation is a well-diversified specialty chemicals company that has established leadership positions in virtually all its principal markets. The company's operations consist of one dominant in-

Great Lakes
Chemical Corporation

dustry segment—chemicals and allied products. It uses unmatched raw materials locations, and technological and manufacturing expertise, to enhance its presence in key international markets, and to develop new products and applications for emerging markets. The company is headquartered in West Lafayette, Indiana, and operates a growing network of sales, production, and distribution facilities worldwide.

"Great Lakes is a vertically integrated manufacturer of a wide range of value-added chemicals that meet specific performance requirements for well defined applications. The company draws on vast reserves of bromine, sodium, furfural and other raw materials to pioneer new technology markets around the world. It has built leadership positions in virtually all its key markets.

"Great Lakes has developed for recreational and industrial markets a broad range of bromine-containing specialty biocides noted for their superior performance, environmental safety, and safe and convenient handling characteristics. The company's Bio-Lab and Bayrol subsidiaries serve recreational water treatment markets throughout North America, Australia, and Europe by supplying a full line of pool and spa sanitizers, as well as pumps, filters, and other equipment. The BL Network, a subsidiary of Bio-Lab, is a full-service distributor to the pool and spa industry, with thirty-two branches located throughout the United States Sunbelt.

"With the U.K.-based Octel Associates, Great Lakes is the world's leading producer of certain antiknock octane boosters for transportation fuels. It has also taken the lead in developing a broad line of high-performance, environmentally friendly petroleum additives for tomorrow's engines. Octel is a fully integrated operation with a strong raw materials base, world-class research and development facilities, and a distribution network that extends to sixty-five countries.

"Great Lakes takes an entrepreneurial approach to identifying new business opportunities that increase the company's technological base, complement existing businesses, and have the potential to meet the company's high performance standards. This approach has taken the company into high-growth areas such as custom synthesis, environmental remediation, oil field services, engineered surface treatments, toxologist testing, and international trading."

Geographically, during 1992 revenues and income were apportioned as follows: The United States 51 percent of revenues and 35.3 percent of income, and foreign operations 49 percent of revenues and 64.7 percent of income.

Great Lakes Chemical Corporation has paid consecutive cash dividends since 1973. Institutions control about 80 percent of the outstanding common shares. Great Lakes Chemical paid a 100 percent stock dividend in 1983, a 100 percent stock dividend in 1989, and a 100 percent stock dividend in 1992.

Total assets: $1.9 billion
Current ratio: 2.3
Common shares outstanding: 71.3 million

	1984	1985	1986	1987	1988	1989	1990	1991	1992	1993
Revenues (Mil.)	283	282	306	501	616	848	1,114	1,348	1,538	1,828
Net Income (Mil.)	36	29	27	56	103	123	141	157	233	273
Earnings per share	.60	.48	.44	.83	1.48	1.76	2.00	2.23	3.27	3.82
Dividends per share	.095	.12	.14	.16	.18	.20	.23	.27	.31	.35
Prices Hi	9.6	11.1	11.1	19.3	16.5	24.0	34.0	58.0	71.4	84.0
Lo	4.3	6.0	7.9	7.5	9.0	12.1	14.1	30.4	50.3	64.5

Hannaford Bros. Co.

145 Pleasant Hill Road
Scarborough, Maine 04074
Tel. (207) 883-2911
Listed: NYSE
Investor contact: Asst. Secretary, Charles H. Crockett
Ticker symbol: HRD
S&P rating: A+

As profiled in its 1992 Annual Report, "Hannaford Bros. Co. is Northern New England's largest food retailer. We are located throughout Maine and New Hampshire, and in parts of Vermont, Massachusetts, and upstate New York. Retail food sales are made through the Company's ninety-three supermarkets operating under the names Shop 'n Save, Alexander's, Martin's, or Sun Foods. Hannaford also operates six wholly-owned retail drug stores under the Shop 'n Save Pharmacy name and thirty-eight separate pharmacies within supermarkets or combination stores. Hannaford also makes wholesale sales to 19 independent customers.

"Of Hannaford's ninety-three supermarkets, more than 75 percent are either new or have been expanded or relocated in the past ten years. During this period, a number of smaller outdated facilities have been closed or sold. Since 1983, Hannaford has opened or acquired forty-eight combination stores ranging in size from 30,000 to 84,000 square feet. These stores offer under one roof the traditional all-department supermarket together with a floral shop, bakery, video rental center, and other shops and services, as well as expanded lines of general merchandise. All but fourteen of these combination stores, as well as an additional four conventional supermarkets, have pharmacy departments. The new stores opened by Hannaford since 1983 also include four superwarehouse stores of 52,000 to 64,000 square feet, operated under the name Sun Foods.

"The principal distribution center, in South Portland, Maine, occupies 521,000 square feet and is well located in Hannaford's marketing territory. It handles a complete line of grocery, dairy, frozen food, produce, and meat products. The distribution center has a dedicated on-line computerized warehouse management system, which efficiently controls the movement of products through the facility, and schedules labor for greater efficiency and productivity.

"Hannaford opened a new distribution center in Schodack, New York, during 1990 to service certain store locations in New York, Vermont, New Hampshire, and Massachusetts.

"Merchandise is transported from Hannaford's distribution facilities by Hannaford Trucking Company, a wholly-owned subsidiary.

"A 200,000 square foot distribution center in Winthrop, Maine, is operated by Progressive Distributors, Inc., a wholly-owned service merchandise subsidiary which for many years has supplied a comprehensive line of health and beauty care products, specialty food items, and some general merchandise to Hannaford's stores. From this warehouse, Progressive also distributes a significant portion of the pharmaceutical items supplied to the company's pharmacies."

Hannaford has paid consecutive cash dividends since 1948 and has increased the cash dividend every year for the past thirty years. Officers and directors control about 35 percent of the outstanding common shares. Hannaford paid a 100 percent stock dividend in 1983, a 50 percent stock dividend in February 1985, a 50 percent stock dividend in August 1985, a 100 percent stock dividend in 1989, and a 100 percent stock dividend in 1992.

Total assets: $795.4 million
Current ratio: 1.9
Common shares outstanding: 41.2 million

	1984	1985	1986	1987	1988	1989	1990	1991	1992	1993
Revenues (Mil.)	714	817	910	1,033	1,262	1,521	1,688	2,008	2,066	2,055
Net Income (Mil.)	11	14	19	24	29	39	42	43	49	57
Earnings per share	.35	.43	.51	.65	.77	.95	1.06	1.08	1.21	1.38
Dividends per share	.098	.12	.13	.14	.16	.18	.22	.26	.30	.34
Prices Hi	3.7	7.1	10.2	13.7	11.8	20.4	20.3	22.8	28.6	25.0
Lo	2.8	3.6	6.2	6.9	8.3	10.7	14.9	16.4	16.0	20.0

John H. Harland Company

2939 Miller Road (P.O. Box 105250)
Atlanta, Georgia 30348
Tel. (404) 981-9460
Listed: NYSE
Investor contact: Vickie P. Weyland
Ticker symbol: JH
R&P rating: A

As profiled in its 1992 Annual Report, "John H. Harland Company and its subsidiaries are major national participants in the financial, commercial, and educational fields.

HARLAND

"Harland's Financial Services Group (FSG) provides products and services that support America's payment system. FSG includes Harland's check printing operations and its Business Services segment. These areas provide documents and accessories to traditional financial markets and emerging non-traditional markets.

"Harland's acquisition of Interchecks in February, 1992, was a move aimed at increasing operating efficiency. The consolidation of Interchecks' plants enhances Harland's nationwide network of production facilities to meet the need of super-regional, regional, and community financial institutions.

"Through commitment to personal service, Harland's FGS remains the leading supplier of financial documents to the brokerage industry and has become a prominent player in serving the credit union movement. Today, Harland maintains its strong position as one of the nation's leading check printers.

"Harland's National Accounts sales specialists serve the top 100 holding companies in the United States. Their focus is on large customers with broad check program needs, including computer support, marketing innovation, and expanded services.

"Harland's Business Services segment offers forms and checks to match accounting programs of leading software providers. For commercial customers, Business Services provides custom short-run computer forms, accounting packages recordkeeping systems, and laser documents. Harland's nationwide Forms Service network provides consistent, reliable, one-stop consulting and analysis of forms needs.

"Harland's Data Services Group (DSG) engages in information recognition, including the collection, processing, and feedback of data. DSG relies on

113

optical mark readers (OMR), optical character recognition (OCR), bar coding, and imaging systems to provide customer solutions in a cost-effective manner.

Scantrol maintained services to the educational market and strengthened application capabilities to commercial, government, and health care markets through the development of new products and services. It increased efficiencies in its European operations. Scantrol consolidated Datascan's production into its U.S. facilities, while maintaining sales and distribution operations throughout Europe."

Harland's financial position is rock solid. In 1992, sales increased for the forty-third consecutive year and dividends for the thirty-ninth straight year. Institutions control approximately 60 percent and insiders 8 percent of the outstanding common shares. Harland paid a 50 percent stock dividend in 1980, a 100 percent stock dividend in 1981, a 100 percent stock dividend in 1985, and a 100 percent stock dividend in 1987.

Total assets: $356.5 million
Current ratio: 3.1
Common shares outstanding: 30.5 million

	1984	1985	1986	1987	1988	1989	1990	1991	1992	1993
Revenues (Mil.)	234	268	293	318	333	345	367	379	445	519
Net Income (Mil.)	27	33	39	48	53	58	57	47	57	53
Earnings per share	.72	.87	1.04	1.26	1.41	1.54	1.52	1.27	1.59	1.62
Dividends per share	.23	.28	.34	.42	.58	.68	.78	.86	.90	.94
Prices Hi	12.4	19.5	25.5	30.8	24.3	25.0	26.1	24.4	27.3	28.1
Lo	8.1	11.9	17.1	16.4	19.3	19.5	17.9	18.0	20.5	20.9

Hershey Food Corporation

100 Crystal A Drive (P.O. Box 810)
Hershey, Pennsylvania 17033-0810
Tel. (717)534-6799
Listed: NYSE
Investor contact: Director of Investor Relations, James A. Edris
Ticker symbol: HSY
S&P rating: A+

As profiled in its 1993 Annual Report, "Hershey Foods Corporation, which includes Hershey Chocolate U.S.A., Hershey Canada Inc., Hershey International,

Hershey Refrigerated Products, and Hershey Pasta Group produces a broad line of chocolate, confectionery, pasta, and other food products.

"Hershey Chocolate U.S.A.'s principal brands include Hershey's, Reese's, Y&S, Kit Kat, and Peter Paul.

"Hershey Canada's major brands include Hershey, Reese, Y&S, Life Savers, Moirs, and Planters.

"Hershey International manufactures chocolate and confectionery products in Germany under the Gubor brand, and in Mexico and Japan under the Hershey's brand. In addition, the Division exports products manufactured by other divisions and monitors licensing of Hershey's products abroad.

"Hershey Refrigerated Products produces and distributes chocolate bar flavor refrigerated puddings throughout the United States.

"Hershey Pasta Group produces eight regional brands of pasta products in the United States: American Beauty, Delmonico, Light 'N Fluffy, P&R, Perfection, Ronzoni, San Giorgio, and Skinner.

"New products made an important contribution to Hershey Chocolate U.S.A.'s sales during 1992. Amazin' Fruit gummy bears fruit candy, the year's principal new confectionery product, was introduced nationally in the summer. Made with real fruit juices, Amazin' Fruit gummy bears come in two varieties of fruit flavors, tropical and original assorted.

"Hershey's Cookies 'n Mint chocolate bar was another important and successful national introduction during 1992. The bar, which is a blend of crunchy chocolate cookie bits in minty Hershey's mild chocolate, was distributed nationally beginning in late 1992.

"Hershey's reduced calorie and fat candy bar was introduced into limited test markets during the fall of 1992.

"Reese's peanut butter was an important source of sales growth for Hershey Chocolate U.S.A.'s grocery line. Building on the success of the Reese's brand as the number-one name in peanut butter candy, Reese's peanut butter entered national distribution in early 1992."

Hershey has increased its cash dividend for nineteen consecutive years. It has paid consecutive cash dividends since 1930. There is both a regular and a Class B common stock issue. Institutions control about 25 percent of the regular shares. The Milton Hershey Schools controls about 30 percent of the regular and 99 percent of the Class B shares. The Class B shares are entitled to ten votes per share, giving the Milton Hershey School effective control of the Company. A 100 percent stock dividend was paid in 1983, and a 200 percent stock dividend was paid in 1986.

Total assets: $2.9 billion
Current ratio: 1.1
Common shares outstanding: 72.4 million
Class B 15.3 million

	1984	1985	1986	1987	1988	1989	1990	1991	1992	1993
Revenues (Mil.)	1,893	1,996	1,635	1,864	2,168	2,421	2,716	2,899	3,220	3,488
Net Income (Mil.)	109	121	133	148	214	171	216	220	243	193
Earnings per share	1.16	1.28	1.42	1.64	2.37	1.90	2.39	2.43	2.69	3.31
Dividends per share	.41	.48	.52	.58	.66	.74	.84	.94	1.03	1.14
Prices Hi	13.8	18.4	30.0	37.8	28.6	36.9	39.6	44.5	48.4	55.9
Lo	9.5	11.8	15.5	20.8	21.9	24.8	28.3	35.1	42.4	43.5

Hillenbrand Industries, Inc.

700 State Street, Route 46 East
Batesville, Indiana 47006-7000
Tel. (812) 934-7000
Listed: NYSE
Investor contact: Asst. Treas., Mark R. Lanning
Ticker symbol: HB
S&P rating: A+

HILLENBRAND INDUSTRIES

As profiled in its fiscal 1993 Annual Report, "Hillenbrand Industries, Inc. is the parent company of six diversified, wholly-owned, and autonomously managed operating companies organized into Funeral Services and Health Care segments.

"Batesville Casket Company, Inc., One Batesville Boulevard, Batesville, Indiana 47006, is a leading manufacturer of protective metal and hardwood burial caskets. The company also manufactures a line of cremation urns and caskets.

"The Forethought Group, Inc., Forethought Center, Batesville, Indiana 47006, is the leading provider of inflation-protected, advance-funeral planning based on life insurance.

"Block Medical, Inc. 5957 Landau Court, Carlsbad, California 92008, is a leading manufacturer of disposable, portable, infusion pumps and ambulatory, electronic, infusion pumps, and related equipment, for use by home care patients.

"Hill-Rom Company, Inc., 1609 State Street, Route 46 East, Batesville, Indiana 47006, is a leading manufacturer of patient care systems, including medical-surgical hospital beds, critical care beds, dynamic sleep surfaces for pressure ulcers, birthing beds, infant warmers, procedural stretchers, power columns, patient room furniture, headwall systems, refurbished hospital beds, nurse communication systems, and patient voice-activation systems.

"SSI Medical Services, Inc., 4349 Corporate Road, Charleston, South Carolina 29405, known to the medical community as Support Systems International (SSI), is a leading provider of specialized therapeutic products and services, including air fluidized and low airloss sleep surfaces for wound and pressure ulcer therapy. SSI also provides products and services for incontinent management, wound irrigation, and the management of pulmonary complications associated with critically ill patients.

"Medeco Security Locks, Inc., 3625 Allegheny Drive, Salem, Virginia 24153, is a leading manufacturer of high-security pick and tamper-resistant mechanical locks, lock cylinders for deadbolts, dropbolts, camlocks, knoblocks, and padlocks–all with patented key control. The company also manufactures high security electronic access control and electronic lock systems."

On August 30, 1993, revenues and operating profits were apportioned as follows: Health Care 60.5 percent of revenues and 53.7 percent of operating income, and Funeral Services 39.5 percent of revenues and 46.3 of operating income.

The Hillenbrand family controls about 60 percent and institutions about 39 percent (including some family-owned shares) of the outstanding common shares. Hillenbrand has paid consecutive cash dividends since 1948. Hillenbrand Industries paid a 100 percent stock dividend in 1962, a 100 percent stock dividend in 1984, a 100 percent stock dividend in 1987, and a 100 percent stock dividend in 1992.

Total assets: $2.3 billion
Current ratio: 2.0
Common shares outstanding: 71.3 million

	1984	1985	1986	1987	1988	1989	1990	1991	1992	1993
Revenues (Mil.)	414	441	587	645	783	872	982	1,084	1,303	1,448
Net Income (Mil.)	38	33	50	56	66	71	76	89	116	146
Earnings per share	.49	.42	.65	.74	.88	.96	1.02	1.22	1.62	2.04
Dividends per share	.13	.14	.14	.18	.20	.25	.28	.29	.35	.45
Prices Hi	6.3	6.8	12.4	15.3	17.9	21.5	24.0	30.4	43.6	48.6
Lo	4.4	4.9	6.1	10.5	11.5	13.3	15.1	17.9	29.3	36.5

Hormel Foods Corporation

1 Hormel Place
Austin, Minnesota 55912-3680
Tel. (507) 437-5950
Listed: NYSE
Investor contact: Vice Pres. & Treas., Robert J. Thatcher
Ticker symbol: HRL
S&P rating: A+

**Hormel Foods
Corporation**

As profiled in its fiscal 1993 Annual Report, "What for 102 years was known as Geo. A. Hormel & Company became known as Hormel Foods Corporation during 1993–a change that more accurately reflects the corporation's growing role and industry presence as a diversified, consumer-branded marketer of value-added products. The new name describes the broad industry arena in which Hormel Foods now competes nationally and internationally, while effectively conveying an image of a corporation that emphasizes product innovation, healthy eating, convenience, and freshness.

"Hormel Foods and its family of subsidiaries manufacture, market, and distribute thousands of processed food products which are known and respected by consumers, retail grocers, foodservice operators, and industrial customers. Many of the company's products are among the best known and trusted in the food industry. They not only enjoy strong brand identification and leading market shares, but address important customer and consumer priorities for high standards of quality, value, and convenience.

"Among the company's principal products are branded, processed meats which are sold fresh, frozen, cured, smoked, cooked and canned. Included are sausages, hams, wieners, and bacon; canned luncheon meats; shelf-stable, microwaveable; entrees, stews, chilies, hash, meat spreads, and frozen processed products. These and other products are sold in all fifty states by sales representatives coordinated from district sales offices located in most of the larger United States cities. These efforts are supported by brokers and distributors.

"A majority of the company's products is sold under the Hormel brandmark. Other well-established trademarks, which are familiar to consumers and have contributed to the Company's established reputation for quality and value, are as follows: Black Label, By George, Cure 81, Curemaster, Di Lusso, Dinty Moore, Farm Fresh, Fast 'N Easy, Frank 'N Stuff, Homeland, Jennie-O, Kid's Kitchen, Layout Pack, Light & Lean, Light & Lean 97, Little Sizzlers, Mary Kitchen, Old Smokehouse, Range Brand, SPAM, Top Shelf, and Wranglers."

Hormel Foods Corporation has paid consecutive cash dividends since 1928. The Hormel Foundation controls about 42 percent, The Hormel Profit Sharing Trust about 6 percent, and institutions about 20 percent of the outstanding common shares. Hormel paid a 100 percent stock dividend in 1985, a 100 percent stock dividend in 1987, and a 100 percent stock dividend in 1990.

Total assets: $1.1 billion
Current ratio: 2.7
Common shares outstanding: 76.9 million

	1984	1985	1986	1987	1988	1989	1990	1991	1992	1993
Revenues (Mil.)	1,455	1,502	1,960	2,314	2,293	2,341	2,681	2,836	2,814	2,854
Net Income (Mil.)	29	39	39	46	60	70	77	86	95	101
Earnings per share	.38	.50	.51	.60	.79	.91	1.01	1.13	1.24	1.31
Dividends per share	.13	.13	.14	.15	.18	.22	.26	.30	.36	.44
Prices Hi	4.3	6.8	8.9	14.8	13.8	16.9	19.8	23.1	24.8	25.5
Lo	3.3	3.8	5.6	8.1	8.8	10.1	14.0	16.0	16.8	20.3

Hubbell Incorporated

584 Derby Milford Road (P.O. Box 549)
Orange, Connecticut 06477-4024
Tel. (203) 799-4100
Listed: NYSE
Investor contact: Director of Public Affairs, Thomas R. Conlin
Ticker symbol: HUB.B
S&P rating: A

As profiled in its 1993 Annual Report, "Hubbell is primarily engaged in the engineering, manufacture, and sale of electrical and electronic products. These products can be divided into three general segments: products primarily used in low-voltage applications, products primarily used in high-voltage applications and products that either are not directly related to the electrical business, or, if related, cannot be classified on a voltage application basis.

Products Used In Low-voltage Applications
Electrical Wiring Devices:
"The Wiring Device Division of Hubbell specializes in the manufacture and sale of highly durable and reliable wiring devices which are supplied principal to industrial and commercial customers. These products, comprising several thousand catalog items, include plugs, receptacles, wall outlets, connectors, adapters, floor boxes and switches.

Lighting Fixtures:
"Hubbell Lighting, Inc. sells lighting fixtures and accessories for both outdoor and indoor applications in the United States, Canada, United Kingdom, Singapore, and elsewhere internationally. Hubbell Lighting has three basic classifications of products—Outdoor, Industrial, and Commercial.

Industrial Controls:
"Hubbell Industrial Controls, Inc. manufactures and sells a variety of heavy-duty electrical control products which have broad applications in the control of industrial equipment processes. These products range from standard and specialized industrial control components to combinations of components that control entire industrial manufacturing processes.

Special Application Products:
"In addition to its other products, Killark Electric Manufacturing Company manufactures and sells weather proof and hazardous location products suitable for explosion proof applications.

Products Used In High-voltage Applications
Insulated Wire and Cable:
"The Kerite Company manufactures and sells premium quality, high performance, insulated electric power cable for application in vital circuits of electric utilities and major industrials. This product line utilizes proprietary insulation systems and unique designs to meet the increasingly demanding specifications of customers.

Electrical Transmission and Distribution Products:

"The Ohio Brass Company manufactures a complete line of polymer insulators, and high-voltage surge arresters used in the construction of electrical transmission and distribution lines and substations.

High Voltage Test and Measurement Equipment:

"Acquired in November, 1992, Hipotronics, Inc. manufactures and sells a broad line of high voltage test and measurement systems to test materials and equipment used in the generation, transmission, and distribution of electricity.

Products Not Classified On A Voltage Basis

Outlet Boxes, Enclosures and Fittings:

"Raco Inc. is a leading manufacturer of steel and plastic boxes used at outlets, switch locations, and junction points, as well as a broad line of fittings for the electrical industry, including rigid conduit fillings, EMT fittings, and other metal conduit fittings.

"Hubbell-Bell, Inc. manufactures a variety of electrical box products, with an emphasis on weather-resistant types suitable for outdoor application.

"Killmark Electric is a leading manufacturer of quality standard and special application enclosures and fillings, including hazardous waste location products for use in installations such as chemical plants, pipelines, grain towers, coal handling facilities, and refineries.

Voice and Data Signal Processing Equipment:

"Pulse Communications, Inc. designs and manufactures a line of voice and data signal processing equipment primarily for use by the telephone and telecommunications industry.

"Hubbell Premise Wiring, Inc. manufactures components used in telecommunications applications for voice and data signals.

Holding Devices:

"The Kellems Division manufactures a line of Kellems grips used to pull, support, and relieve stress in elongated items such as cables, electrical cords, hoses, and conduits. Kellems also makes a line of cord connectors designed to prevent electrical conductors from pulling away from electrical terminals to which the conductors are attached, and wire management products including flexible, non-metallic conduit and fittings, and non-metallic surface raceway products used in wiring and cable harness installations."

Hubbell has both Class A and Class B shares. About 40 percent of the Class A shares are held by trusts for the Hubbell family. Institutions hold about 65 percent of the Class B shares. Hubbell has paid consecutive cash dividends since 1934. Hubbell paid a 100 percent stock dividend in 1981, a 100 percent stock dividend in 1985, a 5 percent stock dividend in 1989, a 5 percent stock dividend in 1990, a 5 percent stock dividend in 1991, and a 5 percent stock dividend in 1992.

Total assets; $874.3 million
Current ratio: 1.6
Common shares outstanding: Class A 5.9 million
Class B 25.4 million

	1984	1985	1986	1987	1988	1989	1990	1991	1992	1993
Revenues (Mil.)	467	521	559	581	614	669	720	756	786	832
Net Income (Mil.)	42	48	54	63	71	79	86	91	78	66
Earnings per share	1.30	1.49	1.69	1.94	2.25	2.52	2.74	2.87	2.45	2.10
Dividends per share	.55	.61	.67	.80	.90	1.12	1.31	1.47	1.59	1.63
Prices Hi	15.1	21.8	29.9	34.5	31.9	41.8	45.0	53.9	59.6	58.9
Lo	11.9	14.4	19.9	21.0	25.0	28.8	31.9	40.1	46.3	50.8

International Flavors & Fragrances Inc.

521 West 57 Street
New York, New York 10019-2960
Tel. (212) 765-5500
Listed: NYSE
Investor contact: Vice Pres. & Treas., Thomas H. Hoppel
Ticker symbol: IFF
S&P rating: A+

As profiled in its 1993 Annual Report, "International Flavors and Fragrances (IFF) is a leading creator and manufacturer of flavors and fragrances used by others to impart or improve flavor or fragrance in a wide variety of consumer products.

"Fragrance products are sold principally to makers of perfumes and cosmetics, hair and other personal care products, soaps and detergents, household and other cleaning products and area fresheners.

"Flavors are sold primarily to makers of dairy, meat and other processed foods, beverages snacks and savory foods, confectionery, sweet and baked goods, pharmaceutical and oral care products, tobacco products, and animal foods.

The company's products utilize both natural and synthetic ingredients.

"On a worldwide basis fragrance sales amounted to approximately 60 percent of total sales, while flavors were 40 percent. This proportion was approximately the same as the previous year, but with fragrance sales showing somewhat greater strength than flavor sales.

"Fine fragrance sales experienced strong growth during the year as a result of the expansion of IFF's market share in this important segment of the business. We participated in several major fragrance launches both in the U.S. and Europe. This trend is also continuing in 1993, as several major international companies, which have purchased existing fragrance and cosmetic houses in the U.S. and Europe, compete with one another on a global basis.

"In the international soap and detergent market, several IFF fragrance wins during the year should result in continuing strong sales growth as these end products are rolled out worldwide. Sales of aroma chemicals, as we predicted last year, recovered smartly and are continuing to grow steadily around the world.

"Flavor sales, while not quite as strong as fragrance, grew solidly on a worldwide basis. A variety of beverage introductions, including 'New Age' beverages, tea-based and sports-oriented drinks containing IFF flavors, resulted in solid gains in this area.

"Nevertheless, the largest single influence on our flavor sales continues to be the trend in all the developed countries toward healthier diets and life styles.

"We continue to search for those new and improved ingredients and processes which afford us a special edge in the marketplace. During 1993, we will spend approximately $77 million on Research and Development."

During 1992, 68.9 percent of revenues and 68.8 percent of profits were derived from foreign markets.

International Flavors & Fragrances has no long term debt. Institutions control over 60 percent of the common shares. It has paid consecutive cash dividends since 1956. It split 3 for 1 in 1993.

Total assets: $1.2 billion
Current ratio: 5.9
Common shares outstanding: 112.1 million

	1984	1985	1986	1987	1988	1989	1990	1991	1992	1993
Revenues (Mil.)	477	501	621	746	840	870	963	1,017	1,126	1,189
Net Income (Mil.)	69	70	86	107	129	139	157	169	171	202
Earnings per share	.63	.63	.76	.94	1.13	1.22	1.37	1.47	1.53	1.78
Dividends per share	.36	.38	.39	.44	.56	.66	.74	.83	.90	1.02
Prices Hi	9.8	13.3	16.3	19.3	18.1	19.1	25.0	34.9	38.7	39.9
Lo	7.6	8.7	11.5	12.4	14.4	16.2	18.2	22.9	31.5	33.0

Johnson & Johnson

One Johnson & Johnson Plaza
New Brunswick, New Jersey 08933
Tel. (908) 524-0400
Listed: NYSE
Investor contact: Asst. Treasurer Investor Relations, Clarence E. Lockett
Ticker symbol: JNJ
S&P rating: A+

As profiled in its 1993 Annual Report, "Johnson & Johnson, with $14.14 billion in sales, is the world's largest and most comprehensive manufacturer of health care products serving the consumer, pharmaceutical, and professional markets. Johnson & Johnson has 84,900 employees and 168 operating companies in 53 countries around the world, selling products in more than 150 countries.

"The consumer segment is the company's largest business segment, representing 34.7 percent of total sales in 1992 and consisting of toiletries and hygienic products, including baby care products, first aid products, nonprescription drugs, and sanitary protection products. Major brands include Act Fluoride Rinse; Band-Aid Brand Adhesive Bandages; Carefree Panty Shields, 'o.b.' Tampons, Stayfree, and Sure & Natural sanitary protection products; Imodium A-D, an antidiarrheal; Johnson's baby products; Monistat7, an over-the-counter product for vaginal yeast infections; Mylanta antacid products; Pedicare children's cold and allergy medications; Piz Buin and Sundown sun care products; Prevent and Reach toothbrushes; Serenity incontinence products; and the broad family of Tylenol acetaminophen products. These products are marketed principally to the general public; they are distributed both to wholesalers and to independent and chain retail outlets.

"The pharmaceutical segment is the most profitable segment; it represents over 50 percent of total operating profit. The segment's principal worldwide franchises are in the allergy and asthma, antifungal, central nervous system, contraceptive, dermatology, gastrointestinal, immunobiology, and biotech fields. These products are distributed both directly through wholesalers for use by health care professionals and to the general public. Prescription drugs include Duragesic, a transdermal patch for chronic pain; Eprex (sold in the U.S. as Procrit), a biotechnology-derived version of the human hormone erythropietin, which stimulates red blood cell production; Ergamisol, a colon cancer drug; Floxin, an antibacterial; Hismanal, the once-a-day less sedating antihistamine; Imodium, an antidiarrheal; Monistat, Sporanox, and Terazol, antifungals; Motilium, a gastrointestinal mobilizer; Orthclone OKT-3, for reversing the rejection of transplanted kidneys; Ortho-Novum group of oral contraceptives; Prepulsid, a gastrointestinal prokinetic; and Retin-A, a dermatological cream for acne.

"The professional segment include sutures, mechanical wound closure products, endoscopic products, dental products, diagnostic products, medical equipment and devices, ophthalmic products, surgical instruments, and medical supplies used principally in the professional fields by physicians, dentists, nurses, therapists, hospitals, diagnostic laboratories, and clinics. Products are distributed to these markets both directly and through surgical supply and other dealers. Products include Vicryl, Prolene and PDS surgical sutures; Proximate surgical staplers; Endopath disposable trocars; Ortho HCV Elisa test system for hepatitis C testing; One Touch II blood glucose monitoring system; Barrier disposable surgical packs, gowns, scrub apparel, face masks and head coverings, and sterile procedure trays; Cidex sterilizing/disinfecting solutions; and Acuvue disposable contact lenses.

"Sales by domestic companies in the consumer products business accounted for 54.6 percent of the total segment and international subsidiaries accounted for 45.4 percent."

During 1992, revenues and operating profits were apportioned as follows: consumer products 34.7 percent of revenues and 20.3 percent of profits, pharmaceuticals 31.6 percent of revenues and 55.4 percent of profits, and professional products 33.7 percent of revenues and 24.3 percent of profits.

Geographically, the United States provided 50.2 percent of revenues and 42.7 percent of profits, Europe 30.9 percent of revenues and 45.7 percent of profits, the Western Hemisphere excluding the U.S. 8.8 percent of revenues and 5.4 percent of profits, and Africa, Asia, and the Pacific 10.1 percent of revenues and 6.2 percent of profits.

The R.W. Johnson Foundation controls 7 percent and institutions about 60 percent of the outstanding common shares. Johnson & Johnson has paid consecutive cash dividends since 1908. It paid a 200 percent stock dividend in 1981, a 100 percent stock dividend in 1989, and a 100 percent stock dividend in 1992.

Total assets: $12.2 billion
Current ratio: 1.6
Common shares outstanding: 642.9 million

	1984	1985	1986	1987	1988	1989	1990	1991	1992	1993
Revenues (Mil.)	6,125	6,421	7,003	8,012	9,000	9,757	11,232	12,447	13,753	14,138
Net Income (Mil.)	515	614	330	833	974	1,082	1,143	1,461	1,625	1,787
Earnings per share	.69	.84	.46	1.21	1.43	1.62	1.72	2.20	2.46	2.74
Dividends per share	.29	.32	.34	.40	.48	.56	.66	.77	.89	1.01
Prices Hi	10.8	13.8	18.6	26.4	22.1	29.8	37.1	58.1	58.8	50.4
Lo	7.0	8.8	11.8	13.8	17.3	20.8	25.6	32.6	43.0	35.6

Kellogg Company
One Kellogg Square (P.O. Box 3599)
Battle Creek, Michigan 49016-3599
Tel. (616) 961-2000
Listed: NYSE
Investor contact: Neil G. Nyberg
Ticker symbol: K
S&P rating: A+

"Kellogg Company, headquartered in Battle Creek, Michigan, is the world's leading producer of ready-to-eat cereal products. The company also manufactures frozen pies and waffles, toaster pastries, cereal bars, and other convenience foods.

"Founded in 1906, Kellogg Company has a heritage of excellence and a reputation for products that contribute to a healthy diet. Kellogg products are manufactured in seventeen countries and distributed in more than 150 countries.

"Kellogg North America's disciplined approach to products development led to the introduction of Kellogg's Low Fat Granola cereal. We also successfully launched Kellogg's Frosted Bran and Kellogg's Rice Krispies Treats cereals, and S'Mores variety of Kellogg's Pop-Tarts toaster pastries in the U.S. Second-year products Kellogg's Nutri-Grain Cereal Bars and Kellogg's Cinnamon Mini-Buns cereal in the U.S., and Kellogg's Cruncheroos cereal in Canada, all achieved excellent growth.

"Through effective advertising, we implemented innovative, value-focused campaigns behind such established products as Kellogg's Corn Flakes, Kellogg's Frosted Mini-Wheats, Kellogg's Corn Pops, Kellogg's All-Bran, and other category-leading cereal brands.

"Kellogg Europe's product lineup continues to grow even stronger. During 1992, we successfully launched Kellogg's Nut Feast cereal and Kellogg's Pop-Tarts toaster pastries in Great Britain and Ireland, Kellogg's Froot Loops and Kellogg's Chombos cereals in Germany, and Kellogg's Froot Loops in France. More product introductions are occurring in 1993, including the launch of Kellogg's Nut Feast in Germany.

"Kellogg's Asia-Pacific's most developed market, Australia, continues to show above-average growth. Other long established markets such as New Zealand and South Africa continue to offer significant growth potential. The fast developing markets of South Korea, Taiwan, Hong Kong, and Singapore continue to show encouraging volume growth. Kellogg Japan, possessing by far the best infrastructure and the highest market share among cereal producers in Japan, is well positioned to respond effectively to this opportunity. Consistent with the company's commitment to global leadership in our business, we reached final agreement in January of 1993 to construct a ready-to-eat cereal plant at Guangzhou, in China's economically progressive Guangdong Province.

"Kellogg Latin America's growth is a shining example of how long-term investments in emerging and developing markets can pay off. Over the decades, Kellogg Latin America has built up an infrastructure of six highly efficient plants. We have marketed an ever-expanding product line and have achieved dominant shares in most markets. In much of Latin America, the name Kellogg is synonymous with high-quality ready-to-eat cereal.

"The similarities between the Kellogg Company and its prime subsidiary, Mrs. Smith's Frozen Foods Co., are striking. Kellogg's is by far the number-one name in ready-to-eat cereal; likewise, Mrs. Smith's two product lines—Eggo frozen waffles and Mrs. Smith's frozen pies—dominate their categories. Year after year, waffles remain the fastest growing category in the freezer case, with the Eggo brand always leading the way."

Geographically, during 1992, revenues and earnings were apportioned as follows: the United States 57 percent of revenues and 66 percent of earnings,

Europe 27 percent of revenues and 21 percent of earnings, and other areas 16 percent of revenues and 13 percent of earnings.

In 1993, Kellogg's sales increased for the 49th consecutive year, earnings were up for the 41st time in 42 years, and dividends were raised for the 37th straight year. Kellogg has paid cash dividends since 1923. The W.K. Kellogg Foundation controls about 34 percent and institutions about 33 percent of the outstanding common shares. Kellogg declared a 2 for 1 split in 1986, and another 2 for 1 split in 1991.

Total assets: $4.2 billion
Current ratio: 1.0
Common shares outstanding: 234.8 million

	1984	1985	1986	1987	1988	1989	1990	1991	1992	1993
Revenues (Mil.)	2,602	2,930	3,341	3,793	4,349	4,652	5,181	5,787	6,191	6,295
Net Income (Mil.)	251	281	319	396	480	470	503	606	683	681
Earnings per share	.84	1.14	1.29	1.60	1.95	1.93	2.08	2.51	2.86	2.94
Dividends per share	.42	.45	.51	.64	.76	.86	.96	1.08	1.20	1.32
Prices Hi	10.7	18.0	29.3	34.4	34.3	40.8	38.8	67.0	75.4	67.9
Lo	6.8	9.6	16.8	19.0	24.5	28.9	29.9	35.0	54.4	47.3

The Limited, Inc.

Three Limited Parkway (P.O. Box 16000)
Columbus, Ohio 43216
Tel. (614) 479-7000
Listed: NYSE
Investor contact: Vice President-Financial and Public Relations,
Alfred S. Dietzel
Ticker symbol: LTD
S&P rating: A+

THE LIMITED, INC.

As profiled in its 1992 Annual Report, "The Limited is principally engaged in the purchase, distribution, and sale of Women's apparel. The company operates an integrated distribution system which supports the company's retail activities. The activities are conducted under various trade names through retail stores and catalogue operations of the company. Merchandise is targeted to appeal to customers in specialty markets who have distinctive consumer characteristics, and includes regular and special-sized fashion apparel available at various price levels. The company's merchandise includes shirts, blouses, sweaters, pants, skirts, coats, dresses, lingerie, and accessories and, to a lesser degree, men's apparel, children's apparel, fragrances, bed, bath, personal care products, and specialty gift items. As of January 30, 1993, the company operated twelve retail divisions and four catalog divisions (Victoria's Secret Catalog, Lane Bryant Direct, Roaman's, and Lerner Direct). The company's wholly-owned credit card bank, World Financial Network National Bank, provides credit services to customers of the retail and catalogue divisions of the company.

"The company also operated Mast Industries, Inc., a contract manufacturer and apparel importer, and Gryphon Development, L.P. Gryphon creates, develops and contract manufactures most of the bath and personal care products sold by the company.

"The following is a brief description of each of the company's operating divisions, including their respective target markets.

"Express (640 stores) brings international women's sportswear and accessories with a distinctive European point of view to fashion-forward women in a spirited continental store environment.

"The Limited (759 stores) offers a full range of fashion-forward, private label sportswear, ready-to-wear, and accessories for women.

"Lerner New York (915 stores) is in the process of upgrading its offering from a budget to a moderate-priced specialty retailer of conventional women's sportswear, ready-to-wear, and coats.

"Lane Bryant (809 stores) focuses on sportswear, ready-to-wear, coats, and intimate apparel for the fashion-conscious, large size woman.

"Victoria's Secret Stores (545 stores) offers lingerie, beautiful fragrances, and romantic gifts in an atmosphere of 'Pure Indulgence.'

"Victoria's Secret Catalogue sells women's lingerie, sportswear, and ready-to-wear.

"Brylane Catalogs is a direct sale catalog business, specializing in misses and larger size fashions for women. Brylane Catalogs, through Lane Bryant Direct, Roaman's, and Lerner Direct, focuses on budget to lower-moderate priced women's apparel.

"Structure (330 stores) offers a men's sportswear collection with a distinct international flavor. The store environment mixes classic Palladian and modern architectural styles to appeal to men with a good sense of fine design.

"The Limited Too (185 stores) offers fashionable casual sportswear for girls wearing sizes 6 to 14.

"Abercrombie & Fitch Co. (40 stores) provides spirited, traditional sportswear for young, thinking men and women.

"Henri Bendel (four stores) offers glamorous and sophisticated women's fashions in an exclusive shopping environment.

"Bath & Body Works (121 stores) provides personal care products for men and women.

"Cacique (71 stores) offers fashion lingerie and gifts in an European shopping environment.

"Penhaligon's (six stores) designs, distributes, wholesales, and retails a variety of perfumes, toiletries, grooming accessories, and antique silver gifts."

Chairman and President Leslie Wexner owns about 30 percent, and institutions about 45 percent, of the outstanding common shares. The Limited has paid very modest cash dividends since 1970. The Limited paid a 100 percent stock dividend in 1982, a 100 percent stock dividend in 1983, a 100 percent stock dividend in 1985, a 100 percent stock dividend in 1986, and a 100 percent stock dividend in 1990.

Total assets: $4.1 billion
Current ratio: 3.1
Common shares outstanding: 363.2 million

	1984	1985	1986	1987	1988	1989	1990	1991	1992	1993
Revenues (Mil.)	1,343	2,387	3,143	3,528	4,071	4,648	5,254	6,149	6,944	7,245
Net Income (Mil.)	92	145	228	235	245	347	398	403	455	391
Earnings per share	.26	.40	.60	.62	.68	.96	1.10	1.11	1.25	1.08
Dividends per share	.04	.05	.08	.12	.12	.12	.16	.24	.28	.36
Prices Hi	4.7	10.6	17.3	26.4	14.0	20.0	25.6	31.6	32.9	30.0
Lo	2.6	4.4	10.3	8.0	8.2	12.6	11.8	21.9	19.3	16.6

Luby's Cafeterias, Inc.

2211 Northeast Loop 410 (P.O. Box 33069)
San Antonio, Texas 78265-3069
Tel. (210) 654-9000
Listed: NYSE
Investor contact: Senior Vice Pres., John E. Curtis, Jr.
Ticker symbol: LUB
S&P rating: A

As profiled in its fiscal 1993 Annual Report, "Luby's Cafeterias, Inc., based in San Antonio, Texas, owns and operates cafeterias in the southern United States. As of August 31, 1993, the company operated a total of 169 units consisting of eleven in Arizona, three in Arkansas, five in Florida, two in Kansas, one in Louisiana, two in Missouri, four in New Mexico, nine in Oklahoma, six in Tennessee, and 126 in Texas. The company has approximately 9,600 employees.

"The company's marketing policy is to combine the food quality and atmosphere of a good restaurant with the simplicity and visual food selection of cafeteria service. Food is prepared in small quantities throughout serving hours and frequent quality checks are made. Each cafeteria offers a broad and varied menu, and normally serves 12 to 14 entrees, 12 to 14 vegetable dishes, 22 to 25 salads, and 19 to 20 desserts.

"The company's cafeterias cater primarily to shoppers and office, or store personnel for lunch, and to families for dinner. The company's cafeterias are open for lunch and dinner, seven days a week. All of the cafeterias sell takeout orders, and most of them have separate food-to-go entrances. Takeout orders accounted for approximately 8 percent of sales in fiscal 1993.

"Each cafeteria cooks or prepares substantially all of the food served, including breads and pastries. The cafeterias prepare food from the same recipes, with minor variations to suit local tastes, although menus are not uniform in all of the company's cafeterias on any particular day.

"Quality control teams, each consisting of experienced cooks and a supervisor, help to maintain uniform standards of food preparation. The teams visit the cafeterias periodically and work with the regular staffs to check adherence to the company's recipes, train personnel in new techniques, and evaluate procedures for possible use throughout the company. The teams also assist in the opening of new cafeterias.

"Each cafeteria is operated as a separate unit under the control of a manager who has responsibility for day-to-day operations, including food purchasing, menu planning, and personnel employment and supervision. Of the 169 cafeteria managers employed by the company, 143 have been with the company for more than ten years. Currently, an individual is employed for a period of seven to ten years before he or she is considered qualified to become a cafeteria manager.

"For the 25th consecutive year, Luby's Cafeterias, Inc. posted record sales and earnings in fiscal 1993.

"Luby's has paid consecutive cash dividends since 1973. Officers and directors control about 15 percent, and institutions about 45 percent, of Luby's outstanding common shares. Luby's paid a 25 percent stock dividend in 1980, a 50 percent stock dividend in 1981, and 25 percent stock dividend in 1983, a 33 1/3 stock dividend in 1984, a 50 percent stock dividend in 1986, and a 50 percent stock dividend in 1990.

Total assets: $302.1
Current ratio: 1.0
Common shares outstanding: 27.2 million

	1984	1985	1986	1987	1988	1989	1990	1991	1992	1993
Revenues (Mil.)	171	196	215	233	254	283	311	328	346	368
Net Income (Mil.)	17	20	22	24	28	29	32	32	33	36
Earnings per share	.63	.72	.80	.87	1.01	1.08	1.17	1.18	1.19	1.31
Dividends per share	.21	.25	.27	.30	.34	.39	.44	.47	.51	.56
Prices Hi	14.3	18.6	19.4	21.9	17.2	18.9	21.3	20.8	23.5	25.9
Lo	10.5	11.9	15.0	13.3	13.5	15.4	15.6	12.0	13.5	19.8

The May Department Stores Company

611 Olive Street
St. Louis, Missouri 63101-1799
Tel. (314) 342-6300
Listed: NYSE
Investor contact: Senior Vice President and Treasurer, Mr. Jan R. Kniffen
Ticker symbol: MA
S&P rating: A+

As profiled in its 1993 Annual Report, "The May Department Stores Company is the country's largest department store retailer and operates quality department store companies nationwide. Our companies and their headquarters are: Lord & Taylor, New York City; Foley's, Houston; Robinsons-May, Los Angeles; Hecht's, Washington,

D.C.; Kaufmann's, Pittsburgh; Filene's, Boston; Famous-Barr, St. Louis; and Meier & Frank, Portland, Oregon.

"Combined, our department store companies serve markets totaling 128 million people across the nation, and each holds a leading position in its region. We operated 301 department stores at fiscal year-end in twenty-nine states and the District of Columbia.

"In addition, May operated Payless ShoeSource, the country's largest chain of self-service family show stores. Payless ShoeSource sold 174 million pairs of shoes in 1993. At fiscal 1993 year-end, 3,797 stores were operated in forty-nine states, the District of Columbia, and Puerto Rico.

"We employ approximately 111,000 associates in forty-nine states, the District of Columbia and twelve offices overseas.

"With the exception of Lord & Taylor, our department store companies today all carry the same merchandise lines, including such prestigious vendors as Estee Lauder, Lancome, Clinique, Prescriptives, Chanel, Clarins, Ralph Lauren, DKNY, Anne Klein II, Polo, Nautica, Hilfiger, Calvin Klein, and Carole Little. These lines are, of course, in addition to our very strong broad-based brands such as Liz Claiborne, Dockers, Levi's, Guess, Nike, Reebok, and many others. Further, all of our department stores have the same merchandise mix and now all carry categories such as furniture and consumer electronics.

"In 1993, we opened thirteen new department stores, with approximately 2 million square feet of retail space, and 220 new Payless ShoeSource stores with over 700,000 square feet of retail space. We remodeled nineteen department stores, including six expansions. In addition, Payless ShoeSource expanded its Payless Kids concept, adding 200 units. By 1993 year-end, 300 stores will operate in this format.

"During the 1993 to 1997 period, we plan to invest $3.1 billion for 108 new department stores, approximately 1,200 new Payless ShoeSource stores and 1,000 Payless Kids stores. This expansion will add more than twenty million square feet of retail square footage."

During fiscal 1993, department stores provided 82.2 percent of revenues and 85 percent of operating income, and Payless ShoeStores provides 17.8 percent of revenues and 15 percent of operating income.

May Department Stores achieved its eighteenth year of record sales and earnings in fiscal 1992. Institutions control about 70 percent of the outstanding common shares. May Department Stores paid a 50 percent stock dividend in 1984, a 100 percent stock dividend in 1986, and a 100 percent stock dividend in 1993.

Total assets: $8.8 billion
Current ratio: 2.6
Common shares outstanding: 248.3 million

	1984	1985	1986	1987	1988	1989	1990	1991	1992	1993
Revenues (Mil.)	6,361	6,825	7,437	7,480	8,874	9,602	10,066	10,615	11,150	11,529
Net Income (Mil.)	327	347	381	444	534	498	500	575	603	711
Earnings per share	1.06	1.11	1.21	1.45	1.81	1.76	1.87	1.94	2.26	2.65
Dividends per share	.39	.46	.51	.56	.63	.70	.77	.81	.83	.90
Prices Hi	10.8	16.3	22.1	25.4	20.0	26.3	29.6	30.2	37.3	46.5
Lo	7.6	9.6	15.0	11.1	14.4	17.3	18.8	18.7	25.8	33.4

McDonald's Corporation

McDonald Plaza
Oak Brook, Illinois 60521
Tel. (708) 575-7428
Listed: NYSE
Investor contact: Vice President, Sharon Vuinovich
Ticker symbol: MCD
S&P rating: A+

As profiled in its 1993 Annual Report, "The McDonald's System is the largest foodservice organization in the world. The company, restaurant managers, franchisees, and joint-venture partners operate more than 14,000 McDonald's restaurants in seventy countries, each offering a limited menu of high-quality food, which can be part of a well-balanced meal plan. McDonald's has pioneered food-quality specifications, equipment technology, marketing and training programs, and operational and supply systems that are considered the standards of the industry throughout the world.

"McDonald's is an operations company, which allows us to deliver customer satisfaction through quality food; fast, friendly service; restaurants known for cleanliness; and a menu that provides value.

"McDonald's restaurants offer a substantially uniform menu consisting of hamburgers and cheeseburgers, including the Big Mac and Quarter Pounder with Cheese, McLean Deluxe sandwiches, the Filet-O-Fish and McChicken sandwiches, french fries, Chicken McNuggets, salads, lowfat milk shakes, sundaes and cones, pies, cookies, and a limited number of soft drinks and other beverages. McDonald's restaurants operating in the United States are open during breakfast hours and offer a full breakfast menu, including the Egg McMuffin and the Sausage McMuffin with Egg sandwiches, hotcakes, and sausage; three varieties of biscuits; no-fat, no-cholesterol Apple-Bran muffins and cereals.

"McDonald's franchising program assures consistency and quality. Two-thirds of our restaurants are franchised to 10,000 owner/operators around the world.

"The company, its franchisees, and affiliates purchase food products and packaging from numerous independent suppliers. Quality specifications are established and strictly enforced for each product. Independently owned and operated distribution centers distribute these products and supplies to most McDonald's restaurants. The restaurants then prepare, assemble, and package these products using specially designed production techniques and equipment to obtain uniform standards of quality.

"Expansion continues to be important to McDonald's growth. We plan to add between 700 and 900 restaurants annually over the next several years."

During 1993, revenues and operating income were apportioned as follows: the United States 53.1 percent of revenues and 54.8 percent of operating income, Europe 30.2 percent of revenues and 27.6 percent of operating income, Canada 7.5 percent of revenues and 5.6 percent of operating income, the Pacific 6.7 percent of revenues and 9.6 percent of operating income, and Latin America 2.5 percent of revenues and 2.4 percent of operating income.

McDonald's has increased earnings and cash dividends each year since 1976. Institutions control about 60 percent of the outstanding common shares. McDonald's paid a 50 percent stock dividend in 1982, a 50 percent stock dividend in 1984, a 50 percent stock dividend in 1986, an 50 percent stock dividend in 1987, a 100 percent stock dividend in 1989, and a 100 percent stock dividend in 1994.

Total assets: $12.0 billion
Current ratio: 0.6
Common shares outstanding: 707.4 million

	1984	1985	1986	1987	1988	1989	1990	1991	1992	1993
Revenues (Mil.)	3,366	3,694	4,143	4,853	5,521	6,066	6,640	6,695	7,133	7,408
Net Income (Mil.)	389	433	480	549	646	727	802	860	959	1,083
Earnings per share	.49	.56	.62	.73	.86	.98	1.10	1.18	1.30	1.46
Dividends per share	.09	.10	.11	.12	.14	.15	.17	.18	.20	.21
Prices Hi	6.3	9.2	12.8	15.3	12.7	17.5	19.3	20.0	25.2	29.6
Lo	4.6	5.7	8.2	7.9	10.2	11.5	12.5	13.1	19.2	22.8

Medtronic, Inc.

7000 Central Avenue NE
Minneapolis, Minnesota 55432-3576
Tel. (612) 574-4000
Listed: NYSE
Investor contact: Director of Investor Relations, Dale F. Beumer
Ticker symbol: MDT
S&P rating: A+

As profiled in its fiscal 1993 Annual Report, "Medtronic, Inc. is a leader in producing therapeutic medical devices to improve cardiovascular and neurological health of patients around the world.

"Founded in 1949 by Earl E. Bakken and the late Palmer J. Hermundslie, Medtronic created the 'pacing' industry, as it is known today, with the development of the first wearable external cardiac pacemaker in 1957. Since then Medtronic has improved the lives of millions of patients through its six businesses: Bradycardia Pacing, Tacharrhythmia Management, Cardiopulmonary, Heart Valves, Interventional Vascular, and Neurological.

"Bradycardia Pacing—Medtronic's core business—develops, manufactures, and markets products designed to treat patients with slow or irregular heartbeats. Products include a wide range of high-quality pulse generators, leads, programmers, and accessories.

"Serving many of the same customers and using many of the same technologies as the Bradycardia Pacing business, Medtronic's Tacharrhythmia Management business develops, manufactures, and markets products for the treating of hearts that beat too rapidly. With the U.S. Food and Drug Administration (FDA) clearance of Medtronic's implantable PCD (pacer/cardioverter/defibrillator) device in February 1993, the company intends to become the acknowledged leader in implantable tacharrhythmia management devices by the mid 1990s.

"Medtronic's Cardiopulmonary business specializes in systems that handle, process, and monitor blood during circulation outside of the body. Its products are designed primarily for open heart surgery, organ transplant, and high-risk angioplasty support application. Medtronic's Maxima membrane oxygenator is the most frequently used membrane bloodoxygenator; in the world; similarly, the company's Bio-Medicus Bio-Pump centrifugal blood pump is utilized more than any other centrifugal blood pump. Medtronic's bypass system features the revolutionary Carmeda BioActive Surface, with unique blood compatible properties.

"Medtronic's Heart Valve business develops, produces, and markets tissue and mechanical replacements for diseased or defective heart valves. Since its introduction in 1977, the Medtronic Hall Mechanical Valve has been a leader in performance and durability.

"Medtronic's Interventional Vascular organization serves interventional cardiologists and catheter laboratory personnel with a range of outstanding percutaneous transluminal coronary angioplasty (PTCA) products. The major products of Medtronic's Interventional Vascular business include several PTCA balloon catheters and guiding catheters. PTCA often serves as an appropriate alternative to bypass surgery and drugs in the treatment of coronary artery disease. PTCA provides effective treatment without general anesthesia and with relatively little trauma, shortened hospital stays, and reduced costs.

"Medtronic's Neurological segment is the second largest of Medtronic's six operating businesses. Today, Medtronic addresses neurological patient needs in two major areas: implantable neurostimulation and implantable drug delivery. The Itrel II spinal cord stimulation system, for example, provides the world's most advanced and flexible neurostimulation treatment. The Itrel II is used primarily for chronic intractable pain caused by failed spinal surgery, reflex sympathetic dystrophy, and chronic limb ischemia. The X-trel system, comprising an implantable receiver and lead system controlled by external radio signals, helps give relief to patients needing higher energy levels to control their pain.

"The SynchroMed infusion system is the only commercially available implantable drug delivery product that is programmed from outside the patient's body. The SynchroMed system is used to administer drugs to the cerebrospinal fluid that bathes the spinal cord for the treatment of severe, chronic pain and spasticity."

During fiscal 1993 revenues were apportioned as follows: pacing 65.7 percent, other cardiovascular products 22.9 percent, and neurological 11.4 percent.

During fiscal 1993 revenues and operating profits were apportioned as follows: The United states 58 percent of revenues and 70.3 percent of operating profits, Europe 29.6 percent of revenues and 17 percent of operating profits, and Canada, Latin America, Japan, and Asia-Pacific 12.4 percent of revenues and 12.7 percent of operating profits.

During fiscal 1993, Medtronic Inc. marked its eighth consecutive year of growth in revenue and earnings. Medtronic has paid consecutive cash dividends since 1977. Institutions control over 70 percent of the outstanding common shares. Medtronic paid a 100 percent stock dividend in 1989, and a 100 percent stock dividend in 1991.

Total assets: $1.3 billion
Current ratio: 2.3
Common shares outstanding: 59.4

	1984	1985	1986	1987	1988	1989	1990	1991	1992	1993
Revenues (Mil.)	391	370	411	515	670	766	866	1,021	1,177	1,328
Net Income (Mil.)	60	38	54	75	87	100	113	133	162	197
Earnings per share	.87	.58	.86	1.25	1.46	1.73	1.92	2.25	2.71	3.32
Dividends per share	.18	.19	.20	.22	.26	.30	.35	.41	.48	.56
Prices Hi	11.2	11.0	23.2	27.2	25.0	35.5	46.0	94.3	104.5	95.5
Lo	6.2	6.4	10.8	16.0	17.2	19.3	29.5	38.5	63.3	51.6

Mercantile Bankshares Corporation

2 Hopkins Plaza (P.O. Box 1477)
Baltimore, Maryland 21203-1477
Tel. (410) 237-5900
Listed: NASDAQ
Investor contact: Suzanne Wolff
Ticker symbol: MRBK
S&P rating: A

As profiled in its 1992 Annual Report, "Mercantile Bankshares Corporation is a multibank holding company organized in 1969 under the laws of Maryland. On January 1, 1993, its principal affiliates were nineteen banks and a mortgage company.

"The affiliated banks are engaged in a general personal and corporate banking business. The corporation's largest bank, Mercantile-Safe Deposit and Trust Company, also provides a full range of trust services.

"The banking affiliates of Mercantile Bankshares Corporation have 144 retail banking offices providing personal banking services. Services include deposit vehicles such as checking accounts, NOW accounts, Money Market Deposit Accounts, Certificates of Deposit, and Individual Retirement Accounts. Loans are made to individuals to meet a variety of consumer needs.

"Each of the corporation's affiliates
gram serving local businesses. The prima.
dium and large companies is centered at N
Company (M.S.D.&T.). Corporate banking sei
ous types of commercial and real estate loans, ac
ment and short-term money market investing.

"The Trust Division of M.S.D.&T. provides se
rations and non-profit institutions. Services for indi
management, estate settlement, living and testamenta
securities. Employee benefit plans, master and directed   ᴄorpo-
rate financial services are provided to businesses. Endo,   ᴜs are managed for non-profit institutions. The Trust Division is also ᴀ ᴄstment advisor to
M.S.D.&T. Funds, Inc., which provides a series of open-ended, no-load mutual
funds.

"Through offices in Maryland and Delaware, Mercantile Mortgage Corporation generates and services real estate mortgage loans and construction
loans, as principal and as agent. Residential and commercial real estate apprais-
als are offered through an appraisal subsidiary."

"Mercantile Bankshares Corporation also operates an insurance agency
(MBC Agency, Inc.) and a real estate company (MBC Realty, Inc.)."

During 1992, loans of $3.5 billion were apportioned as follows: commer-
cial, financial, and agricultural 32.3 percent; real estate-construction 9.1 percent; real estate-mortgage 44.4 percent; and consumer 14.2 percent.

Mercantile Bankshares Corporation has paid consecutive cash dividends
since 1909. Mercantile has increased dividends for the past sixteen consecutive
years. Mercantile paid a 100 percent stock dividend in 1986, a 100 percent
stock dividend in 1989, and a 50 percent stock dividend in 1993.

Total assets: $5.6 billion
Common shares outstanding: 45.9 million

	1984	1985	1986	1987	1988	1989	1990	1991	1992	1993
Net Income (Mil.)	34	37	40	50	58	66	69	71	76	82
Earnings per share	.86	.97	1.04	1.15	1.19	1.33	1.51	1.55	1.67	1.80
Dividends per share	.25	.29	.33	.37	.43	.54	.55	.57	.58	.64
Prices Hi	7.5	12.3	15.7	15.1	13.2	18.4	17.7	19.0	22.2	23.9
Lo	5.3	7.0	11.5	9.3	10.9	11.7	8.9	12.2	18.3	18.0

Merck & Co., Inc.

One Merck Drive (P.O. Box 100)
Whitehouse Station, New Jersey 08889-0100
Tel. (908) 423-1000
Listed: NYSE
Investor contact: Director of Investor Relations, David E. Halter, Jr.
Ticker symbol: MR
S&P rating: A+

As profiled in its 1992 Annual Report, "Merck is a worldwide organization engaged primarily in the business of discovering, developing, producing, and marketing products and services for the maintenance or restoration of health. The company's business is divided into two industry segments: Human and Animal Health Products, and Specialty Chemical Products.

"Human health products include therapeutic and preventive agents, generally sold by prescription, for the treatment of human disorders. Among these are cardiovascular products of which Vasotec, Mevacor, Zocor, Prinivil, Vaseretic, Moduretic, and Aldomet are the largest-selling; anti-ulcerants of which Pepcid and Prilosec are the largest; antibiotics of which Primaxin, Noroxin, and Mefoxin are the largest; vaccines/biologicals of which Recombivax HB (hepatitis B vaccine recombinant) and M-M-R II, a pediatric vaccine for measles, mumps, and rubella, are the largest-selling; opthalmologicals of which Timoptic is the largest; anti-inflammatory/analgesic products of which Indocin, Dolobid, and Clinoril are the largest; and other human health products which include antiparkinsonism products, psychotherapeutics, a muscle relaxant, and Proscar, a treatment for symptomatic benign prostate enlargement, which was introduced in the United States late in the second quarter of 1992.

"Animal health/crop protection products include animal medicinals used for the control and alleviation of disease in livestock, small animals, and poultry. These products are primarily antiparasitics, of which Ivomec, for the control of internal and external parasites in livestock, and Heartguard-30, for the prevention of canine heartworm disease, are the largest-selling; crop protection products; coccidiostats for the treatment of poultry disease and poultry breeding stock.

"The Specialty Chemical Products segment consists of the Kelco Division, Calgon Vestal Laboratories, and the Calgon Water Management Division (which is scheduled to be sold). The company's specialty chemical products

have a wide variety of applications, such as use in
oil exploration, paper, textiles, utilities, and persona
During 1992, sales of human and animal hea
tioned as follows: cardiovasculars 49.4 percent, anti-u
tibiotics 10.4 percent, vaccines/biologicals 5.4 percent,
percent, anti-inflammatories/analgesics 4.8 percent, ot
percent, and animal health/crop protection 9.4 percent.

In 1992, human/animal health products accounted   ..at of
revenues and 97.7 percent of operating income, and spec.   ..cmicals accounted for 6.2 percent of revenues and 2.3 percent of operating income.

Merck has paid consecutive cash dividends since 1935. Institutions control
about 50 percent of the outstanding common shares. Merck paid a 100 percent
stock dividend in 1986, a 200 percent stock dividend in 1988, and a 200 percent stock dividend in 1992.

Total assets: $19.9 billion
Current ratio: 1.0
Common shares outstanding: 1.3 billion

	1984	1985	1986	1987	1988	1989	1990	1991	1992	1993
Revenues (Mil.)	3,560	3,548	4,129	5,061	5,940	6,551	7,672	8,603	9,663	10,498
Net Income (Mil.)	493	540	676	906	1,207	1,495	1,781	2,122	2,447	2,166
Earnings per share	.37	.42	.54	.74	1.02	1.26	1.52	1.83	2.12	1.87
Dividends per share	.17	.18	.21	.27	.43	.55	.64	.77	.92	1.03
Prices Hi	5.5	7.7	14.4	24.8	19.9	26.9	30.4	55.6	56.6	44.1
Lo	4.3	5.0	7.5	13.6	16.0	18.8	22.3	27.4	40.5	28.6

Microsoft Corporation

One Microsoft Way
Redmond, Washington 98052-6399
Tel. (206) 882-8080
Listed: NASDAQ
Investor contact: Raymond B. Ferguson
Ticker symbol: MSFT
S&P rating: B+

As profiled in its fiscal 1993 Annual Report, "Microsoft Corporation operates in
one business segment—the development, production, marketing, and support of

Microsoft ®

a wide range of microcomputer software, including operating systems for personal computers, office machines, and personal information devices; languages; applications programs; and personal computer books, hardware, and multimedia products. Microsoft products are available for all popular personal computers, including Apple computers and computers running Intel microprocessors.

"Microsoft's business strategy emphasizes the development of a broad line of microcomputer software products for business and personal use, marketed through multiple channels of distribution. To accomplish this goal, the company is divided into three main groups: the Products Group, the Sales and Support Group, and the Operations Group.

"The Products Group is comprised of five main divisions, each responsible for a particular area of software development. The Systems Division develops operating systems software, which controls computer hardware, allocates computer memory, schedules the execution of applications software, and manages the flow of information and communication among the various components of the microcomputer system. The company's primary proprietary operating systems for microcomputers are: the Microsoft MS-DOS operating system, the Microsoft Windows operating system, Microsoft Windows for Workgroups, the Microsoft Windows NT operating system, and Microsoft LAN Manager. The Desktop Application Division creates productivity applications. The Database and Development Tools Division creates database products, as well as language programming products and tools. The Consumer Division develops products designed for the home, school, and small business market, including multimedia consumer products. The Workgroup Division develops electronic mail and scheduling products.

"The Sales and Support Group is responsible for building long-term business relationships with customers. This includes marketing products through the U.S., International, and OEM (original equipment manufacturer) markets and providing support for the Company's products through Consulting Services, Product Support Services, and Solutions Providers.

"The Operations Group is responsible for managing business operations and overall business planning. This includes the domestic and international manufacturing operations, and the publishing efforts of Microsoft Press.

"Microsoft has operations in forty-one countries. Revenues from customers outside the United States were more than $2 billion during the past twelve months, representing over 55 percent of total worldwide revenues.

"To serve this global market, we localize all of our products in the languages spoken by our customers.

"During fiscal 1993, revenues by product group were apportioned as follows: Applications software 58 percent, Systems software 34 percent, Hardware 6 percent, and Other 2 percent.

Microsoft has never paid a cash dividend. Officers and directors control about 50 percent of the outstanding common shares (including about 30 percent held by William H. Gates III and 13 percent by Paul G. Allen). Institutions control another 35 percent of the common shares. Microsoft paid a 100 percent stock dividend in 1987, a 100 percent stock dividend in 1991, a 50 percent stock dividend in 1992, and a 100 percent stock dividend in 1994.

Total assets: $3.8 billion
Current ratio: 5.1
Common shares outstanding: 563.0 million

	1984	1985	1986	1987	1988	1989	1990	1991	1992	1993
Revenues (Mil.)	97	140	198	346	591	804	1,183	1,843	2,759	3,753
Net Income (Mil.)	16	24	39	72	124	171	279	463	708	953
Earnings per share	.04	.06	.09	.15	.25	.34	.52	.82	1.21	1.25
Dividends per share	—	—	—	—	—	—	—	—	—	—
Prices Hi	—	2.9	3.8	7.9	9.9	18.0	37.4	44.5	47.5	49.0
Lo	—	1.2	2.7	5.1	5.1	9.4	16.2	32.9	32.8	35.2

NationsBank Corporation

NationsBank Corporate Center
Charlotte, North Carolina 28255
Tel. (704) 386-5000
Listed: NYSE
Investor contact: Director of Investor Relations, Susan C. Carr
Ticker symbol: NB
S&P rating: A-

As profiled in its 1992 Annual Report, "NationsBank is the largest banking company in the South and Southwest, and the fourth largest in the United States. We have full-service banking centers in nine states: Florida, Geor-

NationsBank Corporation

143

gia, Kentucky, Maryland, North Carolina, South Carolina, Tennessee, Texas, and Virginia, plus the District of Columbia. We also provide financial products and services to individuals and businesses in many other states, from New England to the West Coast, as well as in several overseas markets.

"NationsBank, through its various subsidiaries, provides a diversified range of financial services to its customers. These services include activities related to the general banking business, as provided through the General Bank Group (including comprehensive service in the commercial and retail banking fields, the origination and servings of home mortgage loans, the issuance and servicing of credit cards, certain insurance services, and retail brokerage activities); the Institutional Bank Group (including comprehensive service in the corporate and investment banking fields, trading in financial futures through contractual arrangements with members of the various commodities exchanges, and arranging and structuring mergers, acquisitions, leveraged buyouts, private debt placements, international financings and venture capital); international operations through branches, merchant banks or representative offices located in London, Frankfurt, Singapore, Mexico City, Grand Cayman, and Nassau; the Secured Lending Group (including real estate lending, commercial finance and factoring, and leasing and financing a wide variety of commercial equipment); and the Trust Group (including trust and investment management services and private banking services).

"NationsBank conducts its non-banking operations through several subsidiaries, including but not limited to the following: NationsBanc Mortgage Corporation; NationsBanc Securities, Inc.; NationsBanc Commercial Corporation; NationsBanc Leasing Corporation; NationsCredit Corporation, and NationsBanc Capital Markets, Inc.

"In February 1993, we exercised our option to acquire MNC Financial Inc. of Baltimore. In October, we announced a ground-breaking joint venture with Dean Witter creating a new retail securities company—NationsSecurities, A Dean Witter/NationsBank Company. Also in October, we agreed to purchase essentially all of the assets of Chrysler First Inc., which included consumer and inventory finance receivables and 175 lending offices."

During 1993, loans and leases of $92.7 billion were apportioned as follows: commercial 44.2 percent, consumer 18.4 percent, real-estate-mortgage 13.8 percent, real estate commercial 8.9 percent, bank card 4 percent, real estate-construction 3.5 percent, home equity 2.8 percent, leases 2.3 percent, and other 2.1 percent.

NationsBank has paid consecutive cash dividends since 1903. Institutions control about 60 percent of the outstanding common shares. NationsBank paid a 100 percent stock dividend in 1986.

Total assets: $157.7 billion
Common shares outstanding: 271.0 million

	1984	1985	1986	1987	1988	1989	1990	1991	1992	1993
Net Income (Mil.)	119	164	199	167	702	974	595	202	1,145	1,501
Earnings per share	2.04	2.30	2.53	2.03	3.49	4.48	2.61	.76	4.60	5.00
Dividends per share	.59	.69	.78	.86	.94	1.10	1.42	1.48	1.51	1.64
Prices Hi	18.3	23.6	27.8	29.1	29.1	55.0	47.3	42.8	53.4	58.0
Lo	11.5	16.9	20.0	15.5	17.5	27.0	16.9	21.5	39.6	44.5

Newell Co.

29 East Stephenson Street
Freeport, Illinois 61032-0943
Tel. (815) 235-4171
Listed: NYSE
Investor contact: Vice Pres. Finance, William T. Alldredge
Ticker symbol: NWL
S&P rating: A+

As profiled in its 1993 Annual Report, "Newell is a manufacturer and full-service marketer of high-volume consumer products serving the needs of volume purchasers. Newell's basic strategy is to merchandise a multi-product offering of brand-name staple products, with an emphasis on excellent customer service, in order to achieve maximum results with volume purchasers.

"The company's cookware and bakeware business is conducted by the Mirro Division, which manufactures aluminum cookware, bakeware, and kitchen utensils. Mirro products are sold primarily under the brand names of Mirro, Foley, Wearever, Airbake, Airbake 2000, Cushionaire, Concentric Air, and Heat Max.

"Newell's Amerock division offers a broad line of cabinet, window, and bath hardware. These products are sold under the Amerock and Allison brand names and include knobs, pulls, hinges, drawer slides, catches, various window hardware components, towel bars, and tissue holders.

"The company's marker and writing instrument business is conducted by the Sanford Corporation, which manufactures permanent/waterbase markers, highlighters, porous tip pens, dry erase markers, and overhead projector pens. Principal brands names are Sharpie, Vis A Vis, Expo, Major Accent, and Expresso.

Other consumer products include, "Anchor Consumer Glass–tabletop glassware and over bakeware; EZ Paintr–manual paint applicator products; Window Furnishings–drapery hardware, window shades, and alternate window treatments and accessories; Rogers/Keene–office supplies and accessories; Stuart Hall–office supplies, school supplies, and stationary; Intercraft–picture frames; Home Hardware–wall-hung shelving system components and household hardware; Anchor Hocking Plastics–plastic microwave cookware and food storage containers; BernzOmatic–propane and propane/oxygen hand torches and accessories; and Counselor–bath scales.

"During 1992, one customer, Wal-Mart Stores, Inc., accounted for approximately 14 percent of the Company's net consumer sales.

"The industrial segment of Newell Co. consists of Caps & Closures (the company completed the sale of its closures business on December 31, 1992); Anchor Specialty Glass–glass lamp parts, lighting components, meter covers, and appliance covers; and Industrial Plastics–food processing foodservice items."

During 1992, consumer products accounted for 83.1 percent of revenues and 88.4 percent of operating profits, and industrial products represented 16.9 percent of revenues and 11.6 percent of operating profits.

Newell Co. has paid consecutive cash dividends since 1946. Institutions control about 60 percent of the outstanding common shares. Newell paid a 100 percent stock dividend in 1983, a 100 percent stock dividend in 1988, and a 100 percent stock dividend in 1989.

Total assets: $2.0 billion
Current ratio: 1.1
Common shares outstanding: 78.6 million

	1984	1985	1986	1987	1988	1989	1990	1991	1992	1993
Revenues (Mil.)	349	410	474	800	1,087	1,247	1,204	1,259	1,452	1,645
Net Income (Mil.)	18	23	31	50	79	106	126	136	163	165
Earnings per share	.41	.49	.53	.74	1.13	1.43	1.68	1.78	2.10	2.10
Dividends per share	.10	.10	.14	.16	.23	.37	.44	.53	.60	.69
Prices Hi	4.4	5.7	9.2	10.6	14.4	25.0	34.1	45.8	53.0	43.0
Lo	3.3	3.3	5.3	5.5	7.0	13.2	18.5	23.3	33.1	30.8

Old Kent Financial Corporation

One Vandenberg Center
Grand Rapids, Michigan 49503
Tel. (616) 771-5000
Listed: NASDAQ
Investor contact: Senior Vice Pres. and Secretary, Martin J. Allen Jr.
Ticker symbol: OKEN
S&P rating: A+

As profiled in its 1992 Annual Report, "Old Kent Financial Corporation is a bank holding company headquartered in Grand Rapids, with total assets of $8.7 billion. Old Kent is in the business of commercial banking and related services through its sixteen banking affiliates and five non-banking subsidiaries. Old Kent's principal markets for financial services are communities within Michigan ($7.5 billion in assets) and Illinois ($1.2 billion in assets), where its 208 banking offices are located.

Old Kent Financial Corporation

"The services offered by Old Kent's subsidiaries include commercial and retail loans, business and personal checking accounts, savings and individual retirement accounts, time deposit instruments, automated teller machines and electronically accessed banking services, credit and debit cards, money transfer services, safe deposit facilities, cash management, real estate and lease financing, international banking services, credit life insurance, personal investment and brokerage services, and corporate and personal trust services.

"Much of Old Kent's growth has been through acquisition. Old Kent acquired all of the outstanding common stock of the $275 million asset University Financial Corporation (Elgin, Illinois) for a purchase price of $12.5 million, effective January 1, 1993. University Financial Corporation owned First Federal of Elgin F.S.A., which upon acquisition was merged into Old Kent Bank (Illinois). When acquired, University Financial Corporation had approximately $198 million of total deposits. Also acquired were five banking offices located in Elgin, Dundee, and Hampshire, which increased Old Kent's market presence in the northern half of Kane County, Illinois. In addition, Old Kent acquired the rights to service approximately $827 million of residential mortgage loans for third party investors in this transaction.

"On September 27, 1992, Old Kent Bank and Trust Company, Old Kent's largest affiliate, acquired five banking offices located in the Lansing, Michigan area, and their related deposits, which totalled approximately $53 million. The newly acquired offices are located in Lansing, East Lansing, Okemos, and Holt. Old Kent purchased the associated tangible and intangible assets from a federally insured savings bank for $4.6 million.

"Old Kent streamlined its banking offices for reciprocal banking. This means that a customer can do business with any Old Kent banking office as his account is available on computer line."

During 1992, loans of $4.9 billion were apportioned as follows: commercial 25 percent, real estate-commercial 23 percent, real estate-construction 4 percent, real estate-residential 21 percent, home equity 8 percent, and consumer 19 percent.

1992 marked the twentieth consecutive year that Old Kent has increased net income and dividends. Consecutive cash dividends have been paid since 1937. Old Kent paid a 5 percent stock dividend in 1980, a 5 percent stock dividend in 1981, a 50 percent stock dividend in 1984, a 50 percent stock dividend in 1986, and a 50 percent stock dividend in 1992.

Total assets: $9.9 billion
Common shares outstanding: 40.5 million

	1984	1985	1986	1987	1988	1989	1990	1991	1992	1993
Net Income (Mil.)	45	49	61	71	77	85	87	93	111	128
Earnings per share	1.55	1.70	1.81	1.84	1.97	2.15	2.19	2.31	2.75	3.14
Dividends per share	.36	.45	.50	.55	.58	.64	.72	.79	.90	1.07
Prices Hi	10.3	17.3	17.7	17.9	16.7	18.4	19.3	23.6	34.3	37.5
Lo	6.2	9.7	13.9	12.0	12.4	14.9	12.2	14.3	22.5	29.8

The Pep Boys — Manny, Moe and Jack

3111 West Allegheny Avenue
Philadelphia, Pennsylvania 19132
Tel. (215) 229-9000
Listed: NYSE
Investor contact: Senior Vice Pres., Frederick A. Stampone
Ticker symbol: PBY
S&P rating: A+

As profiled in its fiscal 1993 Annual Report, "The company is engaged principally in the retail sale of automotive parts and accessories, automotive maintenance and service, and the installation of parts sold by it through its chain of 357 Pep Boys stores (as of January 30, 1993), having 3,234 service bays. A sustained focus on the automotive aftermarket's three-tiered customer base—the 'do-it-yourselfer,' 'do-it-for-me', and the professional mechanic—holds Pep Boys true to its commitment to provide service and value that exceed its customers' expectation. The company opened twenty-nine warehouse, format automotive supercenters in 1992, and expects to open as many as forty more in 1993.

"The company's automotive product line (approximately 22,000 items) includes: tires; batteries; new and rebuilt parts for domestic and imported cars, including suspension parts, ignition parts, mufflers, engines, and engine parts; oil and air filters, belts, hoses, air conditioning parts, and brake parts; chemicals, including oil, antifreeze, polishes, additives, cleansers, and paints; mobile electronics, including sound systems, alarms, and cellular telephones; car accessories, including seat covers, floor mats, gauges, mirrors, and booster cables; and a large selection of truck and van accessories.

"The company sells oil, transmission fluid, chemicals, paints, and batteries under the Pep Boys name. The company sells antifreeze under the name Pure As Gold. The company sells starters and alternators under the names 'True Blue' and Pro-Start, and water pumps under the names 'True Blue' and Procool. Brakes are sold under the names Shur Grip and Prostop, and tires under the names Cornell and Futura. The company also sells shock absorbers under the names 'ProRyder,' and trunk and hatchback lift supports under the name Prolift. All products sold by the company under the Pep Boys and various other private label names accounted for approximately 19 percent of the company's merchandise sales in fiscal 1993. The remaining merchandise is sold under the brand names of others.

"The company has service bays in 345 of its 357 locations. Each service department can perform a variety of services which include: engine tune-ups, wheel alignments, state inspections, air conditioning service; the repair and installation of parts and accessories including brake parts, suspension parts, exhaust systems, front end parts, ignition parts, belts, hoses, clutches, filters, radios, alarms, sun roofs, cruise controls, and various other merchandise sold in Pep Boys' stores; installation and balancing of tires; and oil and lube jobs.

"All Pep Boys' stores are open seven days a week. Each store with service bays has a manager, a service manager, a parts manager, and two or more assistant managers. A store manager's average length of service with the company is approximately nine years.

"With 357 stores in twenty states, Pep Boys continued to gain market share in fiscal 1993 by entering Alabama and New York, while strengthening its presence in California, Florida, Louisiana, Maryland, Pennsylvania, South Carolina, Texas, Utah, and Virginia. The company expects to enter five additional states in fiscal 1994."

During fiscal 1993, merchandise provided 87.2 percent of revenues and 61.9 percent of operating profits, and automotive services provided 12.8 percent of revenues and 38.1 percent of operating profits.

Pep Boys has paid consecutive cash dividends since 1950. About 15 percent of the common shares are closely held and another 60 percent are controlled by institutions. Pep Boys paid a 6 percent stock dividend in each of the years 1979, 1980, and 1981, a 100 percent stock dividend in 1982, a 200 percent stock dividend in 1983, a 100 percent stock dividend in 1985, and a 200 percent stock dividend in 1987.

Total assets: $1.1 billion
Current ratio: 1.4
Common shares outstanding: 60.1 million

	1984	1985	1986	1987	1988	1989	1990	1991	1992	1993
Revenues (Mil.)	306	348	389	486	554	656	799	885	1,002	1,156
Net Income (Mil.)	16	18	21	28	34	38	35	38	39	55
Earnings per share	.33	.39	.43	.52	.62	.68	.63	.67	.69	.90
Dividends per share	.049	.059	.065	.073	.078	.090	.11	.12	.13	.14
Prices Hi	5.5	9.5	16.1	18.9	15.9	17.3	17.3	19.5	27.4	27.4
Lo	3.9	4.9	8.5	9.5	10.4	10.5	8.5	8.4	15.1	19.9

PepsiCo, Inc.

700 Anderson Hill Road
Purchase, New York 10577-3035
Tel. (914) 253-2000
Listed: NYSE
Investor contact: Vice Pres. Investor Relations, Margaret D. Moore
Ticker symbol: PEP
S&P rating: A+

As profiled in its 1992 Annual Report, "PepsiCo was created in 1965 by the merger of Pepsi-Cola and Frito-Lay. For the next decade, soft drinks and snack foods drove our growth. By the mid-1970s, we were seeking a third growth business that would respond to PepsiCo's skills in marketing and operations.

"We focused on the restaurant business and purchased Pizza Hut in 1977 and Taco Bell in 1978. Both of these chains had huge potential. In 1986, PepsiCo acquired Kentucky Fried Chicken (KFC), another promising chain. With KFC, we had more units than any other restaurant system.

"Back at the turn of the century, when soft drinks were a novelty, our consumers were satisfied with one soft drink—Pepsi Cola—and one way of buying it—at the soda fountain.

"As our consumers changed and wanted more variety, we added new channels of distribution, more packages and soft drinks: Diet Pepsi, Mountain Dew, Caffeine Free Pepsi, Caffeine Free Diet Pepsi, Slice, and Mug.

"Along the way, we expanded into international markets and began distributing 7UP and Miranda outside the U.S.

"In 1992, we formed a partnership with Thomas J. Lipton, and introduced Lipton ready-to-drink teas in unsweetened and sweetened versions; entered an agreement to distribute single-serve bottles and cans of Ocean Spray products in the U.S.; and introduced Crystal Pepsi, a unique-tasting clear cola with 100 percent natural flavors, no caffeine, and no preservatives, in the U.S.

"For as long as most people can remember, Frito-Lay has been the biggest snack chip company in the U.S. The company started about sixty years ago with two brands—Frito's corn chips and Lay's potato chips. Chee-tos cheese flavored snacks came next and then Doritos tortilla chips, our biggest brand in the U.S. By the end of the 1980s, we had eight of the ten largest-selling snack chip brands in the U.S.

"By 1966, we were in six markets outside the U.S. and in some, like Mexico, we had enormous success. In the 1980s, we decided to commit major resources to international snacks and we embarked on an aggressive acquisition program. By 1991, our snack foods were available in twenty-three countries.

"During 1992, in the U.S., we added 11,000 accounts and more than 460 routes; we significantly improved the quality of our leading potato chip brands, Lay's and Ruffles, making them tastier, crisper and crunchier; and we introduced two new varieties of Doritos tortilla chips, two new sizes of Tostitos tortilla chips, and a new flavor of Sunchips multigrain snacks.

"That year, worldwide system sales of Pizza Hut, Taco Bell, and KFC product reached $15.7 billion; the PepsiCo worldwide restaurant system reached 22,336 units; we added a lunch buffet in 2,100 U.S. company-owned Pizza Hut units; Taco Bell expanded testing of Hot 'n Now, a double drive-thru hamburger chain, offering fast service and low prices; and KFC introduced its All You Can Eat Buffet in 675 U.S. system restaurants.

"Also during 1992, our foodservice distribution company that supplies our restaurants with everything required to run a restaurant, added more than 1,200 restaurants to its routes. PepsiCola Food Service now serves nearly 14,000 world-wide, company-owned and franchised restaurants."

During 1992, beverages provided 34.6 percent of revenues and 31.9 percent of operating profits, snack foods provided 27.9 percent of revenues and 39.4 percent of operating profits, and restaurants provided 37.5 percent of revenues and 28.7 percent of operating profits.

Geographically that year, revenues and operating profits were apportioned as follows: the United States 75.3 percent of revenues and 82.3 percent of profits, Canada and Mexico 10.1 percent of revenues and 10 percent of profits, Europe 6.2 percent of revenues and 2.1 percent of profits, and other 8.4 percent of revenues and 5.6 percent of profits.

PepsiCo has paid consecutive cash dividends since 1952. Institutions control over 55 percent of the common shares. PepsiCo paid a 200 percent stock dividend in 1986, and another 200 percent stock dividend in 1990.

Total assets: $23.7 billion
Current ratio: 0.8
Common shares outstanding: 798.8 million

	1984	1985	1986	1987	1988	1989	1990	1991	1992	1993
Revenues (Mil.)	7,059	7,585	9,017	11,018	12,381	15,049	17,516	19,292	21,970	25,021
Net Income (Mil.)	213	544	458	595	762	901	1,077	1,080	1,302	1,588
Earnings per share	.33	.51	.59	.77	.97	1.13	1.37	1.35	1.61	1.96
Dividends per share	.19	.20	.21	.22	.27	.32	.38	.46	.51	.61
Prices Hi	5.1	8.4	11.9	14.1	14.6	21.9	27.9	35.6	43.0	43.6
Lo	3.8	4.5	7.3	8.5	10.0	12.6	18.0	23.5	30.5	34.5

Pfizer, Inc

235 East 42nd Street
New York, New York 10017
Tel. (212) 573-2323
Listed: NYSE
Investor contact: Director of Investor Relatio
Ticker symbol: PFE
S&P rating: A-

As profiled in its 1992 Annual Report, "Pfizer is a researched-based, global health care company with operations in more than 140 countries. Our principal mission is to apply scientific knowledge to help people around the world enjoy longer, healthier, and more productive lives. The company has four business segments: health care, consumer health care, food science, and animal health.

"The company's health care business is comprised of pharmaceutical and hospital products. The company competes with numerous other health care companies in the discovery and development of new, technologically advanced pharmaceutical and hospital products; in seeking use of its products by the medical profession; and in the sale of its product lines to wholesale and retail outlets, public and private hospitals, government, and the medical professional.

"Worldwide sales of Pfizer's pharmaceutical products increased 21 percent in 1992. U.S. and international pharmaceutical revenues advanced 25 percent and 17 percent respectively, principally as a result of strong sales of recently introduced products. These recently introduced products include Unasyn, Sulperazon, Difulcan, Zithromax, Procardia XL, Norvasc, Cardura, Zoloft, Reactine, and Minipress XL, with combined sales accounting for 59 percent of total pharmaceutical sales in 1992. Cardiovascular products are the company's largest therapeutic product line, accounting for 36 percent of pharmaceutical sales.

"In February, the Hospital Products Group completed the sale of Shiley's product lines to Sorin Biomedica, headquartered in Milan, Italy. The remaining businesses were realigned into two divisions—Howmedica and Medical Devices. Howmedica manufactures and markets orthopedic implants. Medical Devices consists of three core businesses—Valleylab (electrosurgery business), Schneider (catheter and stent lines), and American Medical Systems (impotence and incontinence products).

pany's consumer products include proprietary health items, oducts and toiletries, Plax pre-brushing dental rinse, and a number ucts sold in international markets. Among the better-known brands ufactured and marketed by Consumer Health Care are Visine, Visine L.R., Visine Extra and Visine A.C. eyedrops, Unisom Nighttime Sleep Aid and Unisom With Pain Relief, Ben-Gay pain relief ointments, Desitin baby care products, and RID. Other products include Barbasol lines of men's toiletries and Pacquin Hand Cream.

"The company's operations in animal health include the manufacture and sale of animal health products and feed additives. Major products include: veterinary products such as Liquamycin LA-200, a broad spectrum injectable antibiotic; the Banminth, Nemex, and Paratect anthelmintics; Mecadox, an antibacterial for pigs; and Terramycin, a broad spectrum antibiotic used for a variety of animal diseases.

"Pfizer's Food Science segment, formerly known as Specialty Chemicals and Minerals, provides branded ingredients to the global food processing industry. The new name reflects the transformation of our former Specialty Chemicals Group, previously a supplier of commodity products, to a business deriving its sales from research-based healthful food ingredients. Food Science is establishing leadership as the premier ingredient supplier to the low-calorie segment of the food industry."

During 1992, revenues and operating profits were apportioned as follows: pharmaceuticals and hospital products 77.6 percent of revenues and 76.0 percent of profits, consumer health care 5.6 percent of revenues and 20.2 percent of profits, animal health products 7.8 percent of revenues and 2.5 percent of profits, and food science 9 percent of revenues and 1.3 percent of profits.

Geographically, the United States provided 53.8 percent of revenues and 70 percent of operating profits, Europe 23.6 percent of revenues and 24.2 percent of profits, Asia 14 percent of revenues and 1.6 percent of profits, Canada/Latin America 6.5 percent of revenues and 3.2 percent of profits, and Africa/Middle East 2.1 percent of revenues and 1 percent of profits.

In 1992, Pfizer increased revenues for the forty-third, and dividends for the twenty-fifth consecutive year. Institutions control about 65 percent of the outstanding common shares. Pfizer paid a 100 percent stock dividend in 1983, and a 100 percent stock dividend in 1991.

Total assets: $9.3 billion
Current ratio: 1.4
Common shares outstanding: 320.9 million

	1984	1985	1986	1987	1988	1989	1990	1991	1992	1993
Revenues (Mil.)	3,876	4,025	4,476	4,920	5,385	5,672	6,406	6,905	7,230	7,478
Net Income (Mil.)	511	580	660	690	791	681	801	722	811	658
Earnings per share	1.53	1.72	1.95	2.04	2.35	2.02	2.38	2.13	3.25	2.05
Dividends per share	.66	.74	.82	.90	1.00	1.10	1.20	1.32	1.48	1.68
Prices Hi	21.2	28.1	36.4	38.5	30.1	37.9	40.9	86.1	87.0	75.6
Lo	14.7	18.8	23.1	20.6	23.7	27.0	27.3	36.8	65.1	52.5

Philip Morris Companies Inc.

120 Park Avenue
New York, New York 10017
Tel. (212) 880-5000
Listed: NYSE
Investor contact: Vice President and Secretary, Dede Thompson Bartlett
Ticker symbol: MO
S&P rating: A+

As profiled in its 1993 Annual Report, "Philip Morris Companies Inc. is a holding company whose principal wholly-owned subsidiaries, Philip Morris Incorporated, Philip Morris International Inc., Kraft General Foods, Inc., and Miller Brewing Company, are engaged primarily in the manufacture and sale of various consumer products. Tobacco products (mainly cigarettes), accounted for 43 percent of the company's revenues in 1993, food products, beer, financial services, and real estate represent the company's significant industry segments. A wholly-owned subsidiary of the company, Philip Morris Capital Corporation, engages in various financing and investment activities.

"Philip Morris U.S.A. is responsible for the manufacture, marketing, and sale of cigarettes in the United States; subsidiaries and affiliates of Philip Morris International and their licensees are responsible for the manufacture, marketing, and sale of tobacco products outside the United States; and a subsidiary of Philip Morris International is responsible for tobacco exports from the United States. Philip Morris U.S.A.'s major cigarette brands are Marlboro, Benson & Hedges 100's, Merit, Virginia Slims, and Cambridge. Marlboro is the largest selling brand in the United States, with shipments of 124 billion units in 1992.

"In 1992, Kraft General Foods North America was realigned into three operating units: General Foods USA, responsible for General Foods U.S. packaged grocery products, coffee, and certain frozen foods and cultured dairy products businesses; Kraft USA, responsible for Kraft U.S. dry grocery foods, refrigerated foods, and certain frozen products businesses, the processed meat and poultry products business of Oscar Mayer Foods; and Kraft General Foods Commercial, is responsible for U.S. foodservice and food ingredients businesses. Kraft General Foods International is responsible for all of the company's food, coffee, and confectionery businesses outside the United States, Canada, and Latin America.

"General Foods USA is one of the largest processors and marketers of package grocery products in the United States. It is the largest processor and marketer of coffee in the United States, and manufactures and markets a variety of frozen food products. Its principal brands include Maxwell House, Yuban, Sanka, Brim, and Maxim coffees; Jell-O desserts, Post cereals, Log Cabin syrups, Kool-Aid, Entenmann's bakery products, Minute Rice, Stove Top stuffing, Shake 'n Bake coatings, Breyer's ice cream, Sealtest frozen desserts, and, since January 1993, the ready-to-eat cold cereal business of RJR Nabisco Holdings Corp.

"Kraft USA's principal products include cheese and related products; vegetable oil-based products, such as salad dressings and related products; margarine and margarine-type spreads; barbecue sauce; confections; fruit spreads, jellies, and preserves; and packaged pasta dinners. Kraft USA is one of the largest processors and marketers of processed meat and poultry products in the United States. In addition to Kraft, its principal brands include Velveeta, Cracker Barrel, and Churny Cheeses; Miracle Whip salad dressing, Philadelphia Brand cream cheese, Cheez Whiz pasteurized process cheese spread, Seven Seas pourable dressings, Parkay margarine, Birds Eye frozen foods, Oscar Mayer and Louis Rich meat products, and Claussen pickles.

"Kraft General Foods Canada is responsible for manufacturing and marketing packaged grocery, coffee, and cheese products. Major brand names include Kraft, Miracle Whip, Philadelphia Brand, Jell-O, Post, Kool-Aid, Baker's, Parkay, Sanka, and Maxwell House.

"Miller's major products are Miller Lite, the largest selling reduced-calorie beer and second largest selling brand in the United States; Miller High Life; Miller Genuine Draft, which is one of the fastest growing premium beers in the United States; Meister Bräu and Milwaukee's Best, sold in the 'below premium' segment of the United States market; Löwenbräu, brewed and sold in the United States under a license agreement with Löwenbräu München AG; Sharp's, a brewed non-alcohol beverage and Miller Reserve, a super-premium beer introduced in 1992. Miller Lite, Miller Genuine Draft, and Milwaukee's Best are among the top ten selling beers in the United States."

During 1992, revenues and operating profits were apportioned as follows: tobacco products 43.5 percent of revenues and 68.9 percent of operating profits, food products 49.1 percent of revenues and 26.6 percent of operating profits, beer 6.7 percent of revenues and 2.4 percent of operating profits, and financial services .7 percent of revenues and 2.1 percent of operating profits.

Philip Morris Companies, Inc. has paid consecutive cash dividends since 1928. There have been twenty-eight dividend boosts in the past twenty-five years. Institutions control about 60 percent of the outstanding common shares. Philip Morris paid a 100 percent stock dividend in 1979, a 100 percent stock dividend in 1986, and a 300 percent stock dividend in 1989.

Total assets: $51.2 billion
Current ratio: 0.9
Common shares outstanding: 877.2 million

	1984	1985	1986	1987	1988	1989	1990	1991	1992	1993
Revenues (Mil.)	14,102	16,158	25,542	27,650	31,273	44,080	51,169	56,458	59,131	60,901
Net Income (Mil.)	889	1,255	1,478	1,842	2,337	2,946	3,540	3,927	4,939	3,091
Earnings per share	.91	1.31	1.55	1.94	2.51	3.18	3.83	3.25	5.45	4.06
Dividends per share	.43	.50	.62	.79	1.01	1.25	1.55	1.91	2.35	2.60
Prices Hi	10.4	11.9	19.5	31.1	25.5	45.5	52.0	81.8	86.6	77.6
Lo	7.8	9.0	11.0	18.1	20.1	25.0	36.0	48.3	69.5	45.0

Pitney Bowes, Inc.

1 Elmcroft Road
Stamford, Connecticut 06926-0700
Tel. (203) 356-5000
Listed: NYSE
Investor contact: Earnest J. Jackson
Ticker symbol: PBI
S&P rating: A+

As profiled in its 1992 Annual Report, "Pitney Bowes is a $3.4 billion multinational manufacturing and marketing company which provides mailing, shipping, copying, dictating, communications recording, and facsimile systems;

item identification and tracking systems, and supplies; mailroom, reprographics, and related management services; and product financing.

"Pitney Bowes is the worldwide market leader in mailing systems. Pitney Bowes Mailing Systems markets a full line of mailing, shipping, and weighing systems and services to businesses, professionals, nonprofit organizations, and government agencies.

"Pitney Bowes Facsimile Systems is a leading supplier of high-quality facsimile equipment to the corporate market in the United States.

"Pitney Bowes Copier Systems concentrates on serving large corporations with multi-unit installations of its full line of equipment.

"Dictaphone is the worldwide leader in voice processing systems. The company manufactures and markets small work group and central dictation and voice processing systems, communications recorders, and portable and desktop dictation units.

"Pitney Bowes Shipping and Weighing Systems provide parcel and freight information, and automation systems, for the shipping and transportation management function of the logistics market. By providing computer-based systems, scales, parcel registers, and software systems, Pitney Bowes Shipping and Weighing Systems brings efficiencies to both shippers and carriers.

"Monarch Marking Systems is a leading supplier of bar code equipment and technology. Monarch provides bar code marking, tracking, and control systems for retailers and their vendors, as well as bar code tracking and data collection for all types of industries.

"Pitney Bowes Management Services is a leading provider of business support functions, including correspondence, mail, and reprographics management, high-volume transaction mail and related activities, such as facsimile services, supplies distribution, and records management.

"Pitney Bowes Financial Services provides lease financing programs for customers who use products of Pitney Bowes companies, and a variety of other financing programs for creditworthy customers."

During 1992, revenues and operating profits were apportioned as follows: business equipment 69.9 percent of revenues and 60.6 percent of profits, business supplies and service 11.7 percent of revenues and 5.7 percent of profits, and financial services 18.4 percent of revenues and 33.7 percent of profits.

Pitney Bowes has paid consecutive cash dividends since 1934. Institutions control about 75 percent of the common shares. Pitney Bowes paid a 100 percent stock dividend in 1983, a 100 percent stock dividend in 1986, and a 100 percent stock dividend in 1992.

Total assets: $6.8 billion
Current ratio: 0.6
Common shares outstanding: 158.2 million

	1984	1985	1986	1987	1988	1989	1990	1991	1992	1993
Revenues (Mil.)	1,732	1,832	1,987	2,270	2,576	2,876	3,196	3,332	3,434	3,543
Net Income (Mil.)	138	145	166	192	230	180	207	288	312	353
Earnings per share	.88	.92	1.05	1.27	1.54	1.59	1.34	1.85	1.96	2.22
Dividends per share	.26	.30	.33	.38	.46	.52	.60	.68	.78	.90
Prices Hi	9.1	12.5	19.2	25.2	23.8	27.4	26.8	32.8	41.0	44.5
Lo	6.7	8.5	11.4	14.8	16.9	20.5	13.5	19.0	28.0	36.3

PNC Bank Corp.

One PNC Plaza
Fifth Avenue and Wood Street
Pittsburgh, Pennsylvania 15265
Tel. (412) 762-2666
Listed: NYSE
Investor contact: V. P.–Investor Relations, William H. Callihan
Ticker symbol: PNC
S&P rating: B+

As profiled in its 1992 Annual Report, "PNC Bank Corp. has become the nation's tenth largest banking company with more than $51 billion in assets at year-end 1992. It has three banking subsidiaries and 550 offices, spanning five mid-Atlantic and midwestern states (Pennsylvania, Delaware, Ohio, Indiana, and Kentucky) and eighty-five non-banking subsidiaries.

PNC Bank Corp.

"PNC Bank delivers a full range of banking products and services to it customers through four core businesses—Corporate Banking, Retail Banking, Investment Management and Trust, and Investment Banking. Operating within PNC Bank's new line-of-business management, these businesses are delivering an expanded array of high-quality products with increasing efficiency and service capabilities, to meet the unique needs of every customer we serve.

159

"Corporate Banking provides financing, investment, cash management, and administrative and financial services to businesses and government entities. In addition, Corporate Banking maintains banking relationships with many of the largest companies in the U.S., and is a major provider of treasury management products and services.

"Retail Banking provides lending, deposit, investment, payment systems access, and other financial services to consumers and small businesses. Such services are primarily provided through PNC Bank's 550 banking offices located in Pennsylvania, Delaware, Ohio, Indiana, and Kentucky. Certain retail products, including residential mortgages, student loans, and credit cards, are centrally managed to enhance PNC Bank's ability to provide high-quality, low-cost products. Retail Banking serves more than two million households and nearly 70,000 small businesses, operates one of the largest student lending businesses in the U.S., and works closely with other lines of businesses to provide mortgage, investment, corporate, and trust products."

"Investment Management and Trust provides investment advice, asset management, and administrative and custodial services to individuals, institutions, and mutual funds. Additionally, economic and investment research services are sold to more than 225 institutions including brokerage firms, insurance companies, pension funds, and other banks. The corporation ranks as the largest bank manager of mutual funds, the third-largest bank trustee for individuals, the fourth-largest institutional money fund manager, and the six largest bank money manager in the nation.

"Investment Banking includes Asset/Liability Management of PNC Bank as well as underwriting, brokerage, and direct investment services. Full-service brokerage services are provided in ten strategic locations within the retail banking office network through PNC Securities Corp., which ranks as one of the largest bank underwriters of revenue bonds for the health care industry, colleges, and universities. Private equity placements for middle market and smaller companies to finance growth or ownership transactions are provided by Venture Corp. and PNC Equity Management Corp."

During 1992, loans of $26.1 billion were apportioned as follows: commercial 42.1 percent, real estate project 7.5 percent, real estate mortgage 15.7 percent, consumer 30.5 percent, money market .7 percent, lease financing 2.9 percent, and foreign .6 percent.

PNC Bank, via its predecessor banking companies, has paid consecutive cash dividends since the 1860s. Institutions control about 55 percent of the outstanding common shares. PNC Bank paid a 100 percent stock dividend in 1985, and a 100 percent stock dividend in 1992.

Total assets: $62.1 billion
Common shares outstanding: 234.7 million

	1984	1985	1986	1987	1988	1989	1990	1991	1992	1993
Net Income (Mil.)	143	188	286	256	460	377	71	390	427	726
Earnings per share	1.63	1.94	2.22	1.50	2.49	1.99	.37	1.97	2.36	3.14
Dividends per share	.56	.64	.74	.82	.92	1.03	1.06	.80	1.08	1.18
Prices Hi	11.8	17.7	25.5	25.5	23.3	24.5	22.1	24.1	29.1	36.4
Lo	9.1	11.5	17.5	16.6	18.3	19.3	7.9	9.4	23.4	27.0

Policy Management Systems Corporation

One PMS Center
Blythewood, South Carolina 29016
Tel. (803) 735-4000
Listed: NYSE
Investor contact: Executive Vice Pres. Secretary and Treasurer,
Robert L. Gresham
Ticker symbol: PMS
S&P rating: B+

As profiled in its 1992 Annual Report, "Policy Management Systems Corporation (PMSC) is driven by the mission of being the leading provider of automation and information solutions to the worldwide insurance industry.

Policy Management Systems Corporation

"The company offers over 125 business solutions, which include more than ninety application software systems and a wide range of outsourcing, professional and information services, designed to meet the needs of all sectors of the insurance industry.

"The company's primary software systems run on medium and large scale IBM computers, utilizing most IBM operating systems. In addition, a number of systems run on intelligent workstations.

"Most customers licensing the company's software systems use the company's professional services, which are separately charged for and normally provided under separate contracts.

"The company's software products automate most insurance processing functions, as well as various accounting, financial reporting, and cash management functions of insurance organizations. The architecture and technologies contained in the company's software products have undergone dramatic change during the past several years, as the various functions contained in these products have, and continue to be adapted to the company's new generation of integrated systems currently under development, Series III. A primary objective of Series III is the full integration of the information and data gathering, processing, underwriting, claims handling, and reporting processes for providers of all types of insurance to create a true cooperative processing environment where insurance professionals, using advanced intelligent workstations, can process multiple tasks concurrently with minimal clerical support and data entry. Series III provides a seamless flow of information between insurance agents, branch offices, and home office insurance companies.

"The company offers a wide range of information services which are packaged to facilitate efficient review and use and may be ordered and received on an automated basis through the company's nationwide telecommunications network using the company's database products. These information services, which are designed to assist insurance professionals in making better decisions about risk selection, pricing, and claims settlement, currently include motor vehicle (driving record) reports, undisclosed driver information, driver mileage verification, claims histories, credit reports and histories, property inspection and valuation reports, property claims estimating, premium audits, physician reports, and medical histories."

In 1990, an agreement was reached with IBM, whereby IBM designated PMSC as IBM's Insurance Applications Affiliate, the only such company to receive this designation. PMSC has never paid a cash dividend. Institutions, including IBM, control about 75 percent of the common shares. PMSC paid a 100 percent stock dividend in 1983.

Total assets: $659.8 million
Current ratio: 3.6
Common shares outstanding: 22.9 million

	1984	1985	1986	1987	1988	1989	1990	1991	1992	1993
Revenues (Mil.)	85	103	151	180	217	266	346	415	497	453
Net Income (Mil.)	14	14	14	17	20	27	37	48	59	56
Earnings per share	.85	.89	.85	1.05	1.30	1.60	1.92	2.21	2.55	2.46
Dividends per share	—	—	—	—	—	—	—	—	—	—
Prices Hi	31.0	34.8	24.5	30.3	26.0	37.3	43.5	66.4	83.5	87.3
Lo	22.0	16.5	15.0	15.3	18.8	21.8	30.00	39.4	59.8	21.6

Premier Industrial Corporation

4500 Euclid Avenue
Cleveland, Ohio 44103
Tel. (216) 391-8300
Listed: NYSE
Investor contact: Vice Pres. & Secy., Grant C. Grinnell
Ticker symbol: PRE
S&P rating: A

As profiled in its fiscal 1993 Annual Report, "Premier is a full-service, business-to-business supplier of electronic components for industrial and consumer products, essential maintenance and repair products for industrial, commercial, and institutional

PREMIER INDUSTRIAL CORPORATION

applications, and a manufacturer of high-performance fire-fighting equipment.

"Our Electronics Group serves the needs of customers everywhere who need electronic parts to maintain or repair machinery and equipment. Our wide product selection, deep inventories, and speedy service are critical to our customers. We provide them with the widest array of electronic components, all stocked in depth to achieve high order fill rates. We also stock a large selection of mature and hard-to-find products, which often makes us the preferred sources for our customers.

"Our Newark Electronics Division, the nation's leading broad-line distributor, publishes the most comprehensive product source book and reference guide in the industry. Our current catalog lists in excess of 100,000 products from more than 250 manufacturers. All products in the catalog are stocked.

"Our MCM Electronics Division, serving the rapidly expanding consumer and commercial electronics repair market, also uses a comprehensive catalog, updated twice a year, to keep customers informed of additions to its product line. At MCM, we stock a broad line of parts and accessories for the repair and maintenance of electronics products increasingly found in homes, automobiles, and offices.

"Our General Products Group markets thousands of innovative, problem-solving products for use in industrial maintenance, automotive repair, and fire-fighting. As machines and equipment continuously evolve, industries of all types strive to reduce maintenance costs, prolong equipment life, speed repairs and increase safety. Our success is based on a steady stream of problem-solving products that help achieve these goals.

"Some examples of our product innovation efforts during this past year include:

"D-A Lubricant introduced new or reformulated products responding to the demand for higher performance, 'environmentally friendly' oils and lubricants for use on heavy-duty earth moving equipment.

"Kent Industries introduced Ure-Foam for automotive aftermarket use on such applications as sound deadening and sealing water leaks."

During fiscal 1993, revenues and operating profits were distributed as follows: Electronics Distribution 70.2 percent of revenues and 71.8 percent of operating profits, and General Products 29.8 percent of revenues and 28.2 percent of operating profits.

Premier Industrial Corporation has paid consecutive cash dividends since 1950. Insiders control over 60 percent and institutions about 20 percent of the outstanding common shares. Premier paid a 50 percent stock dividend in 1985, a 50 percent stock dividend in 1988, a 50 percent stock dividend in 1990, and a 50 percent stock dividend in 1993.

Total assets: $466.1 million
Current ratio: 8.0
Common shares outstanding: 87.1 million

	1984	1985	1986	1987	1988	1989	1990	1991	1992	1993
Revenues (Mil.)	378	432	435	459	528	596	626	637	641	691
Net Income (Mil.)	38	39	41	48	64	70	75	75	79	88
Earnings per share	.37	.39	.41	.49	.65	.75	.86	.87	.91	1.02
Dividends per share	.087	.10	.11	.12	.15	.20	.24	.28	.31	.34
Prices Hi	7.4	8.6	10.6	14.4	14.8	17.0	18.4	22.1	27.0	30.8
Lo	5.0	5.6	7.5	8.6	10.4	11.3	14.0	14.9	18.0	24.5

Raytheon Company

141 Spring Street
Lexington, Massachusetts 02173
Tel. (617) 862-6600
Listed: NYSE
Investor contact: Senior Vice Pres. & Treas., Herbert Deitcher
Ticker symbol: RTN
S&P rating: A+

As profiled in its 1992 Annual Report, "Raytheon is a diversified, international, technology-based company ranked among the 100 largest U.S. industrial corporations. In 1992 sales were $9.06 billion, with 51.5 percent of that total for the U.S. government.

Raytheon Company

"Raytheon has twenty-one divisional major operating subsidiaries with plants, laboratories, and offices in thirty-eight states, plus the District of Columbia. Overseas subsidiaries and affiliates are located in twenty-two countries, principally in Europe and The Pacific Rim.

"The company has four business segments: Electronics, Major Appliances, Aircraft Products, and Energy and Environmental.

"Raytheon is an internationally recognized leader in the development and production of sophisticated electronics systems and components for the government and commercial markets. Products and markets include tactical missile systems for ground-based, airborne, and ship-launched defense radar systems; satellite communications systems and terminals, air traffic control systems; Doppler weather radar, sonar, and mine hunting systems; military communications equipment; and textbooks and instructional materials for elementary, secondary, and college use.

"As the nation's fifth largest appliance manufacturer, Raytheon's Appliance Group includes three well-recognized names: Amana, Caloric, and Speed Queen. Products and markets include refrigerators, freezers, gas and electric ranges, microwave ovens, dishwashers, air conditioners, and laundry equipment for homes and institutions.

"Beech Aircraft, of Wichita, Kansas, is the world's leading supplier of aircraft for the general aviation market. Products and markets include jet, turboprop, and piston engine aircraft used by individuals, businesses, governments, and regional airlines.

"Raytheon's Energy and Environmental segment represents one of the largest full-line engineering, construction, and technical service capabilities in the world. Products and markets include the design and construction of chemical and petroleum refining plants, power plants, and research and production facilities for the manufacture of specialty chemicals, fertilizers and polymers, pharmaceutical and biotechnology products, mining, metals, and food and consumer products."

During 1992, revenues and income were apportioned as follows: electronics 54.9 percent of revenues and 70.3 percent of income, energy and environmental 19.4 percent of revenues and 13.6 percent of income, aircraft products 13.9 percent of revenues and 13 percent of income, and major appliances 11.8 percent of revenues and 3.1 percent of income.

Raytheon has paid consecutive cash dividends since 1964. Institutions control about 75 percent of the outstanding common shares. Raytheon paid a 100 percent stock dividend in 1992.

Total assets: $7.3 billion
Current ratio: 1.6
Common shares outstanding: 135.2 million

	1984	1985	1986	1987	1988	1989	1990	1991	1992	1993
Revenues (Mil.)	5,996	6,409	7,308	7,659	8,192	8,796	9,268	9,274	9,058	9,201
Net Income (Mil.)	340	376	393	445	490	529	557	592	635	693
Earnings per share	2.01	2.30	2.55	3.06	3.67	4.00	4.27	4.48	4.72	5.11
Dividends per share	.73	.80	.88	.90	1.00	1.10	1.20	1.23	1.33	1.40
Prices Hi	24.4	27.8	35.9	42.4	36.9	42.5	35.6	44.1	53.5	68.5
Lo	17.4	19.6	26.1	28.6	30.5	32.3	28.9	32.9	40.6	50.5

RPM, Inc.
2628 Pearl Road (P.O. Box 777)
Medina, Ohio 44258
Tel. (216) 273-5090
Listed: NASDAQ
Investor contact: Vice Pres. & Treas., Richard E. Klar
Ticker symbol: RPOW
S&P rating: A+

As profiled in its fiscal 1993 Annual Report, "RPM, Inc. is a worldwide producer of specialty chemicals, coatings, and sealants for industrial and consumer markets. The company has approximately 39,000 shareholders, 3,500 employees, and several hundred sales and technical representatives. RPM products are sold in more than 110 countries and are manufactured at thirty-nine plant locations in the United States, Belgium, Canada, Luxembourg and the Netherlands.

"The vast majority of RPM products are used on property which already exists. RPM is not involved to any great degree in new construction and, therefore, is quite recession-resistant. The protection of property may be somewhat deferred, but it cannot be eliminated.

"The markets which RPM serves are primarily in two segments:

"(1) Products sold worldwide to waterproof or rustproof structures, and specialized chemical additives. This segment represents 60 percent of our total business. Typical of the accounts served in this segment of RPM's business are the companies making up the Fortune 500. Our products are also used on manufacturing plants, schools, hospitals, grain-storage facilities, bridges, institutional buildings, and similar-type structures. Some of the companies serving these extensive market areas are Carboline, our largest operating company, and a major supplier of high-performance specialty coatings; Euclid Chemical Company, a quality supplier of concrete and masonry additives and coatings; MA-MECO International, a leader in sealants, deck coatings, and membranes; RPM/Netherlands, B.V., a key supplier of specialized industrial coatings throughout Europe; and Republic Powdered Metals, our founding company that remains a top manufacturer and distributor of waterproofing and corrosion control (Alumination) coatings, and PIB single-ply roofing membranes.

"(2) The balance of our business is products sold to the huge home-owner/'do-it-yourself' and hobby/craft markets. Indicative of the RPM products sold to this market, are Bondex, which is the only nationwide line of household patch and repair products; Testor, the world's best-known line of hobby products; Zinsser, the nation's leading manufacturer of shellac-based products; Wolman, which offers a complete line of wood deck coatings; Petit, Woolsey, and Z-Spar in the pleasure marine market; Ramuc in the residential and swimming pool market; and Craft House, a leading manufacturer and marketer of hobby, craft, and toy products. Typical RPM accounts in the 'do-it-yourself' market would be K-Mart, Ace, HWI, Wal-Mart and Cotter stores."

During fiscal 1993, revenues and net income were geographically apportioned as follows: the United States 88 percent of revenues and 94.7 percent of net income, European operations 10.6 percent of revenues and 5.3 percent of net income, and other foreign operations 1.4 percent of revenues and 0 percent of net income.

RPM has achieved forty-six consecutive years of record sales, record net income and record earnings per share, nineteen years of consecutive cash dividend increases, and nine major stock dividends since 1975. RPM has paid consecutive cash dividends since 1969. It paid a 25 percent stock dividend in 1983, a 25 percent stock dividend in 1984, a 50 percent stock dividend in 1987, a 25 percent stock dividend in 1990, and a 50 percent stock dividend in 1992.

Total assets: $584.6 million
Current ratio: 2.4
Common shares outstanding: 47.3 million

	1984	1985	1986	1987	1988	1989	1990	1991	1992	1993
Revenues (Mil.)	161	223	269	306	342	384	455	500	552	626
Net Income (Mil.)	9	11	13	17	21	25	28	32	34	39
Earnings per share	.31	.33	.36	.41	.51	.57	.65	.68	.73	.83
Dividends per share	.16	.20	.21	.25	.29	.32	.35	.40	.44	.47
Prices Hi	5.0	6.9	8.5	9.2	9.6	10.7	11.9	12.2	18.5	19.4
Lo	3.5	4.7	6.3	5.7	7.3	8.2	8.9	8.3	12.6	16.3

Rubbermaid Incorporated

1147 Akron Road (P.O. Box 6000)
Wooster, Ohio 44691-6000
Tel. (216) 264-6464
Listed: NYSE
Investor contact: S.V.P. Business Development and Investor Relations,
Richard D. Gates
Ticker symbol: RBD
S&P rating: A+

As profiled in its 1992 Annual Report, "Rubbermaid operates in a single line of business—the manufacture and sale of plastic and rubber products for the consumer, institutional, office products, agricultural, and industrial markets. The company was founded in 1920 as the Wooster Rubber Company, which manufactured toy balloons. In 1934, the first rubber dustpan was produced and the company entered the rubber housewares business, which provided the foundation for Rubbermaid's growth and success. The first plastic product, a dishpan, was introduced in the mid-'50s. In 1957, the corporate name was changed to Rubbermaid Incorporated to capitalize on the already widely accepted brand name.

"The Home Products Division, Wooster, Ohio, a continuation of the original housewares business, manufactures and markets such products as bathware, household containers, microwave cookware, tableware, and toolboxes.

"Rubbermaid Commercial Products Inc., Winchester, Virginia, is the outgrowth of the company selling to institutional markets, consumer products such as carts; food service, food storage, and maintenance products; and mopping systems, recycling containers, and refuse control.

"Rubbermaid Specialty Products Inc., established in 1967, has combined Rubbermaid lawn and garden products, casual furniture, and automotive accessories with Gott thermal products acquired in 1985.

"Rubbermaid Office Products Inc., Maryville, Tennessee, formed in 1990, consolidated Rubbermaid Office Products Division with Eldon Industries, acquired in 1990, and MicroComputer Accessories, Inc., a 1986 acquisition.

"The Curver Rubbermaid Group, Goirle, The Netherlands, is a joint venture, formed in 1990, between Rubbermaid's European housewares operation and DSM's Curver operation. It manufactures and markets plastic and rubber housewares, and resin furniture, for Europe, the Middle East, and North Africa.

"The Little Tikes Company, Hudson, Ohio, was acquired in 1984 to enter the childrens products market.

"Other acquisitions include Con-Tact Brand decorative coverings, 1981; SECO Industries, Inc., 1986; Viking Brush Limited, 1987; EWU AG, 1990; CIPSA, 1992; and Iron Mountain Forge Corporation, 1992."

During 1992, revenues and operating profits were apportioned as follows: The United States 89.3 percent of revenues and 93.4 percent of operating profits, and Foreign 10.7 percent of revenues and 6.6 percent of operating profits.

In 1993, Rubbermaid marked the forty-second consecutive year of record sales, the fifty-sixth consecutive year of profitable performance, and the thirty-ninth consecutive year of dividends-per-share gains. Institutions control about 45 percent of the outstanding common shares. Rubbermaid paid a 100 percent stock dividend in 1982, a 100 percent stock dividend in 1985, a 100 percent stock dividend in 1986, and a 100 percent stock dividend in 1991.

Total assets: $1.5 billion
Current ratio: 3.2
Common shares outstanding: 160.4 million

	1984	1985	1986	1987	1988	1989	1990	1991	1992	1993
Revenues (Mil.)	566	671	795	1,015	1,194	1,452	1,534	1,667	1,805	1,960
Net Income (Mil.)	47	57	70	85	99	125	144	163	164	211
Earnings per share	.35	.40	.48	.58	.68	.78	.90	1.02	1.04	1.32
Dividends per share	.098	.11	.13	.16	.19	.23	.27	.31	.35	.41
Prices Hi	5.7	8.8	14.3	17.5	13.5	18.4	22.5	38.3	37.4	37.4
Lo	4.1	5.4	8.3	9.5	10.5	12.5	15.5	18.5	27.0	27.6

Russell Corporation

1 Lee Street (P.O. Box 272)
Alexander City, Alabama 35010-0272
Tel. (205) 329-4000
Listed: NYSE
Investor contact: Treasurer, J. Anthony Meyer, Jr.
Ticker symbol: RML
S&P rating: A-

As profiled in its 1992 Annual Report, "Russell Corporation, founded in 1902, is a vertically integrated international designer, manufacturer and marketer of leisure apparel, activewear, athletic uniforms, better knit shirts, and a comprehensive line of lightweight, yarn-dyed woven fabrics. The company's manufacturing operations include the entire process of converting raw fibers into finished apparel and fabrics. Russell's products are marketed primarily through three sales divisions—Athletic, Knit Apparel and Fabrics—as well as through Cross Creek Apparel, Inc. and Russell Corp. UK Limited, two wholly-owned subsidiaries. Products are marketed to sporting goods dealers, department specialty stores, mass merchandisers, golf pro shops, college book stores, screen printers, distributors, mail order houses, and other apparel manufacturers. The company believes it is the largest manufacturer of athletic uniforms in the United States.

"Russell Athletic is the number one teamwear manufacturer in the United States, producing and selling game practice athletic uniforms for all levels of sports. In 1992, Russell Athletic not only became the official supplier of uniforms for Major League Baseball, but also gained exclusive rights to market authentic game jerseys, under the Major League Baseball Properties' Authentic Diamond Collection, apparel identical to that worn on the playing field.

"In addition to these lines, Russell Athletic continues to produce quality licensed activewear and teamwear for NFL ProLine, Team NFL Collection, and numerous college licenses, and is a leading supplier of NFL authentic jerseys. This division also produces an activewear line consisting of lightweight and fleece products in High Cotton, Pro Cotton, and traditional Russell Athletic knit fabrics.

"The Jerzees brand reflects the American active lifestyle with high-quality imprintable activewear for the value conscious consumer. Jerzees activewear includes sweats, T-shirts, tank tops, knit shorts, and placket shirts for children and adults and is sold through distributors, mass merchandising chains, and other retail outlets.

"Cross Creek Apparel, Inc., a subsidiary of Russell Corporation, manufactures and markets high-quality knit placket shirts, turtlenecks, and rugbys which continue to gain popularity. Whenever professional golfers Hale Irwin, Fred Funk, Jay Haas, Lee Janzen, Tom Lehman, Jeff Maggert, and Craig Perry play a round they will be sporting shirts from the Cross Creek Pro Collection. This line is designed specifically for golfers and is sold in professional golf shops across the country.

"Additionally, Russell produces T-shirts and sweats under the Jerzees and Russell Athletic labels in Europe, where the American casual look is in great demand. And in the increasingly global markets of today, the demand for Russell products is extending beyond Europe into Japan, South America, and Mexico.

"Russell Corporation's marketing efforts also include twenty-six outlet stores in the United States."

Russell Corporation has paid consecutive cash dividends since 1963. The Russell family controls over 45 percent, and institutions about 50 percent, of the outstanding common shares. Russell paid a 100 percent stock dividend in 1981, a 60 percent stock dividend in 1983, and a 100 percent stock dividend in 1986.

Total assets: $1.0 billion
Current ratio: 2.4
Common shares outstanding: 40.4 million

	1984	1985	1986	1987	1988	1989	1990	1991	1992	1993
Revenues (Mil.)	353	385	438	480	531	688	714	805	899	931
Net Income (Mil.)	28	30	43	46	54	64	67	56	82	49
Earnings per share	.70	.74	1.08	1.17	1.36	1.57	1.65	1.38	1.99	1.19
Dividends per share	.15	.15	.16	.19	.23	.28	.32	.32	.34	.39
Prices Hi	9.0	10.0	19.6	20.5	17.8	26.5	31.0	36.3	40.4	36.9
Lo	5.6	6.8	9.3	10.6	11.4	15.6	16.0	19.8	27.8	26.0

St. Jude Medical, Inc.

One Lillehei Plaza
St. Paul, Minnesota 55117
Tel. (612) 483-2000
Listed: NASDAQ
Investor contact: Paul Vetter
Ticker symbol: STJM
S&P rating: B+

St. Jude
Medical, Inc.

As profiled in its 1992 Annual Report, "St. Jude Medical, Inc. serves physicians worldwide with the highest quality medical devices for cardiovascular applications. The company manufactures the world's most frequently implanted heart valve, the St. Jude Medical mechanical heart valve. Since its introduction, more than 400,000 have been implanted.

"St. Jude Medical is headquartered in St. Paul, Minnesota, and has operations in Chelmsford, Massachusetts; St. Hyacinth, Canada; Caguas, Puerto Rico, and Brussels, Belgium, as well as sales and service offices throughout the United States, Japan, and Europe. The company's products are sold in more than seven countries, and its customers include more than 1,500 open heart centers worldwide.

"The company operates through three divisions to focus on the management and growth of its established businesses. The St. Jude Medical Division is responsible for the company's heart valves (mechanical and tissue) and annuloplasty ring products. The Cardiac Assist Division is responsible for the company's intra-aortic balloon pump and centrifugal pump systems. The International Division is responsible for marketing, sales, and distribution of the company's products in Europe, Africa, and the Middle East.

"St. Jude Medical's products include: St. Jude Medical mechanical heart valve; St. Jude Medical heart valve Hemodynamic Plus series; BioImplant tissue heart valve; Toronto SPV tissue heart valve; BiFlex annuloplasty ring; Model 700 intra-aortic balloon pump system; RediFurl, RediGuard, and Taperseal intra-aortic balloon catheters; Lifestream centrifugal pump system and Isoflow centrifugal pump.

"The company manufactures and markets a biofleaflet pyrolytic carbon-coated prosthetic heart valve, which it designed and first sold in 1977. The company's mechanical heart valve consists of four basic components: two leaflets, the valve body or orifice, and the sewing cuff. The company provides a wide range of mechanical heart valve products. Depending on physician preference, cuffs are made from either polyester fiber or polytetraflorethylene fiber.

"The vast majority of our customers worldwide implant both mechanical and tissue heart valves. To serve these customers better—and to leverage our strong, established relationships with cardiovascular surgeons worldwide—we are expanding our presence in the tissue segment of the market.

"St. Jude Medical participates in the growing market for cardiac assist devices with two products: the Model 700 intro-aortic balloon pump (IABP) system and the Lifestream centrifugal pump system. Both of these devices are life-sustaining products that provide short-term assist therapy. Both are marketed worldwide by sales people who are focused specifically on the needs of the specialists and clinicians who use these products."

During 1992, revenues and operating profits were geographically distributed as follows: the United States and Canada 69.1 percent of revenues and 70.9 percent of operating profits, and Europe 30.9 percent of revenues and 29.1 percent of operating profits.

St. Jude Medical initiated cash dividends in 1992. Institutions control about 55 percent of the outstanding common shares. St. Jude Medical paid a 100 percent stock dividend in 1986, a 100 percent stock dividend in 1989, and a 100 percent stock dividend in 1990.

Total assets: $526.8 million
Current ratio: 11.0
Common shares outstanding: 46.4 million

	1984	1985	1986	1987	1988	1989	1990	1991	1992	1993
Revenues (Mil.)	35	26	60	71	114	148	175	210	240	253
Net Income (Mil.)	5.3	(1.1)	12	17	33	51	65	84	102	110
Earnings per share	.14	(.03)	.30	.40	.71	1.07	1.35	1.75	2.12	2.32
Dividends per share	—	—	—	—	—	—	—	—	.30	.40
Prices Hi	2.5	2.9	4.5	7.6	10.8	25.3	36.5	55.5	55.5	42.3
Lo	1.0	1.0	2.4	3.8	5.8	9.6	18.5	27.5	27.5	25.0

Schering-Plough Corporation
One Giralda Farms (P.O. Box 1000)
Madison, New Jersey 07940-1000
Tel. (201) 822-7000
Listed: NYSE
Investor contact: Vice Pres. Investor Relations, Geraldine U. Foster
Ticker symbol: SGP
S&P rating: A+

As profiled in its 1992 Annual Report, "Schering-Plough is a worldwide company engaged in the research, development, manufacturing, and marketing of pharmaceutical and health care products. Products include prescription drugs, vision care, animal health, over-the-counter (OTC) medicines, foot care, and sun care products.

"The company's pharmaceutical operations include prescription drugs, vision care products, and animal health products. Principal prescription drugs include: Celestamine, Claratin, Polaramine, Proventil, Theo-Dur, Trinalin, Vancenase, and Vanceril—respiratory; Eulexin, Garamycin, Intron A, Isepacin, and Netromycin—anti-infective and anticancer; Diprolene, Elocon, Fulvicin, Lotrimin, Lotrisone, Quadriderm, and Valisone—dermatologicals; K-Dur, Nitro-Dur, and Normodyne—cardiovascular; Celestone, Diprosan, Noin, Palacos, Trilafon, and Losec—other pharmaceuticals.

"The company's major vision care product line is contact lenses sold under the Durasoft trademark. The leading product within the Durasoft line is Durasoft Colors, a soft lens that can alter the appearance of eye color. The company sold its domestic lens care business in 1992.

"Animal health biological and pharmaceutical products include antibiotics, vaccines, anti-arthritics, steroids, and nutritionals. Major animal health products are: Gentocin and Garasol—antibiotics; and Banamine, an anti-arthritic.

"Pharmaceutical products also include pharmaceutical chemical substances sold in bulk to third parties for production of their own products.

"The principal product categories in the health care segment are the company's over-the counter (OTC) medicines, foot care, and sun care products primarily sold in the United States. Principal products include: Afrin and Duration, nasal decongestants; Chlor-Trimeton, an antihistamine; Coricidin and Drixoral, cold and decongestant tablets; Correctol and Feen-a-Mint, laxa-

tives; Clear Away and Duo Brand, wart remover; Di-Gel, a
and Femcare for vaginal yeast infections; Dr. Scholl's foo
trimin AF and Tinactin, antifungals; Coppertone, QT, Shaa
Tropical Bland, sun care products; and PAAS egg coloring aı.
ucts."

During 1992, revenues and profits were apportioned as follo   .ma-
ceutical products 82.8 percent of revenues and 86.2 percent of pı .ıts, and
health care products 17.2 percent of revenues and 13.8 percent of profits.

Geographically the United States, during 1992, provided 53.4 percent of
revenues and 61.3 percent of profits; Europe, Middle East, and Africa provided
25.1 percent of revenues and 19.8 percent of profits; Latin America provided
6.8 percent of revenues and 5.9 percent of profits; and Canada, Pacific Area,
and Asia provided 14.7 percent of revenues and 13 percent of profit.

Schering-Plough recorded its seventh consecutive year in which earnings
per share increased at a rate of 20 percent or more. Schering-Plough has paid
consecutive cash dividends since 1952. Institutions control over 60 percent of
the common shares. Schering-Plough paid a 100 percent stock dividend in 1987
and another 100 percent stock dividend in 1990.

Total assets: $4.3 billion
Current ratio: 0.9
Common shares outstanding: 193.6 million

	1984	1985	1986	1987	1988	1989	1990	1991	1992	1993
Revenues (Mil.)	1,874	1,927	2,399	2,699	2,969	3,158	3,323	3,616	4,056	4,341
Net Income (Mil.)	177	193	266	316	390	471	565	646	720	731
Earnings per share	.88	.95	1.08	1.36	1.74	2.09	2.50	3.01	3.60	4.23
Dividends per share	.42	.42	.45	.51	.70	.88	1.07	1.27	1.50	1.74
Prices Hi	10.0	16.8	22.0	27.6	29.8	43.0	50.8	67.1	70.1	71.0
Lo	8.3	8.9	14.0	15.6	22.6	27.8	37.0	40.8	49.9	51.8

ServiceMaster Limited Partnership

One ServiceMaster Way
Downers Grove, Illinois 60515-9969
Tel. (708) 964-1300
Listed: NYSE
Investor contact: Vice Pres. Financial Relations, Maureen P. Gettings
Ticker symbol: SVM
S&P rating: A+

As profiled in its 1992 Annual Report, "ServiceMaster is functionally divided into three operating groups: Management Services, Consumer Services, and International and New Business Development.

"ServiceMaster pioneered supportive management service for health care facilities by instituting housekeeping management services in 1962. Since then, ServiceMaster has expanded its management services. It now provides a variety of supportive management services to health care, education, and commercial customers (including the management of housekeeping, plant operations and maintenance, laundry and linen, grounds and landscaping, clinical equipment maintenance, energy management services, and food service).

"As of December 31, 1992, ServiceMaster was providing supportive management services to approximately 2,300 health care, educational, and industrial facilities. These services were being provided in all fifty states and the District of Columbia, and in fourteen foreign countries.

"ServiceMaster Consumer Services provides specialty services to homeowners and commercial facilities through five companies: Terminix International, L.P. (Terminix); TruGreen-ChemLawn L.P. (TruGreen-ChemLawn); Merry Maids L.P. (Merry Maids); American Home Shield Corporation (American Home Shield) and ServiceMaster Residential and Commercial L.P. (Res/Com). The services provided by these companies include termite and pest control, and radon testing services, under the Terminix service mark; lawn care, tree, and shrub services under the Trugreen and Chemlawn service marks; domestic housekeeping services under the Merry Maids service mark; home systems and appliance warranty contracts under the American Home Shield service mark; and residential and commercial cleaning, and disaster restoration services, under the 'ServiceMaster Res/Com Service' mark.

"The International and New Business Development Group oversees the performance of supportive management services and consumer services in international markets. It also provides management services to hospital-based home health care agencies and, as of December 31, 1992, was servicing forty-five home health care agencies. Likewise, it operates employer or developer sponsored child care centers under the Green Tree service mark. As of December 31, 1992, Green Tree had eleven child care centers in operation, all of which were in the greater Chicago area."

During 1992, revenues and operating profits were apportioned as follows: Management Services 66.4 percent of revenues and 75.2 percent of profits, Consumer Services 32.1 percent of revenues and 56.4 percent of profits, and International and New Business Development 1.5 percent of revenues and -31.6 percent of profits.

ServiceMaster has paid consecutive cash dividends since 1962. Revenues and profits have increased for twenty-two consecutive years. Institutions control about 15 percent of the common shares. ServiceMaster paid a 50 percent stock dividend in 1980, a 50 percent stock dividend in 1983, a 50 percent stock dividend in 1985, a 100 percent stock dividend in 1992, and a 50 percent stock dividend in 1993.

Total assets: $1.1 billion
Current ratio: 1.2
Common shares outstanding: 76.8 million

	1984	1985	1986	1987	1988	1989	1990	1991	1992	1993
Revenues (Mil.)	851	1,002	1,123	1,425	1,531	1,609	1,876	2,110	2,489	2,759
Net Income (Mil.)	30	33	33	60	65	68	83	86	122	146
Earnings per share	.41	.44	.45	.85	.90	.93	1.17	1.19	1.71	1.90
Dividends per share	.29	.35	.38	.67	.75	.78	.82	.85	.87	1.11
Prices Hi	10.6	11.3	11.9	14.3	12.5	10.7	10.6	17.3	19.9	31.0
Lo	8.0	7.7	8.9	9.7	9.9	9.4	8.7	9.7	14.7	17.6

The Sherwin-Williams Company

101 Prospect Avenue N.W.
Cleveland, Ohio 44115-1075
Tel. (216) 566-2000
Listed: NYSE
Investor contact: Vice Pres.—Corporate Planning and Development,
Conway G. Ivy
Ticker symbol: SHW
S&P rating: A

As profiled in its 1992 Annual Report, "Sherwin-Williams celebrated 126 years of doing business in 1992. The company's core business is the manufacture, distribution, and sale of coatings and related products.

"We sell Sherwin-Williams labeled architectural coatings, industrial finishes, and associated supplies through 2,012 company-operated paint and wallcovering stores in forty-eight states and Canada. We also manufacture and sell coatings such as Dutch Boy, Martin-Senour, Kem-Tone, Dupli-Color, and Krylon, plus private label brands to independent dealers, mass merchandisers, and home improvement centers. We produce coatings for original equipment manufacturers in a number of industries, and special-purpose coatings for the automotive aftermarket, and the industrial maintenance and traffic paint markets.

"The Coatings Division manufactures paint and paint-related products for the do-it-yourselfer, professional painter, contractor, industrial and commercial maintenance accounts, and manufacturer of factory-finished products. Sherwin-Williams branded architectural and industrial finishes are manufactured exclusively for the Paint Stores Segment. Dutch Boy, Kem-Tone, Martin-Senour, and Cuprinol branded architectural and industrial finishes are manufactured for distribution by the Consumer Brands Division. Labels, color cards, traffic paint, adhesives, private label and other branded products are manufactured for the Paint Stores Segment, the Consumer Brands Division, and others.

"The Consumer Brands Division is responsible for the sales and marketing of Dutch Boy, Kem-Tone, Martin-Senour, Cuprinol, and private label branded products by a direct sales staff to unaffiliated home centers, mass merchandisers, independent dealers, and distributors. Most of the country's leading retailers are among the division's regional and national customers.

"The Automotive Division develops and manufactures motor vehicle finish and refinish products, which are marketed under the Sherwin-Williams, Martin-Senour, Acme, and Western Automotive Finishes labels in the United States and Canada. The division distributed Standox branded vehicle refinishing paints in the United States and Canada for American Standox, Inc., its joint venture with Herberts GmbH of Wuppertal, Germany.

"The Transportation Services Division provides warehousing, truckload freight and pool assembly, freight brokerage, and consolidation services primarily for the company and for certain external manufacturers, distributors, and retailers throughout the United States.

"The Specialty Division competes in three areas: custom and industrial aerosols, paint applicators, and retail and wholesale consumer aerosols. The division participates in the retail and wholesale paint, automotive, sanitary supply, institutional, insecticide, and industrial markets.

"Products carrying the Sherwin-Williams, Kem-Tone, and related trade names are manufactured and sold around the world through subsidiaries, joint ventures, and licensees. Consolidated foreign operations generally market a full line of products including architectural coatings, industrial maintenance products, automotive repaint finishes, and a variety of home decorative items.

"The Other segment is responsible for the acquisition, development, leasing, and management of properties for use by the company and others. At the end of 1992, the Retail Properties Division owned or leased 205 properties, representing over 1,664,000 square feet of space, which are conducive to the sale of paint and associated products. Retail properties include 123 freestanding buildings, for exclusive use by the Paint Stores Segment, and eighty-two multi-tenant properties, utilized when the basic needs of the paint store can be met and where external rental opportunities can be profitably operated.

"The Non-Retail Properties Division owned or leased twenty-one properties, primarily manufacturing and warehouse facilities for the benefit of the Coatings Segment, at the end of 1992."

During 1992, revenues and operating profits were apportioned as follows: paint stores 61.2 percent of revenues and 64.2 percent of profits, coatings 38.3 percent of revenues and 33.6 percent of profits, and other .5 percent of revenues and 2.2 percent of profits.

Sherwin-Williams posted increased earnings in each of the past sixteen years. After a hiatus of several years, Sherwin-Williams restored its cash dividend in 1979. Cash dividends have increased in each of the past thirteen years. Institutional investors control about 60 percent of the common shares. Sherwin-Williams paid a 100 percent stock dividend in 1983, a 100 percent stock dividend in 1986, and a 100 percent stock dividend in 1991.

Total assets: $1.9 billion
Current ratio: 2.0
Common shares outstanding: 88.5 million

	1984	1985	1986	1987	1988	1989	1990	1991	1992	1993
Revenues (Mil.)	1,454	1,526	1,558	1,801	1,950	2,123	2,267	2,541	2,748	2,949
Net Income (Mil.)	65	75	86	97	101	109	123	128	145	165
Earnings per share	.71	.81	.94	1.08	1.15	1.26	1.41	1.45	1.63	1.85
Dividends per share	.19	.23	.25	.28	.32	.35	.38	.42	.44	.50
Prices Hi	8.1	11.9	16.1	19.3	15.9	17.9	21.1	27.8	32.9	37.5
Lo	5.6	7.0	10.6	10.1	12.0	12.5	15.1	17.6	25.4	29.9

Sigma-Aldrich Corporation

3050 Spruce Street
St. Louis, Missouri 63103
Tel. (314) 771-5765
Listed: NASDAQ
Investor contact: Controller, Kirk A. Richter
Ticker symbol: SIAL
S&P rating: A+

As profiled in its 1993 Annual Report, "Sigma-Aldrich is in two lines of business. Sigma, Aldrich, and Fluka develop, manufacture, and distribute a broad range of biochemicals, organic and inorganic chemicals, diagnostic reagents, and related products. These are used primarily in research and development, in the diagnosis of disease, and as specialty chemicals for manufacturing purposes. B-Line Systems manufactures and sells metal components for strut, cable tray, pipe support, and telecommunications systems. These components are used in routing electrical and mechanical services in industrial installations, and in supporting telecommunications applications.

"Over 71,000 chemical products are now offered to customers, with 10,000 having been added during 1993. The metal product line was also expanded and now contains over 23,000 items.

"Our chemical products are used in research and development, synthesis, analysis, industrial production, and for the diagnosis of diseases. Life science studies, environmental monitoring, and health and medical research are among the fields we serve that are undergoing continuous and rapid changes.

"Metal product lines include strut, cable tray, pipe hangers, and fasteners used as support systems for electrical, telecommunications, and heating and air conditioning services in a wide range of facilities. They are used in new construction, retrofitting, and remodeling. During 1992, B-Line introduced a line of non-metallic cable trays for use in highly corrosive areas, a line of fasteners for isolating vibrations, and telephone racking systems for seismic applications.

"In 1992, new products including ultra pure reagents, environmental standards, and cell culture serums were added in virtually every major chemical category. Sigma Diagnostics added a new line of tests for therapeutic drug monitoring.

"The pending acquisition of Supelco, Inc., a worldwide supplier of chromatography, will fit well with Sigma-Aldrich as both serve the same analytical and research markets, and have well-recognized names and reputations for high-quality products.

"Sigma-Aldrich also offers over 600 technical reference books and an extensive line of laboratory equipment and supplies.

"In 1993, Sigma-Aldrich acquired Supelco, Inc., a worldwide supplier of chromatography products used in chemical research and production, and Circle A.W. Products, a supplier of electrical enclosures, which complements B-Line's comprehensive line of electrical support items."

During 1993, revenues and operating income were apportioned as follows: chemical products 82.9 percent of revenues and 88.8 percent of income, and metal products 17.1 percent of revenues and 11.2 percent of income.

The Bader, Boida, and Fischer families control about 15 percent, and institutional investors about 60 percent, of the outstanding common shares. Consecutive cash dividends have been paid since 1970. Sigma-Aldrich paid a 100 percent stock dividend in 1982, a 200 percent stock dividend in 1986, and a 100 percent stock dividend in 1991.

Total assets: $753.4 million
Current ratio: 4.0
Common shares outstanding: 49.8 million

	1984	1985	1986	1987	1988	1989	1990	1991	1992	1993
Revenues (Mil.)	180	215	253	305	375	441	529	589	654	739
Net Income (Mil.)	24	29	34	42	57	64	71	80	96	107
Earnings per share	.47	.57	.69	.85	1.15	1.29	1.44	1.60	1.92	2.15
Dividends per share	.088	.11	.13	.15	.17	.19	.21	.23	.26	.30
Prices Hi	8.6	14.2	20.1	25.3	25.6	29.8	35.9	53.5	59.3	58.0
Lo	7.2	8.6	13.4	15.1	19.9	21.9	25.0	27.8	41.8	44.5

The J.M. Smucker Company

Strawberry Lane
Orrville, Ohio 44667-0280
Tel. (216) 682-3000
Listed: NYSE
Investor contact: Secretary and General Counsel, Steven J. Ellcessor
Ticker symbol: SJM
S&P rating: A

As profiled in its fiscal 1993 Annual Report, "The J.M. Smucker Company is an Ohio Corporation. The business was begun in 1897 and was incorporated in 1921. The company, generally referred to as Smucker's, has approximately 1,950 employees and operates in one industry—the manufacturing and marketing of food products, including preserves, jams, jellies, fruit-only spreads, marmalades, toppings, fruit butters, low calories spreads, fruit syrups, fruit and fruit products, fruit puree, fruit juice concentrates, peanut butter, industrial fruit products (such as bakery fillings, dairy fillings, cereal fillings, and related items), honey, fruit and vegetable juices, carbonated juice beverages, gift packages, condiments, and frozen, whipped fruit desserts.

"Smucker's markets its fruit spreads and butters under such well-known names as Smucker's, The R.W. Knudsen Family, Dickinson's, Simply Fruit, J.M. Smucker's, Purely the Finest, and Super Spreaders. It markets peanut butter under such brand names as Smucker's, Goober, and Goober Grape. It markets ice cream toppings under such brand names as Smucker's, Special Recipe, and Sundae Syrup. It markets fruit juices and beverages under such names as Smucker's, The R.W. Knudsen Family, Vita Juice, Nice & Natural, and Heinke. Smucker has about 40 percent market share of the jelly and preserve trade.

"Smucker's primary preserve and jelly plant is in Orville, Ohio. Also, it has a specialty jam and jelly manufacturing plant in Ripon, Wisconsin, and satellite manufacturing facilities in Salinas, California, Memphis, Tennessee, Elsenham, England, and Victoria, Australia. Peanut butter is processed in Bethlehem, Pennsylvania. Fruit processing is undertaken at two plants in California, one in Oregon, and one in the State of Washington. Juices are made in Chico, California.

"On June 8, 1993, the company entered into an agreement with Culinar, Inc. of Canada, to acquire their jam, preserve, and pie filling business. As part of the acquisition, the company will obtain a production facility located in Ste.

Marie de Beauce, Quebec. This transaction, which will be financed using internal funds, is expected to be completed during the first quarter of fiscal 1994."

During fiscal 1993, revenues and operating income were geographically apportioned as follows: the United States 92.2 percent of revenues and 99.1 percent of operating income, and Foreign 7.8 percent of revenues and .9 percent of operating income.

The Smucker family controls about 27 percent, and institutions about 50 percent, of the Class A and Class B outstanding common shares. Although the company became publicly owned thirty-four years ago, Smucker family members still own the controlling portion of the Common shares outstanding. The J.M. Smucker Company has paid consecutive cash dividends since 1949. Smucker paid a 100 percent stock dividend in 1983, a 100 percent stock dividend in 1985, a 100 percent stock dividend in 1990 and one Class B (non-voting) common share for each share of Class A in 1991.

Total assets: $294.8 million
Current ratio: 3.0
Common shares outstanding: Class A 14.4 million
Class B 14.8 million

	1984	1985	1986	1987	1988	1989	1990	1991	1992	1993
Revenues (Mil.)	215	230	263	288	314	367	422	455	483	491
Net Income (Mil.)	14	16	16	18	23	28	30	32	34	33
Earnings per share	.47	.54	.54	.61	.78	.94	1.03	1.08	1.16	1.27
Dividends per share	.10	.12	.14	.15	.18	.23	.28	.35	.39	.43
Prices Hi	7.0	12.9	12.5	15.0	15.7	19.5	23.2	38.9	39.0	32.4
Lo	4.5	6.5	9.3	9.8	11.7	14.4	16.1	20.0	24.5	20.3

State Street Boston Corporation

225 Franklin Street
P.O. Box 351
Boston, Massachusetts 02101
Tel. (617) 786-3000
Listed: NASDAQ
Investor contact: V.P. Investor Relations, Susanne G. Clark
Ticker symbol: STBK
S&P rating: A+

> ## State Street Boston Corporation

As profiled in its 1992 Annual Report, "On December 31, 1992, State Street's assets under custody totaled $1.3 trillion. Our role in servicing financial assets is to help our customers execute and control creative, global investment strategies that require the recordkeeping, reporting, analysis, and related services we provide. Information technology is the key to that role.

"Today, we are the largest mutual fund custodian, serving 39 percent of the U.S. funds. We meet the needs of collective investment funds throughout the world. We provide them with a broad array of services, including custody, cash management, securities lending, and treasury services, as well as daily portfolio valuation, and multicurrency portfolio and general ledger accounting.

"For corporate pension plans, public retirement funds, union pension funds, endowments, and foundations, we draw from our total worldwide resources to provide tailored solutions to our customers' servicing needs.

"State Street's treasury centers provide our customers with foreign exchange and multicurrency short-term investment products. During 1992, we opened a treasury center in Luxembourg, which joins our Boston, London, Hong Kong, and Tokyo facilities in providing 24-hour capital markets services around the world.

"Building on our strength as a leading servicer of financial assets, State Street has developed expertise in meeting the investment management needs of institutional investors. Assets under management totaled $111 billion at year-end 1992. State Street is ranked as the third-largest manager of tax-exempt assets in the United States. State Street is also a leading New England trustee and money manager for individuals, endowment funds, and foundations.

"State Street's services for businesses are aimed primarily at New England middle market companies and selected specialized markets. We provide services that meet the specialized requirements of law firms, accounting firms, and other professional firms in New England.

"During 1992, we continued to invest in technology and staff to bring new services to the market and to increase our own productivity. We further increased our systems and programming staff, and added to our operations and process engineering expertise. To ensure that we have the capacity to grow, we established an additional data center in Westborough, Massachusetts."

State Street Boston has paid cash dividends since 1910. Institutions control approximately 70 percent of the outstanding common shares. State Street Boston paid a 100 percent stock dividend in 1983, a 100 percent stock dividend in 1985, a 100 percent stock dividend in 1986, and a 100 percent stock dividend in 1992.

Total assets: $18.7 billion
Common shares outstanding: 75.9 million

	1984	1985	1986	1987	1988	1989	1990	1991	1992	1993
Net Income (Mil.)	49	55	71	83	92	104	117	139	160	180
Earnings per share	.71	.80	.90	1.12	1.25	1.42	1.59	1.86	2.10	2.36
Dividends per share	.13	.15	.18	.22	.26	.30	.34	.39	.46	.52
Prices Hi	5.8	10.4	14.4	18.1	13.9	20.4	21.6	32.1	44.9	49.1
Lo	3.6	5.7	9.6	8.3	9.7	12.8	10.9	15.5	29.3	29.3

Student Loan Marketing Association

1050 Thomas Jefferson Street, N.W.
Washington, D. C. 20007-3871
Tel. (202) 333-8000
Listed: NYSE
Investor contact: V.P. Communications and Investor Relations,
Elizabeth A. Van Houton
Ticker symbol: SLM
S&P rating: A

As profiled in its 1992 Annual Report, "Student Loan Marketing (Sallie Mae) is the major financial intermediary to the nation's education credit market.

"Sallie Mae's primary business for originators is purchasing and subsequently servicing education loans to students and parents, principally federally guaranteed student loans. It also provides operational support and secured funding to originators of education loans, primarily banks. Additionally, it finances academic plant and equipment. In pursuing its business, Sallie Mae has always adhered to a consistent set of management principles to maximize shareholders' value and best serve its market.

"As a secondary market, Sallie Mae counts its bank clients in the hundreds, and its school constituents in the thousands—but its ultimate customers, education loan borrowers, number in the millions.

"More than 40 percent of students today, compared with less than 30 percent just a decade ago, rely—often heavily—on bank-financed, guaranteed education loans to help pay for the education that will assist them in making positive contributions to our society.

"Our introduction in late 1992 of the Great Rewards program—a consumer benefit and reward for good borrower performance—for the first time gave students across the country a real product choice.

"As the first nationally-based program that recognizes responsible student loan repayment habits, Great Rewards enables Stafford loan borrowers to earn a two-percentage-point reduction of their student loan interest rate for making consistent on-time payments for the first four years of repayment. The program has gained the strong support of lenders with Sallie Mae forward-purchase commitments, as they are now able to assure their borrowers of eligibility for the reduced interest rate feature.

"Completing Sallie Mae's array of debt management tools, the SMART AC-COUNT provides a popular repayment option for highly indebted borrowers, enabling them to consolidate their loans for a longer term with lower monthly payments. Today, Sallie Mae has more than 200,000 consolidation loan customers.

"On the technological front, we continue to significantly enhance our CLASS student loan servicing system, the cornerstone of our servicing operations. The CLASS system is the foundation for Sallie Mae's Export SS loan management service for lenders, as well as for Sallie Mae's own servicing capability. Over the course of 1992, we linked the Export SS loan origination function with another eight guarantor agencies, so that we now are connected to twenty-three agencies which guarantee 75 percent of all new business."

Sallie Mae has paid consecutive cash dividends since 1977. Institutions control over 90 percent of the outstanding common shares. Sallie Mae became public in 1983 and paid a $2\frac{1}{2}$ for 1 stock split in 1989.

Total assets: $46.5 billion
Common shares outstanding: 84.1 million

	1984	1985	1986	1987	1988	1989	1990	1991	1992	1993
Revenues (Mil.)	1,160	1,216	1,300	1,582	2,172	3,169	3,503	3,122	2,615	2,417
Net Income (Mil.)	99	123	145	181	225	258	301	345	394	430
Earnings per share	.76	.98	1.23	1.66	2.14	2.53	2.96	3.55	4.21	4.83
Dividends per share	.05	.07	.11	.16	.24	.41	.59	.85	1.05	1.25
Prices Hi	13.9	15.4	27.5	35.9	34.5	53.5	56.5	76.0	76.0	75.3
Lo	8.4	10.0	14.1	24.4	28.0	33.4	32.8	43.6	59.0	39.9

SunTrust Banks, Inc.

25 Park Place, N.E.
Atlanta, Georgia 30303-4418
Tel. (404) 588-7711
Listed: NYSE
Investor contact: James C. Armstrong
Ticker symbol: STI
S&P rating: A+

As profiled in its 1992 Annual Report, "SunTrust Banks, Inc. is a leading banking and financial services company in the Southeast. At year-end 1993, total assets were $40.7 billion. Our three principal subsidiaries—SunBanks, Inc., Trust Company of Georgia and Third National Corporation—operated 624 banking locations in Florida, Georgia, and Tennessee. SunTrust provides a wide range of financial services to a broad and growing customer base. Our primary businesses include traditional deposit and credit services, as well as trust and investment management services. Additionally, we provide investment banking, corporate finance, mortgage banking, factoring, credit cards, discount brokerage, credit-related insurance, and data processing and information services.

"At the end of 1992, shareholders' equity was $2.7 billion, an increase of 6.2 percent from the previous year-end, with an equity-to-asset ratio of 7.38 percent. This does not include the $1 billion in unrealized pre-tax appreciation of the 24,133,248 shares of The Coca Cola Company owned by the company.

"Despite the recessionary dip, SunBanks had its best year ever in 1992. SunBanks' contribution to the SunTrust net income last year was $217.3 million, with an ROA of 1.21 percent. An overall increase in statewide deposit market share resulted from an array of new products with an aggressive business development program using the theme, 'Peace of Mind Banking.' "

The Trust Company of Georgia's contribution to the SunTrust 1992 bottom line was $176.4 million, with an extremely healthy ROA of 1.57 percent. Trust Company Bank, Atlanta, represents about three-fourths of our total Georgia company, both in terms of assets and earnings. Trust Company banks outside Atlanta are heavily dependent on the growth of their local markets which have remained relatively static. Under these conditions, outstanding performance requires close attention to asset quality and expense control.

"SunTrust's subsidiary, Third National Corporation (TNC), has been on a solid track in its return to a stronger balance sheet and improved profitability. In 1992, the TNC contribution to the SunTrust net income was $58.1 and had an ROA of 1.04 percent. With a strong sales orientation matched by conservative banking practices, TNC is well positioned to move to a new plateau of success. The addition of First United Bancorp, Inc. of Florence, Alabama, will augment TNC's markets."

During 1992, loans of $22.8 billion were apportioned as follows: commercial 34.8 percent, real estate-construction 4.5 percent, real estate-residential 24.7 percent, real estate-commercial 18.8 percent, lease financing 1.6 percent, credit card 3.2 percent, and consumer 12.4 percent.

Consecutive cash dividends for the holding company have been paid since 1985. Consecutive earnings and dividend increases on the predecessor banking companies go back many years. Institutions control over 55 percent of the outstanding common shares. SunTrust paid a 100 percent stock dividend in 1986.

Total assets: $40.7 billion
Common shares outstanding: 122.5 million

	1984	1985	1986	1987	1988	1989	1990	1991	1992	1993
Net Income (Mil.)	—	167	242	283	309	337	350	377	404	474
Earnings per share	—	1.65	1.83	2.17	2.38	2.61	2.75	2.88	3.13	3.77
Dividends per share	—	.57	.61	.65	.70	.78	.86	.94	1.03	1.16
Prices Hi	—	20.4	28.0	27.8	24.5	26.9	24.3	40.0	45.6	49.6
Lo	—	13.6	17.3	17.0	18.5	19.8	16.5	20.5	33.5	41.1

Synovus Financial Corp.

901 Front Avenue Suite 301 (P.O. Box 120)
Columbus, Georgia 31902-0120
Tel. (706) 649-2197
Listed: NYSE
Investor contact: Director of Investor Relations, Richard B. Illges
Ticker symbol: SNV
S&P rating: A+

As profiled in its 1992 Annual Report, "Synovus Financial Corp. is a $5.2 billion asset, multi-financial services company headquartered in Columbus, Georgia. Synovus owns thirty-one community banks in Georgia, Alabama, and

Florida. Synovus affiliate banks operate under a decentralized management structure. Each bank has its own name, Chief Executive Officer, and Board of Directors. Our banks take deposits and lend money in the communities they serve.

Synovus Financial Corp.

"Our decentralized management structure places the ultimate responsibility of each bank on the shoulders of its management team. Our banks make decisions locally, providing a substantial incentive for our bankers to achieve superior results. Synovus provides support in the form of loan administration, bond portfolio management, marketing, legal counsel, audit, human resources, and operations to each affiliate bank.

"Synovus owns 80.7 percent of Total System Services, Inc. (TSYS), the second largest credit card processing company in the world. TSYS provides card processing services to 114 banks and 30 million cardholders across North America. Synovus also owns Synovus Securities, Inc., a full-service retail brokerage firm specializing in portfolio management for fixed-income securities.

"During 1992, Synovus completed its largest merger ever with the affiliation of First Commercial Bancshares, Inc. (FCB) of Jasper, Alabama. First Commercial (FCB) and its five affiliate banks are a significant addition to the Synovus family. First Commercial's flagship bank is the First National Bank of Jasper. We anticipate that FCB will continue to grow in Alabama, which has a history of being an excellent state for banking.

"Synovus Data Corp., a wholly-owned general bank data processing subsidiary of Synovus, provides general bank data processing services to Synovus and its banking subsidiaries."

During 1992, loans of $3.6 billion were apportioned as follows: commercial, financial and agricultural 36.5 percent; real estate-construction 6.1 percent, real estate-mortgage 38.8 percent, and consumer 18.6 percent.

Synovus, via its predecessor banks has paid consecutive cash dividends since 1891. Columbus Bank & Trust Co. controls about 15 percent, officers and directors about 15 percent, and institutions about 10 percent of the outstanding common shares. Synovus paid a 100 percent stock dividend in 1984, a 50 percent stock dividend in 1985, a 50 percent stock dividend in 1986, a 50 percent stock dividend in 1988, and a 50 percent stock dividend in 1993.

Total assets: $5.6 billion
Common shares outstanding: 66.7 million

	1984	1985	1986	1987	1988	1989	1990	1991	1992	1993
Net Income (Mil.)	12	16	19	24	27	31	35	41	61	74
Earnings per share	.33	.40	.46	.54	.58	.67	.70	.76	.92	1.11
Dividends per share	.10	.12	.15	.16	.19	.22	.25	.27	.31	.37
Prices Hi	4.5	8.9	10.5	11.1	10.0	13.0	12.7	12.5	16.5	20.4
Lo	2.9	3.6	7.0	6.4	7.7	7.5	8.3	8.7	11.1	15.0

SYSCO Corporation

1390 Enclave Parkway
Houston, Texas 77077-2099
Tel. (713) 584-1390
Listed: NYSE
Investor contact: Executive Vice Pres. Finance & Administration,
E. James Lowrey
Ticker symbol: SYY
S&P rating: A+

As profiled in its fiscal 1993 Annual Report, "SYSCO Corporation is the largest marketer and distributor of foodservice products to the 'away-from-home-eating' industry in America. Operating from distribution facilities nationwide, the company provides its products and services to approximately 245,000 restaurants, hotels, schools, hospitals, and other institutions. SYSCO's distribution network covers virtually the entire continental United States and includes all of its largest cities, as well as the Pacific Coast region of Canada. SYSCO operates 104 distribution facilities within the United States and two in Canada. The company's fleet of approximately 4,100 delivery vehicles consists of tractor and trailer combinations, vans, and panel trucks, most of which are either wholly or partially refrigerated for the transportation of frozen or perishable foods.

"The foodservice industry consists of two major customer segments—'traditional' and 'chain restaurants.' Traditional foodservice customers include restaurants, hospitals, schools, hotels, and industrial caterers. SYSCO's chain restaurant customers include regional pizza and French-style bakery operations, and national hamburger, chicken and steak chain operations.

"The traditional foodservice segment includes businesses and organizations which prepare and serve food to be eaten away from home. Products distributed by the company include a full line of frozen foods, such as frozen meats, fully prepared frozen entrees, frozen fruits, vegetables, and desserts, and a full line of canned and dry goods. In addition, SYSCO's broader line of product offerings includes such items as fresh meat, imported specialties, and produce. The company also supplies a wide variety of nonfood items, including paper products such as disposable napkins, plates, and cups; tableware, such as china and silverware; restaurant and kitchen equipment and supplies; medical/surgical supplies and cleaning supplies. SYSCO distributes both nationally-branded merchandise and products packaged under its own private brand.

"The company's SYGMA Network subsidiary specializes in customized service to chain restaurants. Certain traditional foodservice operations also provide service to this market segment. SYSCO's sales to the chain restaurant industry consist of a variety of food products necessitated by the increasingly broad menu of chain restaurants. The company believes that consistent product quality, and timely and accurate service are important factors in the selection of a chain restaurant supplier."

During fiscal 1993, revenues were apportioned as follows: restaurants 60 percent, hospitals and nursing homes 13 percent, schools and colleges 7 percent, hotels and motels 6 percent, and other 14 percent.

SYSCO has paid consecutive cash dividends since 1970. Officers and directors control about 6 percent and institutions about 60 percent, of the outstanding common shares. In fiscal 1993, SYSCO completed its 18th consecutive year of higher earnings. SYSCO paid a 50 percent stock dividend in 1980, a 100 percent stock dividend in 1982, a 100 percent stock dividend in 1986, a 100 percent stock dividend in 1989, and a 100 percent stock dividend in 1992.

Total assets: $1.1 billion
Current ratio: 1.9
Common shares outstanding: 191.3 million

	1984	1985	1986	1987	1988	1989	1990	1991	1992	1993
Revenues (Mil.)	2,312	2,628	3,172	3,656	4,385	6,851	7,591	8,150	8,893	10,021
Net Income (Mil.)	45	50	58	62	87	108	132	154	172	202
Earnings per share	.27	.29	.33	.35	.45	.60	.73	.83	.93	1.08
Dividends per share	.043	.048	.05	.065	.075	.085	.10	.12	.17	.26
Prices Hi	4.9	5.9	8.5	10.4	9.8	16.8	19.2	23.7	27.8	31.0
Lo	3.3	4.0	5.7	5.7	6.5	9.2	12.8	15.0	20.5	22.3

Teleflex Incorporated

630 West Germantown Pike Suite 450
Plymouth Meeting, Pennsylvania 19462
Tel. (215) 834-6301
Listed: AMEX
Investor contact: Investor Relations, Janine Dusossoit
Ticker symbol: TFX
S&P rating: A+

Teleflex Incorporated

As profiled in its 1992 Annual Report, "Teleflex is a leading manufacturer of products and services for the automotive, marine, industrial, aerospace, and medical markets worldwide. The company uses its extensive engineering capabilities in mechanical and electromechanical devices, plastics extrusion and molding, and metallurgy to solve customer problems. Teleflex employs more then 8,000 people in more than sixty units worldwide.

"The company's business is separated into three segments—Aerospace Product and Services, Medical Products and Commercial Products."

"The Aerospace Products and Services Segment serves the aerospace, defense, and turbine engine service markets. Its businesses design and manufacture precision controls and systems for both military and commercial applications, and provide sophisticated coating and repair services for turbine engine manufacturers, operators, and overhaulers. Aerospace operates seventeen plants, most of them in the U.S. and Europe.

"The Aerospace Products and Services Segment consists of two major product lines: Aerospace/Defense and Sermatech.

"The Aerospace/Defense segment manufactures and services mechanical and electromechanical control systems for commercial and military aircraft, space vehicles, ground support equipment, missiles, and naval vessels; electrical actuation systems and cargo handling components and systems.

"Sermatech International manufactures sophisticated coatings for gas turbine engine components, and does highly-specialized repairs for critical components such as fan blades and airfoils.

"The Medical Products Segment manufactures and distributes a broad range of invasive disposable and reusable devices for the urological, gastroenterological, and anesthesiological markets worldwide. It also manufactures general and specialized surgical instruments used principally in thoracic; ear, nose and throat; and cardiovascular procedures. Medical has more than twenty production and distribution facilities in twelve countries.

"Rusch International and TFX Medical manufacture and distribute invasive disposable and reusable medical devices such as latex catheters, endotracheal tubes, laryngoscopes, face masks, tracheostomy tubes; general and specialized surgical instruments such as scissors, forceps, vascular clamps, needle holders, and retractors; and, standard and custom-designed components which are sold to other original equipment manufacturers.

"The Commercial Products Segment serves the automotive, pleasure marine, outdoor power equipment and fluid transfer markets. Products are manufactured and marketed worldwide to a broad spectrum of customers. This segment operates seventeen manufacturing facilities located in the United States, Canada and England.

"Automotive products consist of automatic and manual transmission shift controls; accelerator, cruise, and park lock controls; deck lid and hood release cables; and heat resistant fuel system hose.

"Marine products consist of mechanical and hydraulic steering systems; throttle and shift controls; electrical gauges and instrumentation; and electronic navigation systems. About 60 percent of sales are to original equipment manufacturers.

"Industrial products consist of light duty cables for outdoor power equipment and certain other applications; flexible fluroplastic hose used in underground tank connectors, food processing plants, and the chemical industry; and heat-shrinkable tubing for home appliances."

During 1992, revenues and operating profits were apportioned as follows: Aerospace Products and Services 31.3 percent of revenues and 23.9 percent of profits, Medical Products 31.6 percent of revenues and 37.8 percent of profits, and Commercial Products 37.1 percent of revenues and 38.3 percent of profits.

1992 marks Teleflex's fiftieth year of operation. Teleflex has paid consecutive and increased cash dividends since 1977. Institutions control about 50 percent of the outstanding common shares and another 23 percent are closely held. Teleflex paid a 100 percent stock dividend in 1986 and a 50 percent stock dividend in 1991.

Total assets: $640.6 million
Current ratio: 2.1
Common shares outstanding: 17.1 million

	1984	1985	1986	1987	1988	1989	1990	1991	1992	1993
Revenues (Mil.)	156	175	218	272	328	360	444	483	570	667
Net Income (Mil.)	11	13	16	20	24	27	29	30	32	34
Earnings per share	.72	.84	1.01	1.20	1.48	1.63	1.73	1.77	1.87	1.95
Dividends per share	.14	.15	.18	.22	.26	.31	.35	.39	.42	.45
Prices Hi	10.7	13.6	20.0	23.3	20.3	25.9	24.1	34.4	39.5	38.3
Lo	7.1	8.9	13.3	11.6	14.3	18.8	16.6	19.6	25.0	27.8

Thermo Electron Corporation

81 Wyman Street (P.O. Box 9046)
Waltham, Massachusetts 02254-9046
Tel. (617) 622-1000
Listed: NYSE
Investor contact: Chief Financial Officer, John N. Hatsopoulos
Ticker symbol: TMO
S&P rating: B+

ΙΈ Thermo Electron

As profiled in its 1992 Annual Report, "Thermo Electron Corporation develops, manufactures, and markets environmental, analytical, and test instruments, alternative energy power plants, low-emission combustion systems, paper- and waste-recycling equipment, and biomedical products. The company also operates power plants, provides services in environmental sciences and analysis, thermal waste treatment, does specialty metals fabrication and processing, as well as research and product development in unconventional imaging, laser technology, and direct-energy conversion.

"Thermo Electron's various businesses are organized into majority-owned subsidiaries and wholly-owned operations. Shares of Thermo Electron are traded on the New York Stock Exchange; all of its majority-owned public subsidiaries are traded on the American Stock Exchange.

"Ever-increasing regulatory demands on industry continue to benefit our Thermo Instrument Systems, Inc. subsidiary. Thermo Instrument's presence in the high-performance liquid chromatography systems marketplace increased significantly with the February 1993 purchase of Spectra-Physics Analytical, Inc. Thermo Instrument has become the leader in mass spectrometry techniques. With the addition of Nicolet Instrument Corporation in August 1992,

we became the industry leader in Fourier transform in.
try.

"Alternative-energy Systems, formerly known as
ment, has been renamed to reflect the expanding scope
participation in a rapidly changing marketplace. The coi
ergy Systems Corporation subsidiary now operates six agric
fueled electric power plants, which represent approximate.
total on-line capacity in the U.S. biomass-power market.

"We acquired FES, Inc., a subsidiary of Carrier Corporauon, in October
1992. FES is a leading supplier of specialized refrigeration equipment used in
food processing, and in the chemical, pharmaceutical, petroleum refining, and
liquified-gas storage industries.

"The company's Thermo Process Systems Inc. subsidiary designs, manufactures, installs, and sells computer-controlled, custom-engineered, thermal-
processing systems used to treat primary metals and metal parts. In 1992, the
Holocroft division of our Thermo Process Systems Inc. subsidiary secured major orders for its metallurgical processing systems from long-time customers, including nearly $4 million worth of equipment to be installed in various Ford
Motor plants.

"Aqueous cleaning systems by our Napco subsidiary are used at Eastman
Kodak Co. in place of chemical solvents during the production of medical-imag-
ing processors. These cleaning systems are often used in conjunction with
Napco's electroplating lines, which process components ranging from surgical
needles the size of a human hair to thirty-ton steel slabs for industrial equipment.

"During 1992, Thermo Cardiosystems moved a step closer to commercial
approval of its HeartMate–air-powered heart-assist device–with the submission
of 19 patient-years worth of data to the U.S. Food and Drug Administration for
review. On average, one or two implants of the HeartMate System are performed
every week at any one of seventeen U.S. medical centers now using this advanced lifesaving technology.

"One of our International Technidyne subsidiary's fastest-growing products is its tenderfoot incision device, which provides a safer, quicker, and more
comfortable alternative to the traditional 'heel stick' used to draw blood samples from infants.

"Our Thermadynamics, Inc. subsidiary manufactures a family of proprietary, medical-grade polyurethanes for catheters and tubing used in drug-deliv-
ery and fluid-transfer systems.

"Our Soil-Recycling Services business expanded its network of sites across
the United States, increasing from two centers last year to six by the end of
1992. Thermo Process Systems, Inc. is now the leading U.S. supplier of services

.ermal treatment of soil contaminated by petroleum products leaking underground tanks.

"Work aimed at commercializing advanced products in medical imaging and avionics progressed at ThermoTrex Corporation, our principal long-term research and development operation. Most significantly, a clinical test unit of ThermoTrex's sonic CT (computed tomography) system is nearing completion. This system will be applied for breast imaging as a tool in early cancer detection and, with supplemental hardware, for blood-flow measurement to diagnose and monitor peripheral vascular disease. Lasercom, a space-based laser communications system by our ThermoTrex subsidiary, will transfer up to one billion bits of information per second between aircraft."

During 1992, revenues and income were apportioned as follows: instruments 36.8 percent of revenues and 68.6 percent of income, Alternative-energy Systems 23.4 percent of revenues and 2 percent of income, Process Equipment 16.9 percent of revenues and 16 percent of income, Biomedical Products 6.1 percent of revenues and 1.4 percent of income, Services 12 percent of revenues and 9.7 percent of income, and Advanced Technologies 4.8 percent of revenues and 2.3 percent of income.

Thermo Electron Corporation has never paid a cash dividend. Institutions control approximately 55 percent of the outstanding common shares. Thermo Electron paid a 50 percent stock dividend in 1984, a 50 percent stock dividend in 1985, a 50 percent stock dividend in 1986, and a 50 percent stock dividend in 1993.

Total assets: $2.5 billion
Current ratio: 3.0
Common shares outstanding: 47.9 million

	1984	1985	1986	1987	1988	1989	1990	1991	1992	1993
Revenues (Mil.)	253	286	359	420	541	623	721	806	949	1,250
Net Income (Mil.)	5.7	11	16	21	23	27	35	47	59	77
Earnings per share	.30	.45	.55	.67	.77	.86	1.09	1.31	1.51	1.75
Dividends per share	—	—	—	—	—	—	—	—	—	—
Prices Hi	6.6	10.3	15.3	19.1	13.9	25.2	23.5	31.3	31.7	43.3
Lo	4.1	5.3	8.9	6.7	8.5	12.7	14.5	17.2	25.0	31.4

Tootsie Roll Industries, Inc.

7401 South Cicero Avenue
Chicago, Illinois 60629
Tel. (312) 838-3400
Listed: NYSE
Investor contact: President, Ellen R. Gordon
Ticker symbol: TR
S&P rating: A

As profiled in its 1992 Annual Report, "Tootsie Roll Industries, Inc. has been engaged in the manufacture and sale of candy since 1896. This is the only industry segment in which the company and its consolidated subsidiaries operate, and is its only line of business. A majority of the company products are sold under the

**Tootsie Roll
Industries, Inc.**

registered trademarks 'Tootsie,' 'Tootsie Roll,' or 'Tootsie Pop.' The principal product of the company is the familiar 'Tootsie Roll,' a chocolate-flavored candy of a chewy consistency, which is sold in several sizes and which is also used as a center for other products in the line including 'Tootsie Pops,' a spherical fruit or chocolate-flavored shell of hard candy on a paper safety stick, and 'Tootsie Pop Drops,' a smaller-sized version of the 'Tootsie Pop' without the stick. The company and its predecessors have manufactured the 'Tootsie Roll' product to substantially the same formula and sold it under the same name for over ninety years. The company's products also include 'Tootsie Roll Flavor Rolls' and 'Tootsie Frooties,' multiflavored candies of chewy consistency.

"The company also manufactures and sells molded candy drop products under the registered trademark 'Mason' and 'Tootsie,' including 'Mason Dots,' and 'Mason Crows.'

"The company's wholly-owned subsidiary, Cella's Confections Inc., produces a chocolate covered cherry under the registered trademark 'Cella's.'

"In 1988, Tootsie Roll Industries, Inc. acquired Charms Company. This candy manufacturer produces lollipops, including bubble gum-filled lollipops, and hard candy. The majority of the company's products are sold under the registered trademarks 'Charms,' 'Blow-Pop,' 'Blue Razz,' and 'Zip-A-Dee-Doo-Da-Pops.'

"The company's products are marketed in a variety of packages designed to be suitable for display and sale in different types of retail outlets and vending machines. They are distributed through approximately 100 candy and grocery brokers, and by the company itself, to approximately 15,000 customers throughout the United States. These customers include wholesale distributors of candy and groceries, supermarkets, variety cooperative grocery associations, membership club stores, vending machine operators, and fund-raising religious and charitable organizations."

Tootsie Roll Industries has no long-term debt. It has both a regular and Class B common stock issue. The Class B common stock is transferable on a one-for-one basis with the regular common stock shares. However, the Class B common shares have ten votes per share as against one vote per share for the regular common shares. Melvin J. Gordon, Chairman and Chief Executive Officer, and his wife, Ellen R. Gordon, President and Chief Operating Officer, control about 35 percent of the regular and about 65 percent of the Class B Common shares. Tootsie Roll Industries has paid consecutive cash dividends since 1942. It has paid a 3 percent stock dividend every year since 1964. Also, it paid a 50 percent stock dividend in 1986 and a 100 percent stock dividend in 1987.

Total assets: $303.9 million
Current ratio: 2.2
Common shares outstanding: 7.3 million
Class B 3.5 million

	1984	1985	1986	1987	1988	1989	1990	1991	1992	1993
Revenues (Mil.)	93	107	111	115	129	179	194	208	245	260
Net Income (Mil.)	8.9	11	13	15	17	20	23	25	32	35
Earnings per share	.80	1.02	1.17	1.34	1.52	1.86	2.08	2.44	2.95	3.26
Dividends per share	.10	.12	.15	.18	.19	.20	.20	.23	.27	.35
Prices Hi	8.7	15.9	21.3	27.6	29.8	33.3	44.4	68.7	79.6	83.4
Lo	2.6	6.5	13.2	16.8	22.4	21.0	27.6	32.6	56.4	64.5

Torchmark Corporation

2001 Third Avenue South
Birmingham, Alabama 35233-2186
Tel. (205) 325-4200
Listed: NYSE
Investor contact: M. Klyce
Ticker symbol: TMK
R&P rating: A+

As profiled in its 1992 Annual Report, "Torchmark Corporation, an insurance and diversified financial services holding company, was incorporated in Delaware on November 19, 1979, as Liberty National Insurance Holding Company. Through a reorganization effective December 20, 1980, it became the parent company for the businesses operated by Liberty National Life Insurance Company (Liberty), of Birmingham, Alabama; Globe Life And Accident Insurance Company (Globe), of Oklahoma City, Oklahoma; United American Insurance Company (United American), of Dallas, Texas; Waddell & Reed, Inc. (W&R), of Kansas City, Kansas; and United Investors Life Insurance Company (UILIC), of Birmingham, Alabama, along with their respective subsidiaries which were acquired in 1981. The name Torchmark Corporation was adopted July 1, 1982. Family Service Life Insurance Company (Famlico), of Dallas, Texas, was purchased in July 1990.

"Torchmark's insurance subsidiaries—Liberty, Globe, United American, UILIC, and Famlico—write a variety of individual, nonparticipating ordinary life products. These include permanent (whole life) insurance in the form of interest-sensitive and traditional products, term life insurance, and variable life insurance. Individual life insurance products are sold through a variety of distribution channels, including home service agents, independent agents, exclusive agents, and direct response.

"Liberty, Glove, United American, and American offer an assortment of individual health insurance products. These products are generally classified into three categories: (1) Medicare Supplement, (2) cancer, and (3) hospital, surgical, accident, and other. United American Medicare Supplement products are sold by United America, Globe, Liberty, and W&R agents. They provide reimbursement for certain expenses not covered under the national Medicare program.

"Torchmark offers, through Liberty Fire and its subsidiaries, industrial fire insurance, collateral protection insurance, and personal and commercial property and casualty coverages. Liberty Fire is also active in the domestic reinsurance business, underwriting both quota-share business and catastrophic business.

"Torchmark's mutual fund operations are carried out by W&R, a subsidiary of United Management, which markets and manages the sixteen mutual funds in the United Group of Mutual Funds, and the five mutual funds in the Waddell & Reed Fund, Inc. (W&R Funds).

"Torchmark engages in energy operations through Torch Energy Advisors Incorporated (Torch Energy) of Houston, Texas, and its subsidiaries. Torch Energy is a wholly-owned subsidiary of United Management. Torch Energy manages oil and gas properties and investments, primarily in the form of limited partnerships, for affiliated Torchmark companies as well as for unrelated institutions."

During 1992, revenues and operating income were apportioned as follows: individual life 32.3 percent of revenues and 45.1 percent of operating income, individual health 47.3 percent of revenues and 27 percent of operating income, annuities 1 percent of revenues and 3 percent of operating income, property and casualty insurance 5.8 percent of revenues and 2.4 percent of operating income, financial services 9.2 percent of revenues and 19.3 percent of operating income, and energy 4.4 percent of revenues and 3.2 percent of operating income.

Torchmark has increased earnings and dividends for thirty-eight consecutive years. Institutions control about 50 percent of the outstanding common shares. Torchmark paid a 100 percent stock dividend in 1985, and a 50 percent stock dividend in 1992.

Total assets: $7.6 billion
Common shares outstanding: 73.8 million

	1984	1985	1986	1987	1988	1989	1990	1991	1992	1993
Revenues (Mil.)	1,127	1,362	1,555	1,590	1,537	1,629	1,787	1,907	2,046	2,117
Net Income (Mil.)	132	167	206	193	182	211	229	246	265	298
Earnings per share	1.08	1.47	1.82	1.91	2.07	2.59	2.85	3.13	3.58	4.01
Dividends per share	.30	.35	.53	.67	.73	.83	.93	1.00	1.07	1.08
Prices Hi	11.4	17.9	25.7	24.5	22.3	39.2	38.3	39.5	58.4	64.8
Lo	6.1	9.8	14.1	14.5	15.9	20.0	25.4	30.9	36.0	41.1

Tyson Foods, Inc.

2210 West Oaklawn Drive (P.O. Box 2020)
Springdale, Arkansas 72762-6999
Tel. (501) 290-4000
Listed: NASDAQ
Investor contact: Vice Pres. & Treasurer, Wayne Britt
Ticker symbol: TYSNA
S&P rating: A

As profiled in its fiscal 1993 Annual Report, "Now the world's largest fully-integrated producer, processor, and marketer of poultry-based food products, Tyson has expanded into other center-of-the-plate proteins, replicating the pattern it developed in  poultry. By focusing on higher-profit, further-processed foods, Tyson has built one of America's fastest growing companies. Tyson products are sold through the foodservice, retail, wholesale club, and international marketing channels.

"Since 1973, Tyson has completed sixteen transactions involving business acquisitions and major purchases of business assets. Tyson's 66 processing plants, 24 feed mills, 35 hatcheries, 39 fishing vessels, approximately 6,000 contract poultry and swine growers, and some 50,000 hard-working team members stand as testament to Tyson's aggressive growth philosophy.

"This philosophy has made Tyson the world's largest producer, processor, and marketer of poultry. About 90 percent of the company's poultry production is value-enhanced. Tyson is the largest poultry-based, pet food ingredients supplier. The company also operates one of the largest farrow-to-finish swine operations in the U.S., and is one of the country's largest tortilla manufacturers.

"Tyson is the leader in manufacturing and marketing fully cooked, breaded, and unbreaded poultry products to the foodservice and retail markets.

"Beef is an emerging protein line with some 600 products. Its Quik-to-Fix chicken-fried-steak line is an industry leader in the foodservice market. Tyson also has a full line of precooked school products to meet low-fat criteria. Tyson now markets a complete line of further-processed pork, with further-processed cured meats, including hams, bacon, and ethnic sausage, and portion-controlled fresh pork.

"Seafood was added to the Tyson's family products in late 1992, with the acquisition of Arctic Alaska Fisheries Corporation and Louis Kemp Seafood Company. Louis Kemp's Crab Delights and Lobster Delights products claim a 77 percent share of the retail prepackaged market in this category. The company has also developed about 100 further-processed fish products in the past year."

During fiscal 1993, Tyson increased earnings for the thirteenth consecutive year. Tyson has two common stock issues, namely A and B. The Class B shares have ten votes per share and are 99 percent owned by the Tyson family, which maintains both financial and management control of the business. Consecutive cash dividends have been paid since 1972. Institutions control about 30 percent of the outstanding common shares. Tyson paid a 100 percent stock dividend in 1983, a 150 percent stock dividend in 1985, a 100 percent stock dividend in 1986, a 50 percent stock dividend in 1987, and a 100 percent stock dividend in 1991.

Total assets: $3.3 billion
Current ratio: 1.5
Common shares outstanding: Class A 78.8
Class B 68.5

	1984	1985	1986	1987	1988	1989	1990	1991	1992	1993
Revenues (Mil.)	750	1,136	1,504	1,786	1,936	2,538	3,825	3,922	4,169	4,707
Net Income (Mil.)	18	35	50	68	81	101	120	145	161	180
Earnings per share	.16	.29	.39	.53	.64	.78	.90	1.05	1.16	1.22
Dividends per share	.005	.008	.012	.019	.02	.02	.02	.03	.04	.04
Prices Hi	1.4	4.8	12.8	12.0	10.2	13.1	17.8	23.3	24.9	27.1
Lo	1.0	1.9	4.3	5.4	5.5	7.4	11.4	13.9	15.3	19.3

UST Inc.

100 West Putnam Avenue
Greenwich, Connecticut 06830-9984
Tel. (203) 661-1100
Listed: NYSE
Investor contact: Mgr. Investor Relations, Mark A. Rozelle
Ticker symbol: UST
S&P rating: A+

As profiled in its 1992 Annual Report, "UST is a holding company for four wholly-owned subsidiaries: United States Tobacco Company, International Wine & Spirits Ltd., UST Enterprises Inc., and UST International Inc. Through its subsidiaries, the company is a leading producer and marketer of moist smokeless tobacco products, including Copenhagen, Skoal, Skoal Long Cut, and Skoal Bandits.

"Other consumer products produced and marketed by UST subsidiaries include premium wines from Washington state and from California's Napa Valley, sold nationally through our Chateau Ste. Michelle, Columbia Crest, Conn Creek, and Villa Mt. Eden wineries.

"Our two flagship brands, Copenhagen and Skoal, continue to be recognized as leaders within the moist smokeless tobacco category.

"Copenhagen, introduced in 1822, continues to be the world's best-selling brand of moist smokeless tobacco. Copenhagen is a true American original and is one of the oldest packaged consumer brands still in use in the United States.

"Skoal, launched in 1934, continues to hold the distinction of being America's favorite wintergreen-flavored, moist smokeless tobacco.

"The phenomenal success achieved with Copenhagen and Skoal has paved the way for Skoal Long Cut, now the second-largest selling and our fastest-growing brand of moist smokeless tobacco. Designed for consumers who prefer a longer cut product, Skoal Long Cut is offered in wintergreen, mint, straight, and classic flavors.

"Our Skoal Bandits line of products offers the convenience of enjoying tobacco in individual portion packs. Skoals Bandits are available in wintergreen, mint, straight, and classic varieties.

"UST markets America's best-selling imported pipe tobacco—Borkum Riff—and produces and markets Don Tomas premium hand-made cigars from Honduras. Other dry smokeless tobaccos include Rooster, Red Seal, Bruton, CC, and Devoe. Chewing tobacco is sold under the WB Cut name. Other products include smoker's accessories such as Dr. Grabow Pre-smoked and Mastercraft imported pipes, plus Dill pipe cleaners.

"Stimson Lane Ltd., a subsidiary of International Wine & Spirits, markets premium varietal wines produced by our Chateau Ste. Michelle and Columbia Crest wineries in Washington state, and our Villa Mt. Eden and Conn Creek wineries, located in California's Napa Valley.

"In the second quarter of 1992, Domaine Ste. Michelle Blanc de Blanc was introduced, a companion product to the highly successful Champagne Brut. In its second year of national distribution, Domaine Ste. Michelle has become one of the largest producers of *methode champenoise* sparkling wine in the United States.

"In the first quarter of 1992, Villa Mt. Eden introduced two new lines of wine in six western states and was named a 'Winery of the Year' by *Wine & Spirits* magazine.

"UST Enterprises and its subsidiary, Cabin Fever Entertainment, which develops, produces, and markets video programming with an American theme, continued to emerge as a creative and innovative niche business."

During 1992, revenues and operating profits were apportioned as follows: tobacco 84.4 percent of revenues and 97.2 percent of operating profits, wine 7.2 percent of revenues and .9 percent of operating profits, and other products 8.4 percent of revenues and 1.9 percent of operating profits.

UST has increased earnings for thirty-three consecutive years. It has paid consecutive cash dividends since 1912, and has increased cash dividends in each of the past twenty-two years. Institutions control about 55 percent of the outstanding common shares. UST paid a 200 percent stock dividend in 1983, a 100 percent stock dividend in 1987, a 100 percent stock dividend in 1989, and a 100 percent stock dividend in 1992.

Total assets: $706.2 million
Current ratio: 3.1
Common shares outstanding: 215.7 million

	1984	1985	1986	1987	1988	1989	1990	1991	1992	1993
Revenues (Mil.)	444	480	518	576	619	682	765	907	1,044	1,110
Net Income (Mil.)	84	94	104	131	162	190	223	266	313	349
Earnings per share	.36	.41	.46	.56	.70	.82	.98	1.18	1.41	1.71
Dividends per share	.18	.22	.25	.30	.37	.46	.55	.66	.80	.76
Prices Hi	5.4	4.9	5.6	8.0	10.5	15.4	18.3	33.9	35.4	32.8
Lo	3.9	3.6	3.8	4.9	6.0	9.6	12.4	16.4	25.4	24.4

The Valspar Corporation
1101 Third Street South (P.O. Box 1461)
Minneapolis, Minnesota 55415
Tel. (612) 332-7371
Listed: NYSE
Investor contact: Vice Pres. Finance, Paul C. Reyelts
Ticker symbol: VAL
S&P rating: A+

The Valspar
Corporation

As profiled in its fiscal 1993 Annual Report, "The Valspar Corporation is one of the five largest North American manufacturers of paints and coatings. Founded in 1806 as the manufacturer of America's first varnish, Valspar's products include consumer paints sold to the do-it-yourself market; packaging coatings for the food and beverage industries; industrial coatings for a broad spectrum of OEM markets; and specialty products including resins, colorants, floor coatings, and industrial maintenance and ma-

204

rine coatings. Headquartered in Minneapolis, Valspar operates twenty-one manufacturing plants throughout North America and licenses its technology worldwide.

"The Consumer Coatings group manufactures and distributes a full line of latex and oil-based paints, stains, and varnishes serving primarily the do-it-yourself market. Its products are marketed under proprietary brands (Colony, Valspar, Enterprise, Magicolor, McCloskey, BPS, and Masury) and under private labels.

"The Industrial Coatings group manufactures and distributes, primarily in the United States and Canada, decorative and protective coatings for applications to wood, metal, and plastic substrates. The company is a major supplier of finishes to the furniture and wood paneling industry.

"The Packaging Coatings group is the largest coatings supplier to the rigid packaging industry in North America, and a major licensor of the related technology to coatings companies throughout the world. Packaging coatings for application to food and beverage can bodies and ends comprise the largest volume of sales by this group.

"The Special Products group is engaged in the production and marketing, primarily in the United States, of resins and emulsions for heavy-duty maintenance and marine coatings, high-performance floor coatings for industrial and commercial use, colorants, and colorant systems."

During fiscal 1993, revenues were apportioned as follows: Consumer Coatings 30 percent, Industrial Coatings 23 percent, Packaging Coatings 27 percent, and Special Products 20 percent.

Valspar has increased earnings for eighteen consecutive years and has raised cash dividends for fourteen consecutive years. It has paid consecutive cash dividends since 1964. Officers and directors control about 15 percent, and institutions about 65 percent, of the outstanding common shares. Valspar paid a 100 percent stock dividend in 1984, a 100 percent stock dividend in 1987, and a 100 percent stock dividend in 1992.

Total assets: $337.0 million·
Current ratio: 1.7
Common shares outstanding: 21.5 million

	1984	1985	1986	1987	1988	1989	1990	1991	1992	1993
Revenues (Mil.)	224	347	345	449	480	527	571	633	683	694
Net Income (Mil.)	11	12	15	18	18	23	27	28	34	40
Earnings per share	.48	.49	.63	.80	.81	1.04	1.22	1.27	1.57	1.85
Dividends per share	.10	.11	.13	.16	.20	.22	.26	.30	.36	.44
Prices Hi	5.1	7.7	12.1	20.3	14.8	18.3	20.0	29.8	36.5	41.5
Lo	3.8	4.8	7.4	10.7	10.6	11.9	14.7	17.9	27.6	30.4

Walgreen Company

200 Wilmot Road
Deerfield, Illinois 60015
Tel. (708) 940-2500
Listed: NYSE
Investor contact: Vice Pres. & Treasurer, W. Lynn Earnest
Ticker symbol: WAG
S&P rating: A+

Walgreens

As profiled in its fiscal 1993 Annual Report, "Walgreen Co. is the leader of the U.S. chain drugstore industry in sales, profit, and technology use. Sales for 1993 reached $8.3 billion, produced by 1,836 drugstores—including fourteen RxPress (pharmacy only) stores—located in thirty states and Puerto Rico. Seventy percent of these stores have been opened or remodeled in the last five years.

"Founded in 1901, Walgreen has 58,000 employees and 28,000 shareholders. Its drugstores serve nearly two million customers daily and average $4.5 million in annual sales per unit. That's $462 per square foot, among the highest in the chain drug industry. Walgreen drugstores are served by seven major distribution centers and four photo-processing plants.

"Walgreen presently fills 7 percent of all prescriptions in the United States. Despite lower inflation, prescription sales during the year climbed a healthy 15.7 percent to top $3 billion. They are now nearly 40 percent of total Walgreen sales—up from 28 percent just five years ago.

"The 149 new drugstores opened during fiscal 1993 were nineteen more than projected, and included ten new stores in Indianapolis and three RxPress

(Pharmacy only) stores in Spokane. These are new markets for Walgreen, and we are exceeding sales projections in both.

"In addition to entering such new markets as Cleveland and Buffalo, we plan to open 175 new drugstores across the country in fiscal 1993-1994. By 1996 we'll be opening 200 stores a year, and expect to operate 3,000 drugstores by the end of this decade.

"Walgreen participates in the relatively new dynamic of managed-care pharmacy through our pharmacy mail service subsidiary, Walgreen Healthcare Plus. This subsidiary, started in 1992, had an excellent year, and we expect its strong growth to accelerate. Its state-of-the-art Orlando, Florida, mail-service facility opened last September and is exceeding our sales plans.

"To further handle this 30 percent annual growth rate business, we plan to open a new and larger pharmacy mail service facility in Tempe, Arizona. Scheduled to begin operation in September 1994, it will have an initial capacity of 7,500 prescriptions per day."

During fiscal 1993, revenues were apportioned as follows: prescription drugs 38 percent, nonprescription drugs 14 percent, cosmetics and toiletries 9 percent, general merchandise 25 percent, tobacco products 4 percent, and liquor and beverages 10 percent.

During fiscal 1993, Walgreen achieved its nineteenth consecutive year of record sales and earnings. Walgreen has paid dividends in every quarter since 1933, and has raised dividends eighteen times in the past sixteen years. Institutions control about 50 percent of the outstanding common shares. Walgreen split two-for-one in 1982, paid a 100 percent stock dividend in 1983, a 100 percent stock dividend in 1985, and split two-for-one in 1991.

Total assets: $2.5 billion
Current ratio: 1.7
Common shares outstanding: 123.1 million

	1984	1985	1986	1987	1988	1989	1990	1991	1992	1993
Revenues (Mil.)	2,745	3,162	3,661	4,282	4,884	5,380	6,047	6,773	7,475	8,295
Net Income (Mil.)	85	94	103	104	129	154	175	195	221	222
Earnings per share	.70	.77	.84	.84	1.05	1.25	1.41	1.58	1.78	1.98
Dividends per share	.18	.22	.25	.27	.30	.34	.40	.46	.52	.60
Prices Hi	11.3	15.1	19.8	22.9	18.7	25.1	26.6	38.6	44.5	44.6
Lo	7.2	10.8	12.1	12.4	13.6	15.6	19.9	24.6	30.4	35.4

Wal-Mart Stores, Inc.

702 Southwest 8th Street (P.O. Box 116)
Bentonville, Arkansas 72716-8611
Tel. (501) 273-4000
Listed: NYSE
Investor contact: Finance and Treasurer, D. Randy Laney
Ticker symbol: WMT
S&P rating: A+

WAL-MART

As profiled in its fiscal 1993 Annual Report, "Wal-Mart Stores, Inc. is a merchandiser, operating as of January 31, 1993, 1,880 discount department stores (including 30 Supercenter stores), 256 warehouse clubs, 64 warehouse outlets, and four hypermarkets.

"The company operates Wal-Mart stores (including Supercenters) in forty-five states and Puerto Rico. The average size of a Wal-Mart store is approximately 81,000 square feet, and store sizes range between 30,000 and 196,000 square feet of building area. The company operates Wal-Mart Supercenter stores in nine states, and the average size of a Supercenter store is 165,000 square feet.

"The company operates Sam's Clubs in forty-one states. The average size of a Sam's Club is approximately 120,000 square feet, and club sizes generally range between 90,000 and 150,000 square feet of building area.

"Wal-Mart stores are generally organized with thirty-six departments and offer a wide variety of merchandise, including apparel for women, girls, men, boys, and infants. Each store also carries curtains, fabrics and notions, shoes, housewares, hardware, electronics, home furnishings, small appliances, automotive accessories, garden equipment and supplies, sporting goods, toys, cameras and supplies, health and beauty aids, pharmaceuticals, and jewelry.

"Sam's offers bulk displays of name brand hardgood merchandise, some softgoods, and institutional-size grocery items. Each Sam's also carries jewelry, sporting goods, toys, tires, stationery, and books. During fiscal 1993, Sam's began experimenting with fresh bakery, meat, and produce departments, and currently has 131 clubs with fresh food departments.

"McLane's offers a wide variety of grocery and non-grocery products, including perishable and non-perishable items. The non-grocery products consist primarily of tobacco products, hardgood merchandise, health and beauty aids, toys and stationery. Western Merchandisers offers a wide variety of prerecorded music and video, hardcover and paperback books, and related accessories. Both of these companies are wholesale distributors that sell their merchandise to a variety of retailers, including the company's Wal-Mart stores and Sam's Clubs.

"The company endeavors to meet or undersell local competition. Wal-Mart stores maintain uniform prices, except where lower prices are necessary to meet local competition. Sales are primarily on a self-service, cash-and-carry basis, with the objective of maximizing sales volume and inventory turnover while minimizing expenses."

Wal-Mart has increased earnings for thirty consecutive years. It initiated cash dividends in 1973 and has increased its dividend every year since 1977. The Walton family controls about 40 percent, and institutions about 30 percent, of the outstanding common shares. Wal-Mart paid a 100 percent stock dividend in each of the following years: 1980, 1982, 1983, 1985, 1987, 1990, and 1993.

Total assets: $26.4 billion
Current ratio: 1.6
Common shares outstanding: 2.3 billion

	1984	1985	1986	1987	1988	1989	1990	1991	1992	1993
Revenues (Mil.)	6,401	8,451	11,909	15,959	20,649	25,811	32,602	43,887	55,484	67,968
Net Income (Mil.)	271	327	450	628	837	1,076	1,291	1,608	1,995	2,333
Earnings per share	.12	.15	.20	.28	.37	.48	.57	.70	.87	1.02
Dividends per share	.013	.018	.022	.03	.04	.06	.07	.09	.11	.17
Prices Hi	3.0	4.4	6.7	10.7	8.8	11.2	18.4	25.0	33.0	34.1
Lo	1.9	2.4	3.7	5.0	6.1	7.5	10.1	14.3	25.1	23.0

Wilmington Trust Corporation

Wilmington Trust Center
Rodney Square North
1100 North Market Street
Wilmington, Delaware 19890-0001
Tel. (302) 651-1000
Listed: NASDAQ
Investor contact: Executive Vice Pres., Ted T. Cecala
Ticker symbol: WILM
S&P rating: A+

As profiled in its 1992 Annual Report, "Wilmington Trust Corporation and the Bank's subsidiaries provide a full-range of banking and related services to individual and corporate customers in the Delaware region. Founded in 1903, the company attributes much of its success to the expansion of trust

> # Wilmington Trust Corporation

and custody service over the past ninety years. Our experience in providing highly personalized trust and custody services to generations of prominent families has led Wilmington Trust to become the ninth-largest personal trust institution in the nation. We serve these customers from Delaware and two offices in Florida.

"The bank historically has concentrated its banking activities within the state of Delaware and, to the extent permitted by the laws of such states, in nearby regions of southeastern Pennsylvania, southern New Jersey and northeastern Maryland.

"The bank directly originates or purchases residential first mortgage loans. These are secured principally by properties located in Delaware, Pennsylvania, New Jersey, and Maryland. The bank generally services loans which it originates or purchases and which are not subsequently resold.

"The bank also originates loans secured by mortgages on commercial real estate and multi-family residential real estate. Such loans generally involve greater risks than one-to-four family residential mortgage loans. Since payment of loans secured by commercial and multi-family residential properties often is dependent on the successful operations and management of those properties, repayment of these loans may be subject to a greater extent to adverse conditions in the real estate market or the economy generally than loans secured by one-to-four family residential properties.

"The bank also makes other types of commercial loans to businesses located in its market area. Lines of credit, term loans, and demand loans are offered to finance, among other things, working capital, accounts receivable, inventory, and equipment purchases. Typically, such commercial loans have terms not exceeding seven years, and bear interest at rates fluctuating with a designated interest rate.

"The bank makes loans and participates in arrangements to finance the construction of residences and commercial real estate. The bank also originates loans for the purchase of unimproved property to be used for residential purposes. The bank's residential and commercial construction loans generally have terms of twenty-four months or less, and interest rates which adjust from time to time in accordance with changes in a designated interest rate. Residential and commercial construction loans afford the bank the opportunity to increase the interest rate sensitivity of its loan portfolio, and to receive yields higher than those obtainable on permanent residential mortgage loans. These higher yields correspond to the higher risks associated with construction lending.

"The bank offers both secured and unsecured personal lines of credit, installment loans, home improvement loans, direct and indirect automobile loans, student loans, and credit card facilities. The bank views such consumer lending as a basic part of the program to provide a wide range of financial services to its customers.

"The corporation, through its subsidiaries, also performs corporate trust and custodial services for both institutional and individual clients. The bank serves as trustee in equipment leasing transactions and asset securitizations. Through its Personal Financial Services Department, Corporate Financial Services Department, and Investment Management Department, the bank acts as trustee. executor, administrator, guardian, and custodian, and provides fiduciary services for employee benefit plan trusts. The corporation also assists corporate clients in establishing and maintaining Delaware-chartered investment holding companies."

During 1992, loans of $3 billion were apportioned as follows: commercial, financial and agricultural 28.8 percent, real estate-construction 3.9 percent, mortgage-commercial 21 percent, mortgage-residential 23.1 percent, and installment loans to individuals 23.2 percent.

Wilmington Trust has paid consecutive cash dividends since 1914. Institutions control about 40 percent of the outstanding common shares. Wilmington Trust paid a 100 percent stock dividend in 1983, a 100 percent stock dividend in 1985, a 100 percent stock dividend in 1986, and a 100 percent stock dividend in 1992.

Total assets: $4.6 billion
Common shares outstanding: 37.0 million

	1984	1985	1986	1987	1988	1989	1990	1991	1992	1993
Net Income (Mil.)	25	31	39	47	56	61	69	73	78	83
Earnings per share	.68	.83	1.02	1.21	1.45	1.59	1.81	1.92	2.09	2.24
Dividends per share	.22	.28	.32	.39	.46	.59	.72	.80	.88	.98
Prices Hi	5.5	9.5	12.8	18.0	15.8	23.2	22.5	29.0	29.4	31.0
Lo	3.9	5.5	9.2	10.0	11.5	13.3	15.2	18.0	22.6	24.8

WMX Technologies, Inc.
3003 Butterfield Road
Oak Brook, Illinois 60521
Tel. (708) 572-8800
Listed: NYSE
Investor contact: Vice Pres. & Treas., James E. Koenig
Ticker symbol: WMX
S&P rating: A-

As profiled in its 1992 Annual Report, "The mission of Waste Management Inc. is to be the acknowledged worldwide leader in providing comprehensive environmental, waste management and related services of the highest quality to industry, government, and consumers using state-of-the-art systems responsive to customer needs, sound environment policy, and the highest standards of corporate citizenship.

"Waste Management of North America, Inc. is the leading provider of integrated solid waste services in North America. It serves local government, business, and industry. Services include commercial and residential collection, transfer and disposal of solid and special wastes, collection and processing of recyclable materials, medical waste collection and disposal, and special events resources including portable sanitation.

"Chemical Waste Management, Inc., headquartered in Oak Brook, Illinois, is the nation's leading provider of comprehensive hazardous and low-level radioactive waste services. Services include hazardous waste reduction, recycling, collection, transportation, treatment, thermal destruction, and disposal.

"Wheelabrator Technologies, Inc. is a multi-faceted environmental services company. Based in Hampton, New Hampshire, it is North America's leading operator of trash-to-energy and cogeneration facilities. It is one of the nation's leading suppliers of contract operation and maintenance services for water and waste water treatment facilities, and it also provides a range of air pollution control technologies and capability for industry and utilities.

"Waste Management International Inc. is the leading international provider of solid and hazardous waste management and related services. Based in London, it conducts essentially all of the company's waste management operations located outside North America.

"Rust International Inc. (operations began January 1, 1993), formed from units of Chemical Waste Management, Wheelabrator Technologies, and The

Brand Companies, is a leading provider of environmental and infrastructure engineering and design, construction and consulting services, headquartered in Birmingham, Alabama."

During 1992, revenues and operating income were apportioned as follows: solid waste 49.2 percent of revenues and 58.7 percent of income, hazardous waste 17.4 percent of revenues and 10.2 percent of income, environmental services 16.9 percent of revenues and 16.4 percent of income, and international operations 16.5 percent of revenues and 14.7 percent of income.

Waste Management has increased dividends each year since initiation in 1976. Institutions control about 55 percent of the outstanding common shares. Waste Management paid a 200 percent stock dividend in 1981, a 100 percent stock dividend in 1985, a 100 percent stock dividend in 1987, and a 100 percent stock dividend in 1989.

Total assets: $16.3 billion
Current ratio: 1.0
Common shares outstanding: 483.5 million

	1984	1985	1986	1987	1988	1989	1990	1991	1992	1993
Revenues (Mil.)	1,315	1,625	1,998	2,729	3,528	4,414	6,034	7,551	8,661	9,136
Net Income (Mil.)	143	172	371	227	464	562	685	606	850	453
Earnings per share	.37	.43	.88	.73	1.02	1.22	1.49	1.23	1.86	.93
Dividends per share	.096	.11	.14	.18	.23	.29	.35	.42	.50	.58
Prices Hi	6.0	9.5	15.0	24.3	21.4	35.9	45.5	44.4	46.6	40.3
Lo	3.5	5.5	8.6	13.9	15.8	20.4	28.6	32.6	32.0	23.0

Wm. Wrigley Jr. Company

410 North Michigan Avenue
Chicago, Illinois 60611-4287
Tel. (312) 644-2121
Listed: NYSE
Investor contact: Vice Pres.–Corporate Affairs & Secretary, William M. Piet
Ticker symbol: WWY
S&P rating: A+

As profiled in its 1992 Annual Report, "The company's principal business is the manufacture and sale of chewing gum, both in the United States and abroad.

"The company's brands manufactured and available in the United States are: Wrigley's Spearmint, Doublemint, Juicy Fruit and Big Red, which account for a majority of the company's sales volume; Freedent, a specially formulated chewing gum which does not stick to most types of dental work, is available in three flavors and Extra, a sugarfree chewing gum containing Nutrasweet brand sweetener, which is available in four flavors and as bubble gum.

"Except for Big Red, which has limited availability overseas, these six Wrigley brands are also available in many international markets in various flavors. Additional brands manufactured and marketed abroad are: Arrowmint, Cool Crunch, Dulce 16, Juicy Fruit and P.K., chewing gums in sugar coated pellet form, Freedent and Orbit sugarfree gums, and Big Boy, Hubba Bubba and Big G, all standard bubble gum products.

"The company's six largest markets outside of the United States in 1992 were Australia, Canada, Germany, Philippines, Taiwan, and the United Kingdom.

"Finished chewing gum is manufactured in four factories in the United States and eight factories in other countries. Three domestic wholly-owned associated companies manufacture products other than finished chewing gum. The Amurol Products Company manufactures and markets primarily children's bubble gum items, including Big League Chew, Bubble Tape, and other uniquely packaged confections. Amurol markets Hubba Bubba in the United States under a licensing agreement with the parent company. Various non-gum items, such as a line of suckers, dextrose candy, liquid gel candy, and hard roll candies are an important part of Amurol's total business. Reed's, maker of individually wrapped hard roll candies, was acquired by Amurol Products Company in 1989. The principal business of L.A. Dreyfus Company is the production of chewing gum base for the parent and wholly-owned associated companies. Northwestern Flavors, Inc. processes flavorings and rectifies mint oil for the parent and associated companies."

For 1992, the geographic breakdown of sales and operating profit was as follows: The United States 56.6 percent of sales and 58.5 percent of profits, Europe 28.6 percent of sales and 28.7 percent of profits, and Other 14.8 percent of sales and 12.8 percent of profits.

Wrigley has no long-term debt. There are two classes of common shares, regular and Class B. The Wrigley family controls over 25 percent of the regular common and over 45 percent of the Class B common. Wrigley has paid consecutive cash dividends since 1913. Wrigley paid a 100 percent stock dividend in 1980, a 200 percent stock dividend in 1986, a 100 percent stock dividend in 1988, and a 200 percent stock dividend in 1992.

Total assets: $815.3 million
Current ratio: 3.2
Common shares outstanding: 90.6 million
Class B 25.8 million

	1984	1985	1986	1987	1988	1989	1990	1991	1992	1993
Revenues (Mil.)	591	620	699	781	891	993	1,111	1,149	1,287	1,429
Net Income (Mil.)	40	43	54	70	87	106	117	129	141	175
Earnings per share	.31	.34	.43	.56	.73	.90	1.00	1.09	1.27	1.50
Dividends per share	.16	.17	.21	.28	.36	.45	.49	.55	.62	.75
Prices Hi	3.3	5.3	8.7	11.8	13.8	17.9	19.8	27.0	39.9	46.1
Lo	2.5	3.2	4.6	6.5	10.7	11.8	14.6	16.4	22.1	29.5

Bibliography

Babson-United Investment Advisors, Inc. *United & Babson Investment Report.* Babson-United Building, 101 Prescott Street, Wellesley Hills, Massachusetts 02181.

Growth Stock Outlook, Inc. *Growth Stock Outlook.* P.O. Box 15381, Chevy Chase, Maryland 20815.

Malkiel, Burton G. *A Random Walk Down Wall Street* (1973). W.W. Norton Company, 500 Fifth Avenue, New York, New York 10110.

Moody's Investors Service, Inc. *Moody's Bank & Finance Manual,* vols. 1 & 2. 99 Church Street, New York, New York 10007.

Moody's Investors Service, Inc. *Moody's Handbook of Common Stocks.* 99 Church Street, New York, New York 10007.

Moody's Investors Service, Inc. *Moody's Handbook of OTC Stocks.* 99 Church Street, New York, New York 10007.

Moody's Investors Service, Inc. *Moody's Industrial Manual,* vols. 1 & 2. 99 Church Street, New York, New York 10007.

Moody's Investors Service, Inc. *Moody's OTC Industrial Manual.* 99 Church Street, New York, New York 10007.

National Association of Investors Corporation. *Better Investing.* P.O. Box 220, Royal Oak, Michigan 48068.

Standard & Poors, Corporation. *Outlook.* 25 Broadway, New York, New York 10004.

Standard & Poors, Corporation. *Standard & Poors Corporation Records.* 25 Broadway, New York, New York 10004.

Standard & Poors, Corporation. *Stock Guide.* 25 Broadway, New York, New York 10004.

Standard & Poors, Corporation. *Stock Reports.* 25 Broadway, New York, New York 10004.

Train, John. *Dance of the Money Bees* (1974). Harper & Row, Publishers, Inc. 10 East 53rd Street, New York, New York 10016.

Train, John. *Preserving Capital and Making It Grow* (1983). Clarkson N. Potter, Inc. Publishers, New York, New York 10016.

Walden, Gene. *The 100 Best Stocks To Own in America.* (3rd edition, 1993). Dearborn Financial Publishing, Inc., 520 North Dearborn Street, Chicago, Illinois 60610-4975.

Wall Street Transcript Corporation, "Wall Street Transcript." 99 Wall Street, New York, New York 10005.

Index